JOURNEYS IN INDUSTRIOUS ENGLAND

From Cambridge

To go to Oxford or Abingdon in the winter time the Hill Country way is best.

From Cambridge we went to Wilson and so to Royston a faire town with a great market for corne in the stores from thence to London.

Soe we went out of London Road thwarting the fields under the Edge of the Hills in Hartford Shire to a town called Oaken in a way thither we have a Causways way lately made & railed in by the present Earle of Salisbury this town is so called from the fruitfulnes of oakes my Companion told me there nold but one in the Parish he also told me by meanes of the Hare Warren there being holes to let the Hares through they are not very plentifull in the fields there about.

From Oaken we went to Dunstable in the way thither we have a high roune Hill out of from the maine ridge of mountaines the are in Hartford shire this Hill may be seen upon one way laid in Summer heat and Harvest

Dunstable is a pretty good market town in Hartford shire It hath a faire church in it and the ruines of an Abboy or a religious House Sit under in a plaine under the Hills having Sergi holes about it where the poore theire Cattle good tacker to have the greatest offtem for birds of that kinde in London. And some people of this town are very curious in mgking Steele Hats & other workes of that nature

From Dunstable you may go to Tring through Aylsbury or else leaving Aylsbury a mile or more on the right hand go to farne and so to Oxford.

A page from a Baskerville manuscript with variations in handwriting and an experiment in the heading for a journey. (Transcript page 114)
British Library MS Add 70523 f14r

THOMAS BASKERVILLE

Journeys in Industrious England

and Writings Personal and Topographical

EDITED BY

Anthea Jones

THE HOBNOB PRESS

First published in the United Kingdom in 2023

by The Hobnob Press,
8 Lock Warehouse, Severn Road, Gloucester GL1 2GA
www.hobnobpress.co.uk

British Library Cataloguing in Publication Data
A catalogue record for this book is available from the British Library

ISBN 978-1-914407-51-2

Typeset in Adobe Garamond Pro 11/14 pt.
Typesetting and origination by John Chandler

CONTENTS

MAPS AND ILLUSTRATIONS

FOREWORD

'IT WAS BY a side entrance,' her editor observed, 'that Celia Fiennes slipped unobtrusively into the world of letters'. Short extracts from an anonymous manuscript volume appeared in print in 1812, and a fuller version was incompletely transcribed and published in 1888. A few historians noticed and cited it, including G.M. Trevelyan and the Webbs, but not until 1947 did her work receive the scholarly edition that it deserved.[1] And in consequence she has taken her place alongside Leland, Defoe and Cobbett as one of the inquisitive travellers whose eye-witness descriptions of their surroundings so much enrich our social history.

Thomas Baskerville (1630-1700), an older contemporary of Fiennes (1662-1741), has had to wait somewhat longer. A portion of his travel journals was published obscurely and with omissions in 1893, and some of his description of Oxford in 1905, but neither these nor his hitherto unpublished writings have received much attention from scholars, and none from the general reading public. Yet his journeys, which make up the largest portion of the present edition, and which were undertaken only a few years before Fiennes, cover many parts of England; and in his descriptions of what he did and saw he displays the same keen curiosity and enthusiasm as has earnt Fiennes the affection from readers that her work now enjoys. It is to be hoped that the painstaking work of Dr Jones in transcribing, editing and annotating Baskerville's surviving writings for publication in this edition will accord him similar recognition.

Topographical and travel writing has a very long history, which can be traced back to classical antiquity, notably the guide to Greece by the Hellenistic writer Pausanius. Medieval England's topographers were rarely travellers, content or compelled to derive their information second-hand from written sources of dubious accuracy, or from guesswork. Generally regarded as

---

1   C. Morris (ed.), *The Journeys of Celia Fiennes* (Cresset Press, 2nd edn., 1949), xiii-xv; A McRae, *Literature and Domestic Travel in Early Modern England* (Cambridge, 2009), 174-209.

the first to record his journeys was William Worcestre (or Botoner), a 15th-century agent and peripatetic secretary for a Norfolk landowner. But it was the polymath John Leland (*c.*1503-1552), traversing England and Wales in the service of Henry VIII, and then on his own initiative, who should take the credit as founder of English topographical writing. His expeditions, year after year, discovered in town and countryside, 'a hole worlde of thinges very memorable,' but eventually drove him insane.

Later Tudor topographers ('chorographers' was their preferred term) tended to restrict their perambulations to a smaller compass – Kent, Leicestershire or London – or adopted an encyclopaedic structure, in Latin prose (William Camden) or mellifluous verse (Michael Drayton); or they wove a narrative around their maps (John Norden and John Speed). After 1600 a new breed was less high-minded. Thomas Coryate, John Taylor, Richard Braithwaite and their ilk brought a picaresque flavour to tourism – as it was becoming – by mimicking the great sea-dog explorers of the new world with derring-do in the old.

A new spirit of enquiry emerged as improving roads had begun to make travel easier by about 1700, and we enter the world of the inquisitive Celia Fiennes and the ideologically driven Daniel Defoe, whose *Tour* became, through multiple editions (from 1724 to 1779), the standard guidebook for the 18th-century English (and Welsh) explorer. Recording in one's diary the aristocratic grand tour around Europe was becoming fashionable, and when that was not feasible a journey to the picturesque Lakes or the Wye valley had to suffice. And so travel diaries and pedestrian tours of limited interest proliferated from the 1790s and through the 19th century.

Baskerville's importance, in this procession of sightseers, is on one level that he is earlier than most, ahead of Fiennes by a decade or more, and a mature man of the world when she is an adventurous young woman. But more than that, he shares with her, despite his portrait's dour appearance, an affable temperament and an insatiable interest in whatever and whoever he happens upon. Whether it be the cultivation of saffron or cider apples, the waterworks at Worcester or the market at Norwich, the annoying persistence of Doncaster stocking-sellers, the Northampton inn saved from burning by beer, the ploughman's dexterity or the Harrogate women's complexions – Baskerville investigates and reports. He suggests improvements that could be made to the Uffington white horse, he marvels at the view from Cotswold heights, but also finds himself with his companions benighted there in fog. He has a rags-to-riches tale of a York midwife, and tells a touching story of a girl's young fiancé lost to smallpox. He calls on members of his extensive family, and befriends anyone with his surname. He is a clubbable man, who enjoys good food, drink and company.

The ten journeys 'in industrious England' – our title, not his – are the main components of his surviving writings presented here. But he also made lists of London taverns, set about describing Oxford colleges, collected miscellaneous biographical material about his family and others, and essayed to write even worse doggerel verse than John Taylor about rivers and landscapes. A thoroughly likeable, entertaining and occasionally infuriating travelling companion, now rediscovered from a distant age.

John Chandler

Once I was alive, and had Flesh did thrive
But now I am a Skellitan . at 70

A shadows fly, So houres dye,
And dayes do span, the age of man
In Month of AUGUST Twenty nine
ffirst began my Mourning Time
Thousand Six hundred thirty nine
I number Yeares then sixty nine
Yet I drudge on as said before
There Time when Time shall be no more
Ascend Birth I had I say
January Eleventh day
In that Circle Fifty two Weeks
Thousand Six hundred fixty Six
A Ray of Light I saw that day
Enter my heart with heat and joy
Saying these words unto me then
King of Ierufalem .

*Thomas Baskerville commissioned an engraving to go in the publication of his writings
but then used it to produce a surprising broadsheet with a record of his birthday.
(Reproduced by permission of Abingdon School)*

Even such is time who takes on trust
Our youth our Joyes and all we have
And payes us but with age and dust
Who in the darke and silent grave
When we have wandered all our wayes
Shuttes up the story of our dayes
But from that age that grave that dust
The Lord will rayse me up I trust.
W.R.

    Sir Walter Raleigh
    Oxford, Bodleian Libraries, MS. Rawl. D. 859 f.85b

1
INTRODUCTION

The Manuscripts

THOMAS BASKERVILLE'S SURVIVING writings seem mainly to have been put together in 1682 or 1683 from notes made or given to him in earlier years; these dates are mentioned quite frequently. Thomas Hearne, who knew Baskerville, understood that he intended to publish his writings, and that he 'had written fair in two large Folios', and had an engraving made of his portrait with publication in mind. Indeed, Hearne says he had approached Lichfield, a publisher.[1] Baskerville did not continue with this project, although he was obviously preparing a substantial amount of material. In his account of his home parish of Sunningwell, then in Berkshire but now in Oxfordshire, he expressed a wish to inform his successors about the trees planted by his father Hannibal and himself near the church. But it may be that the birth of a son altered his approach, giving him hope that he would pass on information in person about his family and kin. His first son died in 1685, possibly soon after birth. A second son, Matthew Thomas Baskerville, was born in 1687. Thomas Baskerville died aged 70 years in November 1700. Matthew died aged 33

---

1 *Remarks and collections of Thomas Hearne* (1906), 215, 221,240, 241, 257.

years in February 1721, and at this point it appears that Thomas Baskerville's writings were still in his house at Bayworth, with his collection of books and manuscripts.

Hearne walked over to Sunningwell on the 2nd March 1731.

> What I chiefly went for was to see the two Folio MSS. written by old Baskerville ... The Books are not neer full, three Parts in 4, or thereabouts, being left Blank, and perhaps there may be about 12 Quire of Paper in both Volumes. 'Tis a Medley of merry stuff.

Various antiquarian collectors visited Bayworth, and also the house 'over against the Town-Hall in Oxford' to see Matthew Baskerville's executor, a farrier named Giles. Hearne was one who wished to buy but found Mrs Giles hostile to his approaches, though he said he would have purchased all the manuscripts. Other collectors were more successful.

Richard Rawlinson, a book collector, was abroad when Thomas's son Matthew died, but at some date he acquired one of the two Folio volumes.[2] It was donated to the Bodleian library, reference MS Rawl. D. 810, together with the large number of books and manuscripts in his collection. As Hearne suggested, this folio volume does have a number of blank pages, though not a large number. The second folio volume seems to have disappeared. Rawlinson also collected ninety loose papers comprising some written by Thomas Baskerville and some by his father Hannibal, with a number of letters from Hannibal's mother and from other correspondents. Three letters are from Thomas to his father. These papers are also in the Bodleian library, catalogued MS. Rawl. D. 859. One of the papers written by Thomas Baskerville is a draft of a section written more neatly in the main Rawlinson volume.

Two more manuscript books of Baskerville's writings have survived but not in large Folio volumes. One Timothy Thomas of Christ Church made a list of Baskerville's books 'with a Design to secure some for my Ld Harley', and as well as books, at some point one manuscript now in the British Library came into Harley's collection, reference British Library, MS Harl. 4716. This is a thin narrow folio. A third manuscript, also now in the British Library, came into the Portland family library at Welbeck Abbey and is also in the British Library, reference MS Add 70523. These two manuscripts, with the exception of the pages of travels in verse, give an impression of being drafts, with many alterations; text here, too, was copied more neatly into the Rawlinson volume in at least one instance. The main Rawlinson volume, on the other hand, is a

2   ODNB.

very clean copy with hardly any alterations or corrections, and could well have been prepared for printing.

All three manuscripts contain a variety of material. Hearne thought Baskerville was mad to consider printing his writings;[3] but substantial sections from two of the manuscripts were printed two hundred years later, which would have gratified him. The manuscripts also contain material as yet unpublished, of which most is presented here; even so, there will be a small amount of material still not in print. Baskerville would no doubt have clasped the two editors round the waist if he had known that these writings, too, were to be published more or less simultaneously in two quite different books.[4]

Her Majesty's Historical Manuscript Commission (HMC), in Appendix part II to their *Thirteenth Report* in 1893 published a transcription from the Welbeck Abbey manuscript, in which Baskerville described his journeys across England at intervals during the years 1649 to 1681. The Commission omitted small amounts of material, particularly the listing of places which Baskerville rode through or past, thus removing insight into which roads he followed, and avoiding many of the problems of his spelling of place-names. The HMC report has been mentioned by academic researchers and writers, though without quoting very much detail. A new edition of the text forms a major component of this book, including material which HMC omitted.

A few years later, in 1905, the Oxford Historical Society published material concerning the University from the Rawlinson folio volume in which it forms the largest component. It was transcribed by H Baskerville of Oriel College (where Hannibal, Baskerville's father, was enrolled) and was published in *Collectanea IV,* volume XLVII in the Oxford Historical Society's series. The volume omitted some parts of the manuscript not directly about Oxford, in particular his account of his family and kin, which is presented here. Baskerville seems to have planned a survey of all the colleges, and at some stage allocated three folios per college; whether he decided not to pursue the project further, or whether he did not have opportunity to gather further material, the last ten colleges and the six halls have a minimum of information and several blank pages.

---

3   *Remarks and collections of Thomas Hearne* (1906) 221.
4   See his greeting of Tom Hyde in Chapter 6 'Miscellaneous Writings'. John Blair has written a chapter on 'Thomas Baskerville on the upper Thames: verse and prose by a seventeenth-century maverick' in a volume edited by Martin Henig and Nigel Ramsay (Archaeopress, forthcoming). A mutual friend alerted us to the fact that quite independently we were both working on Baskerville's writings.

Baskerville had persuaded a number of friends and acquaintances to help him and he probably copied verbatim into the volume the material which they gave him. He, and an assistant, also copied out, on some twelve folios, brief biographies of fellows of Balliol drawn from the history of the college by Henry Savage, published about 1660.[5] A friend lent Baskerville this book. On the earlier colleges, however, he had a great deal of information, while every now and again offering the reader a diversion from the serious business of describing the university by writing about some incident or exploration prompted by a reference to a particular college fellow. Two of the more extended diversions, not published in the *Collectanea* volume, are set out here in a chapter devoted to his 'Miscellaneous writings'.

The third manuscript, British Library, MS Harl. 4716, has not hitherto been published. It contains a mixed bag of contents. Part, a narrative in verse of his travels westward from his home at Bayworth in Sunningwell, appears to have been ready for publication; there are almost no alterations or corrections. The rest of the volume contains material on the Civil War, and a draft of a short section copied up neatly in the Rawlinson volume. Bound in at the end of these sections there is a separate booklet listing taverns in London street by street. This section is in a rather poor hand, while the spelling matches the poor writing. Nonetheless it contains a fascinating account of the many London taverns, and is here presented with a modernised version side by side with the original.

Amongst the loose papers collected by Rawlinson are three letters signed by Thomas Baskerville, each of which is in a different hand. One of the letters was written for him and he then signed it, or else he was experimenting with very different styles of writing. There is also a copy of his will, in the same printed style as one of the letters.

Editing Thomas Baskerville's writings

THE THRUST OF this edition is to make the text as readable as possible while largely maintaining the original orthography and as little punctuation as is reasonable to make meanings clear. HMC's standardised spelling removed the period flavour of the text, while *Collectanea's* editor reproduced all the original English spellings but modernised the punctuation. Different problems occur in each of the three manuscripts, and more editorial intervention is needed in some parts than others; not all the manuscripts were written in the same hand, and some were more 'modern' than others. The variations in hand-writing might suggest that some parts were dictated to another to write, and the use of

5   Savage, *Balliofergus.*

a new quill or a sharpened quill may have made a difference to the appearance of other parts. Baskerville himself appears to have cultivated more than one style of hand-writing.

Baskerville's spellings are here presented without alteration. His spelling of personal names can make identification difficult, while his spelling of place-names can be even more puzzling. It is quite a challenge to identify some of the place-names. There were not many sign posts until the Turnpike Commissioners made a practice of erecting them,[6] nor name boards on the approaches to towns, and though he may have had maps to guide him, they did not name every small place of which he took notice; only major place names in his text are as usually spelled today. Baskerville mentions that in some places he relied on local people to tell him the name of a place, as in St Albans and on his journey to the north, and his spellings may be phonetic and influenced by local dialects. Names can often be spelled in diffferent ways on each occasion they are referred to. Brought up in the Essex county town of Chelmsford, the local pronunciation of this name, 'Chumsford', is not far from Baskerville's reference to 'Chansford'. He also tells us that he wrote up at least one account of a journey from notes which got blotted in the rain. A modern version of each place-name is given in a footnote without interrupting the flow of the text.

In writing his neat copy, Baskerville's handwriting was upright, rounded and rather mannered and formal. He frequently wrote a capital letter at the beginning of a line even when in the middle of a sentence; it can be difficult to know whether he intended a capital letter or not and is a matter of judgement where to present one in the printed transcript. Other parts of the manuscripts are written in a more cursive and less formal style and contain a minimum of capital letters. His puncuation was erratic and he was sparing in his use of both commas and full stops.[7] A new paragraph was indicated with a new line, but in the less polished parts of one of the manuscripts every sentence started on a new line; these are only taken as paragraphs where the meaning suggests one. Sometimes he used a colon instead of a full stop, but also indicated a shortened name with a colon. Dates were often separated with a stop on either side, but these stops have not been transcribed. He very rarely inserts a possessive inverted comma. Baskerville writes as though talking to the reader personally,

6   Moir, *The Discovery of Britain* (1964), 9.
7   Thomas Baskerville's usage can be compared with his father, Hannibal's, some of whose writings are preserved in Bodleian Library, MS Rawl. D. 859. There is little modern-style punctuation there either, but Hannibal's spelling is a little more regular.

and could run on breathlessly without pausing. It is a pity to remove all the characterful features of his text, so most of his punctuation is left as written and only a minimum of modern usage introduced.

Conventional abbreviations employed by scribes writing in Latin were adopted in English, and Baskerville's formal hand made extensive use of them. Abbreviations were discussed and illustrated in Essex Record Office publication No. 21 (1954) by Hilda E P Grieve, *Exampes of English Handwriting 1150-1750.* These abbreviations are expanded or extended in this edition, but names or titles when abbreviated are not altered. The most frequently used abbreviations are:

y=th; ye=the; yn=then; yt=that; &=and; wch=which; wth=with
Abbreviated titles: Bp, Col, Lrd, Sr, are also expanded.
li after a number = £

A missing letter is very occasionally discreetly inserted within brackets where there is clearly a scribal slip, and a missing word is inserted within square brackets. Inserted or altered words are taken as the text without indicating the earlier version. Substantial additions to the text, however, often in a brown ink rather than the black ink of most of the text, are placed within angled brackets < >.

The name Baskerville is spelled in a number of different ways, Baskervyle, Baskervile, Baskervill, Baskerville. The modern spelling of the name is Baskerville.

The Manuscripts

Oxford, Bodleian Libraries, MS. Rawl. D. 810.
Oxford, Bodleian Libraries, MS. Rawl. D. 859. Miscellaneous papers attributed to Hannibal Baskerville.
Courtesy of the British Library board:
British Library, MS Harl. 4716. Miscellaneous writings.
British Library, MS Add. 70523. An account of journeys in England.

Baskerville frequently quotes sums of money, which can be compared with other sums to give a sense of the relative value. He was impressed by the modest charge made by the innkeeper at Withington for one night's lodging for seven men, meals, and fodder for the horses, which was 17 shillings (*see* Chapter 4 Journey 6, and Chapter 5). As far as a modern equivalent can be calculated, using the MeasuringWorth website, this might be equivalent to

£130 to £143, maybe enough for one horse's feed today; in terms of average earnings it might equate to £2,060, perhaps a more realistic comparison.[8]

> 20 shillings (s) = £1
> 12 pence (d) = 1 shilling
> 1 shilling since decimalisation is 5p and £1 = 100p

8   https://www.measuringworth.com; as employed by Floud in *An Economic History of the English garden* (2019).

The hill which Baskerville would have seen riding from Bayworth to Sunningwell, and the view of the North Wessex Downs from the site of Bayworth house.

2
LIFE AND KIN

The Baskerville Family

THOMAS BASKERVILLE WAS aware of an extensive set of relationships. As he journeyed round England, he referred to his kinship with owners or residents whose houses he passed near or sometimes stayed in. An account of this network of family was written almost at the beginning of the large Rawlinson folio volume, and it occupies most of nine closely written pages. The detail of his cousinage documents vividly the demographic conditions of the seventeenth century and would have provided Peter Laslett with a good illustration of *The World we have Lost*: so many marriages terminated by the death of one of the partners after a few years of marriage, so many children dead before they reached adulthood, so many second and third marriages.[1] As a result, many had step-brothers or sisters, as was the case with Thomas Baskerville's father Hannibal and Thomas himself. Many marriages appear to have been 'suitable' to the social position of the partners, and as far as Hannibal's mother was concerned, her second marriage though fitting her social position was disastrous; there is, though, one example of a second marriage which is unusually described as with the man's first love.

The Baskervilles were 'gentry'.[2] During the visitation of Berkshire in 1665-6 'Hanybal Baskerville of Bayworth' was summoned to appear 'personally before Elias Ashmole, Windsor-Herald at Armes, on Thursday 16 March by Eight of the clock' at the house of Edward Hart being the New Inn in Abbington'. Hannibal was armigerous. Interest in the family pedigree was necessary if a man wished to bear arms and be accounted a gentleman, and the Baskerville family of Eardisley had a notable pedigree reaching back to the eleventh century. Hannibal offered notes about his family for the Visitation, preserved amongst his papers, and afterwards noted that Ashmole listed all

1 Laslett, *The World we have Lost* (1971).
2 Heal and Holmes, *The Gentry* (1994) : this Baskerville family matches the detailed criteria in chapters 1 and 2.

his children, 'dead and alive' (seven sons and two daughters) but not some of his relations.[3] He traced his ancestry from Sir James Baskerville of Eardisley, who died in 1485, but Elias Ashmole's pedigree traced his descent from Henry Baskerville of the City of Hereford, and noted that Thomas Baskerville was 'son and heir' to Hannibal, and was aged 34. There were no further visitations after 1688. Ashmole was paid 37s 6d. Hannibal had been summoned 40 years before, but did not have his pedigree until after 1629 when he married his cousin Mary. Amongst his papers are notes on other relations whom he had known, many from the Scudamore family because his mother had married Sir James Scudamore after the death of his father Sir Thomas Baskerville.

An account of Hannibal's birth and christening was found by Thomas and copied into the large folio book, but either he did not find or did not copy any further details of Hannibal's life, although there is an (incomplete) account of his early years, as he was moved from one house to another. The main focus of Hannibal's account was the sufferings of his mother; he referred to several periods of separation followed by reconciliations.[4] Only in the last year of her life, he wrote, did she live contentedly at Bayworth, and was buried in Sunningwell on 17 October 1632. Thomas would not have remembered her as he was only two years old. Thomas referred to his grandmother's second marriage and the Scudamore children, but did not make any comment on the acrimonious marriage. He did mention that her brother lived at Clowerwall or Clearwell, and typically in the summer of 1684 he went to see the house.[5]

Amongst Hannibal's papers there are five folios relating to Sir Walter Raleigh, including copies of two letters he wrote to his wife, his speech on the scaffold and the poem he wrote on the night before his execution, quoted at the beginning of the book.[6] The Bodleian catalogue notes that the wording is 'evidently more correct' than printed versions. There is also a short account of his final actions and words as he prepared to die, written by someone who witnessed the scene in person. The link with Hannibal was most probably through his mother, Mary Throckmorton, daughter of Sir Thomas Throckmorton of Tortworth in Gloucestershire, as Thomas Baskerville noted; Raleigh had clandestinely married one Elizabeth or Bess Throckmorton, a lady-in-waiting at Elizabeth 1's court, and his letters reveal his great love for

3 Oxford, Bodleian Libraries, MS. Rawl. D. 859 ff.70 & 71; The four visitations of Berkshire [The Harleian Society] (1907-8).
4 Oxford, Bodleian Libraries, MS. Rawl. D. 859 ff.3b-6b. Hannibal wrote on the backs of several letters from his mother.
5 See below.
6 Oxford, Bodleian Libraries, MS. Rawl. D. 859, f.85b, f.68b.

her. These papers are not in Mary Throckmorton's hand, as seen in letters she wrote to Hannibal.

Thomas Baskerville set down a great deal about his family's history, yet in all the words he wrote about his family and their extensive connections, usually without dating the vital events, he wrote very little about himself. His story has to be pieced together from the occasional incidental brief references to his experiences in his writings. Even his birth date is not certainly known, but has been deduced from hints including in a verse on the broadsheet used by James Caulfield: it says that he was born in 'August 29' which has been interpreted as August 1629; it also states that he was 69 in 1699 which suggests a birth in 1630.[7] The Herald's Visitation noted that on 16 March 1664/5 he was 34 years old. Hannibal's marriage licence was dated 4 November 1629, and this suggests that his first child was born in 1630.[8] 'August 29' should therefore probably be read as 29th August, in which case he was still 34 at the time of the Herald's Visitation but would have been 35 on 29 August 1665.

This birth date is supported by comments in the midst of Baskerville's writing about Oxford.[9] Under Corpus Christi College, he referred to 'Mr Coward', a Somersetman, with an estate at East Penard, four miles from Worminster 'in St Cuthbert's parish, Wells, where I was born'. The connection was tenuous; Christopher Coward was rector of Kingston Seymour from 1668 until his death in 1699, the location of a story about a bad inn.[10] Writing about Queen's College, Baskerville mentioned Dr Barlow, a bishop of Lincoln, which typically reminded him that another Barlow, 'a great lover of my father and mother, Dean of Wells, Anno Dmi 1630, was one of my Godfathers, Mr Thomas Lyte of Lytes Cary Somerset ... was the other.' Ralph Barlow was Dean of Wells between 1621 and his death in 1631. Thomas may have been baptised in the cathedral, or in St Cuthbert's church, the parish and civic church for the City of Wells; his brother William was baptised in St Cuthbert's in 1633 and so was his sister Constance in 1640, who died young and was buried in Somerton.[11] Baskerville also mentions that he went to school in Wells.[12]

---

7 Caulfield, *Portraits, Memoirs, and Characters* (1790-95). The date of the Visitation would have beeen Old Style.
8 Kingsley, *Landed Families*.
9 Bodleian Library, MS Rawl. D. 810 f.59 and f.67b.
10 Christopher Coward, gentleman commoner 1653-1660, prebendary of Wells Cathedral, 1664. BHO Foster; CCEd.
11 Kingsley, *Landed Families*; the monument in Sunningwell records the burial dates of Thomas Baskerville's brothers and sisters, and of his mother and father. It was erected by Thomas, 'now Lord of this mannour', in 1680.
12 Bodleian Library, MS Rawl. D. 859 ff.7b.

His mother, whose first marriage was to a Somersetshire man, John Morgan, apparently had a house in the area, and Hannibal went to live there with her; in his account of his early life he wrote that he lived at Bayworth until he was married.

In the same way only a few details of Baskerville's later life are mentioned, and dates are sparse. In 1649, a short time after the beheading of Charles I, he journeyed to Southampton and took ship to Newfoundland, an English settlement founded in 1610; he would then have been 19 years old. At this time there were five more boys living in Bayworth, and one daughter.[13] Was he being sent to make his fortune? It is not clear why he went, but his description of the English part of the journey was written up in the 1680s along with the other journeys he had made over the previous thirty years.[14] There is no information on when he returned, but he was perhaps fortunate not to be at home in 1656 when three of Hannibal's children died. He was certainly back in England before 1662 when he travelled through Essex.[15]

A few years before this he and his brother Henry sailed to Barbados, probably about 1655. Again he gave no reason for going, and typically he mentioned this incidentally in his account of Tom Hyde's adventures.[16] There is no indication that the Bayworth Baskervilles had an interest in Barbados, although Thomas and Henry expected to see two of their brothers when they arrived, but found Robert had died.[17] There is some suggestion that Thomas and Henry went as seamen, perhaps to earn wages and gain experience, being encouraged to follow in the steps of Hannibal's father. Sir Thomas Baskerville was appointed in 1595 as colonel-general in command of the land forces accompanying Sir Francis Drake and Sir John Hawkins on their last expedition to the Indies; when Drake died he succeeded to the command of the expedition and brought it home.[18] Sir Thomas became General of the English forces in France, and died on a military expedition to Picardy 1597, a few weeks after Hannibal's birth, and was buried in the new Quire in St Paul's, where a monument containing his epitaph was consumed in the Great Fire of London; Hannibal or Thomas had copied the epitaph and it was recut and placed on the wall in St Leonard's church, Sunningwell beneath the memorial

13 Kingsley, *Landed Families*.
14 Journey 5 in HMC transcript of British Library, MS Add. 70523, f.29v.
15 See Chapter 4 'Journeys in Industrious England'.
16 See Chapter 6 'Miscellaneous Writings'.
17 Robert was aged 19 when he died in 1654. A Humphrey Baskerville owned slaves in Jamaica when he died in 1688 but was from a different Baskerville family. Centre for the Study of the Legacies of British Slavery. UCL https://www.ucl.ac.uk/lbs/
18 ODNB.

to Thomas's parents and siblings. The monument is topped with a carving of the Baskerville coat of arms.

Thomas Baskerville may not have lived at Bayworth until after his father's death in 1668. His mother had died in 1644 leaving Hannibal with a large young family, so Thomas was possibly sent away from home when quite young. During the 1660s he lodged for some time with Mr Thomas Stevenson (sometimes spelled Stephenson) in Stanton Harcourt, as did Thomas Baker rather later, who became a close friend and accompanied him on his journey to Norwich.[19] Three surviving letters from Thomas to his father are dated 1663, 1664, and 1666, two of which were written from Stanton Harcourt.[20] One letter refers to him being happily settled there and another refers to his father forbidding him to call at Bayworth, which may have been because of illness in the house; Thomas's brother William died in 1665.

There were attempts to place Thomas as a gentleman in another house, but he preferred a more modest and less expensive life with Mr Stevenson and spent his time fishing. He was godfather to Thomas Stevenson's son Thomas who was probably born while he was living there, and who later helped him with his study of Oxford colleges.[21] This house was called Morage or Mooridge and appears to have belonged to the Baskervilles; after one journey Thomas refers to setting plants in 'our garden' there. For two or three years also he lived in Compton Dundon Parsonage house, Somerset, a prebend of Wells Cathedral with 'a woman of good understanding' who was looking after her mother's house, but he did not give a date. She was called Penbrook Sydney, her mother's maiden name was Constance Huntley.[22]

His personal family was not one Thomas Baskerville wrote about, and indeed all his writings appear to have been done early in the 1680s before he had any children. His will, made in 1694, of which a copy or draft is in the collection of papers in MS Rawl. D.859, suggests a conscientious man anxious to look after the people to whom he became related. He recorded that Mary Hunny or Honey, a member of a local family, looked after him for some years, probably his housekeeper, and that she bore him two sons. Other evidence shows that the first was probably born in 1685 and died in infancy, buried in Sunningwell as the bastard son of Mary Honey; the second, Matthew Thomas,

---

19 For Thomas Baker see Chapter 3 'Oxford'.

20 Bod. MS Rawl. D. 859 ff.58, 60, 61. See below.

21 Thomas Stephenson, son of Thomas, of Staunton Harcourt, Oxon, p.p. Christ Church, matriculated 8 March, 1677-8, aged 16, B.A. 1681, M.A. 1684. He died before 1683. BHO Foster.

22 Bodleian Library, MS Rawl. D. 810 f4b.

who outlived his father, was born in 1687.[23] The baptism register of Holy Trinity, Clapham, records his birth date, 21 September and his christening 11 October 1687, the son of Thomas Baskervile and Mary his wife. Baskerville's will also refers to Mary as his wife, but it appears that he did not marry her until 1698. His marriage legitimised and facilitated his son's inheritance of Bayworth and Sunningwell. He knew from his father's experience how tricky inheritance could sometimes be: Hannibal had a lengthy dispute with his step-father, Sir James Scudamore, before he was able to occupy the estate which his father had purchased.[24]

Bayworth House and Estate

There is a brief description of Bayworth during Hannibal's occupation of the house, and another from the period immediately after the death of Matthew Thomas. Anthony à Wood visited Bayworth in Lent 1658 with Thomas Smith M.A. (who had been ejected from his clerkship of Magdalen college by the visitors in 1648).[25] They went 'to a private and lone house in or neare to Bagley wood, between Oxon. and Abendon, inhabited by the lord of Sunningwell called Hannibal Baskervyle, esq.' Hannibal was acquainted with Smith, and also with Wood because while a student at Brasenose, he used to visit the house of his kinswoman Lady Scudamore, and Wood's mother lived nearby. It is interesting that Hannibal visited a Scudamore although his mother's second marriage to Sir James Scudamore was most unhappy. The visitors went up 'a paire of stairs' to a pretty oratory or chappel, which Hannibal had either created or refurbished, equipped with velvet cushions and carpet, which had had painted windows, 'but defaced by Abendon soldiers (rebells) in the grand rebellion.'[26] The chapel was used; James Eglesfeild of Abingdon wrote on 2 April 1664 saying that he would be ready on Good Friday at 9 o'clock to administer the sacrament to Hannibal in his own house.[27]

On the occasion of Wood's visit, Thomas Smith played the organ and sung, and his music was appreciated by Hannibal, though Wood 'found him

---

23 At the end of the account of the Huntley family, there is a note of the date TB's mother was born, and the names of his two sons, also of Mary's parents. See below.

24 Sir James Scudamore had granted a 60-year lease of Sunningwell and Bayworth. Hannibal won the legal cases and gained possession, and from that time he 'lived constantly' there until he was married. Bodleian Library, MS Rawl. D. 859 , f.6.

25 Anthony A Wood *Athenae Oxonienses* (1813), xxxiii-xxxiv.

26 TB also refers to this in Chapter 3 'Oxford' apropos the windows of Christ Church, where he names the artist.

27 Bod. MS Rawl. D. 859 f.62. James Eglesfeild (*sic*) MA matriculated 1619, Queens College Oxford; vicar of St Helen's, Abingdon (1661-1675). BHO Foster.

to be a melancholy and retir'd man'. His melancholy may have been a natural result of his misfortunes, losing his wife in 1644 and six of his children before Wood's visit, three in 1656; two more children pre-deceased him, and only Thomas survived him. Wood is the source of the story that Hannibal built a barn-like building for wandering beggars, and hung a bell at his back door for them to ring when they wanted anything; Hannibal was several times indicted at Abingdon sessions for harbouring beggars. He told Wood he gave a third or fourth part of his estate to the poor. In November 1619, just after he came of age, he had 'made a vowe ... to give money unto pious uses and unto poore'; in July 1636 he computed that he had given £198 up to the 16th November 1629.[28] Thomas was more sociably inclined than his father, but he, too, was a serious man and two and half pages in the Rawlinson folio volume contain a series of short moral reflections. His will also refers to a religious experience in 1666.

Hearne, another observer who recorded his visits to Bayworth, described the manor as 'a brave estate' and 'all belong'd to Baskerville as did also the Presentation to the Parsonage of Sunningwell'. He noted that Baskerville 'mightily improv'd the estate'. A very few comments by Baskerville incidentally display his interest in the estate. A letter to his father included a recommendation to improve the length of the hop poles, and on his travels he acquired cuttings of fruit trees and plants and noted that they were growing well at Bayworth. A note in British Library, MS Harl. 4716 [f.15b] confirms the large number of trees growing at Bayworth:

> September the 26: 1693. Mr Thomas Baskervile Lord Master of Bayworth house and orchards about it, in which are some 1000s trees most of them at full growth and Mr Thomas Ellis schoolmaster of Sunningwell, we two did overlook the trees in the orchards and could find or gather no more than 41 aples; 103 crabs and about 20 pears.

Wood also visited Bayworth in Thomas's time, 'to refresh his mind with a melancholy walke, and with the retiredness of the place, as also with the shady box-arbours in the garden'. Baskerville did not write much about his house at Bayworth, but he did mention the blessing of living near hills, with good air, and the views to be obtained, and also the 'beauty' of his gardens.[29] As he journeyed round England, he gave high praise to 'delicate' walks and gardens. His awareness and enjoyment of hills was nurtured by his home. Unhappily

28 Bodleian Library, MS Rawl. D. 859 f.9.
29 See his will and the description of Sunningwell below.

Matthew Thomas did not continue to nurture the estate, and shortly before his early death he sold the house to Sir John Stonehouse of Abingdon, who did not occupy it but left it to fall down.

Bayworth house was on rising ground, and apparently faced south, so taking advantage of the view to the hills now designated the North Wessex Downs. Aerial photographs suggest that the house consisted of a central hall range with two cross-wings, standing behind a forecourt.[30] A limited excavation has shown that the courtyard was constructed of well-laid pitched limestone blocks, and contained a well; beyond was a road similarly constructed, which continued in the direction of Abingdon.[31] It suggests that a house on this site had been built during the period in which Abingdon Abbey had complete control of the estate. Bayworth was a significant estate (10 hides) belonging to the abbey in 1086, divided into three holdings; during the fourteenth century these holdings were surrendered back to the abbey. There are references in the abbey's accounts to the 'keeper' of Bayworth, whose house if on this site would have been conveniently accessible from Abingdon. After the suppression of the abbey in 1538, Bayworth became linked with the manor of Sunningwell, which the abbots had kept in their own hands from the mid-thirteenth century, and Sir Thomas Baskerville bought both manors.[32]

The comments by both Wood and Hearne emphasise that the house was very old. Wood wrote that Bayworth 'is an old house, situated in a romancy place, and a man that is given to devotion and learning, cannot find out a better place'. Hearne described the house as 'a brave old thing, full of conveniences, and as pleasant a Place as need be desired.' Some 20 years later, when Hearne went there again, he recorded 'the old house of the Baskervilles is now almost quite gone to ruin, the family of the Baskervilles being (as I have noted formerly) exstinct;'[33] to have delined so dramatically in 20 years implies a very old house. Early in the present century another house has been built a little lower down the hill, but the site of Baskerville's house remains just under the surface of the ground.

~~~

30 Kingsley, *Landed Families*.
31 *South Midlands Archaeology* 34 (2004), 54-5. I'm grateful to Paula Levick who led the excavation for giving me a copy of this report.
32 *VCH (Berks)* 4.
33 *The remains of Thomas Hearne* (1965) 318. TB expressed some scepticism that his brother William was the father of twins see Family History below 'A note of her childbearing'.

FAMILY HISTORY

Oxford, Bodleian Libraries, MS. Rawl. D. 810 ff.2b to 6b

The account is mostly written in a clear, large and mannered hand, making it difficult to distinguish capital and lower case initial letters. A draft of a small part is amongst papers in MS Rawl. D.859. The popularity of certain Christian names, for example Constance, made for confusion which Baskerville was aware of, and he tried to tie the person he was writing about to her maiden name, spouse or parents. His energy in maintaining links with many distant relations, and indeed with friends and acquaintances, must have relied on diligent exchanges of letters as well as his habit of journeying and visiting.

Headings have been inserted, and some punctuation.

Baskerville, Morgan, Huntley, Lyte of Lytes Cary

MARY BASKERVILLE WAS the first born of Nycholas Baskervyle And Constance Huntley. Shee was born the sixth of January in the year 1602. Shee was married to John Morgan of Wormister in the county of Somerset at the age of [blank] and had by him two sonnes and one daughter. John (still liveing Anno 1683) William and Mary (both defunct).

After his death shee remained a widdow seaven yeares, and then was married on the 5th day of November to Hannyball Baskervyle in the parish Church of Dinder in Somersettshier by William Hunt then Curate there, and vicar of the Cathedrall Church of St Andrewes in Wells.[34] By him shee had Seaven Sonnes and Two Daughters, and dyed the 21th of March 1643 [1644].

A note of her child bearing

She had by John Morgan 3 Children named John Mary and William. John married the widdow of James Godwin of Wells in Somerset and had Issue by her 4 daughters vizt Gartrude Alice Barbara and Mary Anna. Gartrude (now dead) was married to Captn Richard Prater of Nunny-Castle who hath by her two Sonnes and one daughter. Alice (now dead) was married to a Farmer who lives upon Mendeep above Wells Shee had Children. Barbara married to Mr Parker A Kentish Gent who hath Issue by her at this present 83 - one sonne and two daughters. Mary Anna was married to Thomas Lyte, Son of Thomas Lyte of Martock in Som'rset and hath att present by her 3 Children. [*see on*]

---

34 William Hunt, vicar choral at Wells 1619, prebendary 1622, curate Dinder 1629, died 1639. CCEd.

Mary Morgan was marryed to Captn John Ivye a Wiltsh' Gentle[man] and had Issue by her - Mary, William, John, Thomas and Gartrude. Thomas was taken captive by the Turks about 68 and by their severe usage hee dyed amongst them. John about 77 went a volunteer to Virginia to assist his Majesty against the Rebellious Insurrection of Bacon, and the Rebells there, and dyed in that Country,[35] but the other 3 are still in beeing.

William Morgan (now defunct) marryed Barbara Hodges of Wedmore the daughter of Captn: Hodges and had Issue By her - William, Penbrooke, and Thomas, all which are dead; but William before hee dyed married Mrs Mary Cotherington daughter of the Widdow Cotherington of Todington in Gloucester sheire by whom hee had a daughter but shee is dead, and Williams Wife is now married to Mr Weeks Huntley of Boxwell.

By Hannyball Baskervyle her 2d Husband shee had Thomas, yet alive 1683[36], all the rest viz Nicholas 3rd Henry 2nd William Gartrude Robert George Constance and James are dead. But William by Mary the daughter of Ambrose Stevenson had Twinns (as shee sayes by him) a Sonne and a daughter named William and Mary.

Constance Huntley's three marriages:
Baskerville, Sydney, Lyte

Constance Baskervyle sister of Mary Baskervyle, and 2d daughter to Captn: Nicholas Baskervyle (and Constance Huntley her mayden name his wife) was marryed to Henry Lyte of Lytes Cary in the county of sommersett Gent: the Eldest Son of Thomas Lyte of the place abovesaid, which Thomas Lyte marryed Constance, or Huntly, first wife of Captn: Nicholas Baskervyle, 2d of Sir John Sidney [see below] and 3d wife to the said Thomas Lyte.

By each Husband Shee had 3 Children. By Baskervyle her first Husband Shee had Mary William and Constance By Sidney her 2d Barbara John and Penbrook. By Lyte her third and last Husband Shee had George Constance and Elizabeth. Here we may remember that Thomas Lyte the Father, and Henry Lyte his Son marryed Mother and daughter much about the same time. But to return. This Thomas Lyte her last Husband was a worthy man, and well read in Heraldry, for hee undertook a tedious task in that kinde of Learning - to draw down the Genealogy of King James from Brute, and great princes in England Scotland and Wales and Ireland wth an acco. of the most memorable and

35 Nathaniel Bacon led an unsuccessful rebellion in 1675-6 against the Governor of Virginia, Sir William Berkeley, because settlers wanted protection against the Indians and to occupy their land, and were also suffering from low tobacco prices.
36 The writer.

remarkable things which happened in that large space of time; this work beeing a curious pen-man hee drew on Bellam [vellum] or parchment, illustrating it with the figures of men women and other things agreeable to the History. Hee drew with his pen on parchment 2 of these Geneologyes, one hee presented to King James, who gave him a fair Jewell of Gold in which was sett a Cross of rich diamonds and as I remember, for I was a Child when I saw itt, wth the Kings picture on the other side of it.[37] The other Genealogye set in a frame about 3 yards each square is now to bee seen in the great parlor at Lytes Cary house in Sommersetshier, where now, 1683, lives Henry Lyte the Grand-Son of that Tho. Lyte, who is at present a Leiut Collo: for that part of the County. But to proceed this Tho. Lyte (beeing a great lover of my father Hannibal Baskervyle[38]) hee was my God-father. The other was Dean Barloe of Wells.[39] This Tho. Lyte was the husband of 2 Wifes the which I remember, because of his posyes in their wedding rings. That in the first wifes Ring - was - Lytes Love is little worth - Shee was, as they say, a pretty little woman, and her mayden name was Worth. Constance his 2d wife's this: Constance bee constant, and thy Lyte resplendant. Hee dyed some yeares before the late civill warrs between the King and parliament in England. But his 2d Wife my Grand-Mother did live after him many yeares. Hee was while hee lived a Justice of the peace of good repute in that part of the County where hee dwelt.

The family of Henry Lyte

A N ACCOUNT OF the Issue of Henry Lyte Son of Tho. Lyte by Constance his wife the daughter of Captn Nicholas Baskervyle.

Henry Tho Paul John Edmond - daughters - Constance Hester, Francis, Mary, Elizabeth, Rebecca.

Henry the Eldest Son and now 1683 the present possessor of Lytes Cary, Marryed [blank] the daughter of Mr Hypsley of Enbrow on Mendeep[40], by whome hee hath Issue now alive. Eleven Children vizt. Margarett, Constance, Henry, Katherine, Francis, Phebe, John, Rebecca, Elizabeth, Gartrude, Thomas.

Henry his Eldest Son is lately married, his wifes Maiden Name wee doe not

37 This 'nugget' of information has been repeated in VCH Somerset 3 'Charlton Mackrell', drawn from Proceedings of the Somerset Arch Soc vol 38 p59-73 and vol 204 p124-5.

38 Again shows that the notes were written by TB though possibly based on notes amongst Hannibal's papers.

39 Ralph Barlow was Dean of Wells cathedral 1621 until his death on 20/7/1631. CCEd.

40 Emborough on Mendip.

yet know.

Margaret is marryed to Mr Tho. Harryss a Lawyer in Glastonbury, who hath 2 Children by her now alive.

Constance was marryed to Mr Tho. Cook of Shepton, who is now dead, but left one Child yet alive.

Katherine marryed Mr Tho Cooth of Shepton, who hath Children by her.

Tho. Lyte, who lives now at Martock 5 miles from Lytes-Cary married Gertrude the daughter of [blank] a Gent. as I think of Wiltsh., who hath Issue now alive by her a son and a daughter.

Tho. his son was a Schollar of Trinity Colledge in Oxford, who has marryed Mary Anna the daughter of my Brother Lieut. Collo. John Morgan and has Issue by her 3 Children - Tho. Mary and Anna. Hee hath now a parsonage in Sommersetshier at a Town called [blank].[41]

Constance is lately marryed to a Gold-Smith in Crookhorn, whose Name is.

Paul Lyte served an apprentishipp in Bristol but could not fadge to set up there, but came home again to his Father, who lookt very Severely upon him haveing so many Children to provide for. But upon my return from Barbados going thither to present a Token was sent to him by his Sisters Tennant from thence I took an occasion to incourage my Unckle to venture £100 with my Cosin Paul to Barbadoes; hee did it, and Paul went thither who is now, 83, by his own endeavours and the marriage of a wealthy widdow become a rich man. Hee is a major, a man of good esteem in that Iland and as Mr Pulton a Sea-Man told mee, who brought mee a Letter and Token from him, a Governor of one of the Kings forts in Carlile Bay, hee hath as hee writt in a Letter lately to me by this woman 3 Children.

John Lyte serv'd an apprentish in Bristoll, and is still alive there this present, 83, but being not able to keep his Trade going, hee fell upon In-keeping, and so gets a pretty good livelyhood. By his ingenuity hee has contriv'd a mault-mill turn'd by a mastiffe dogg in a great wheel which also when hee pleaseth Chymes a tune on small Bells. His mannor is at the great Fayres of Bristol viz. St Paul and St James' to hire a consort of musick in his house for that time, which drawes plenty of people thither to eat drink and bee merry; beeing in Town in the time of St James fayre which doth last 3 weeks or more, I went to see him and saw his mault-mill and this jollity.

---

41 Thomas Lyte, Rector of Bleadon, Somerset, 15/12/1682 (gentleman scholar of Trinity 1671-2). BHO Foster. TB never uses the designation step-brother. TB visited Thomas Lyte at Bleadon see Chapter 3 'Oxford': Corpus Christi.

John Lyte marryed the sister of Mr Roots a Gent. in Barbadoes an acquaintancee of mine when there, for hee was then a suitor to my Cozin Mall Tennant a handsome young woman, and did after marry her.
John Lyte had 9 Children by his wife of which are still alive, Henry Elizabeth Mary Constance.

Edmond Lyte was also an apprentice in Bristoll to an ire-monger; hee was marryed and set up his trade. Did live well when I saw him there, but is since dead, and had no Children by his wife.

Constance the eldest daughter of Henry Lyte and Constance his wife was marryed to Mr Brown of Chiltorne, who had Issue by her, a son and a daughter that I have seen. His son was marryed, his wife is now dead, hee lives now on his Fathers Estate in Chilthorn. His daughter Constance is as my Cozin Ivy tells mee, likely to bee marryed to Mr Jones a Parson and Chaplain to Dr Mew, the present Bishop of Bath and Wells.[42] Constance the wife of Mr Brown, the Father, after after (*sic*) his death, was marryed to Mr Giles Lock of Charlton, but is now defunct.

Hester was marryed to Mr Marwood a Devonshier Gent. who had Issue by her, but shee and her Children are all dead.

Frances dyed a Mayd. [space] Mary marryed Mr Robert Brown, the Brother of Mr John Brown of Chilthorn and Unckle to the present Mr John Brown, and hath Issue by him.

Elizabeth was marryed to Mr Stocker a Lawyer in Sommerton, who as I think had Children by her after Bettys death, Mr Stocker Marryed Rebecca his sister and hee lives now wth her att Long Sutton in Sommersettshier and he hath now alive 1 Son and 4 daughters.

The family of Constance Huntley and Sir John Sydney

THE ISSUE OF Sir John Cidney by Constance Huntly her mayden name, Baskervyle her first Husbands name [space] Cidney her second Husbands name. This Cidney had 3 Children by her according to birth Barbara, John and Penbrook. Barbara yet alive is marryed to Paul Dayrell, a Gt. who hath an Estate att Denton by Cudsdown in Oxford shier. They have Issue now alive, Alice, Penbrooke and Mary; Alice and Penbrook are mayds, Mary is marryed to Mr Peirce of Denton and they live there in a fair house built by Peirce Bishop of Bathe and Wells[43] the Grand-father of this young man.

---

42 Peter Mew(s) 1673-84 (translated), bishop of Bath and Wells 1673, and of Winchester 1684-1706; in 1685 he was in arms against the rebels headed by the Duke of Monmouth. CCEd.

43 Bishop: Peirs/Pearce, William (1632-1670), bishop of Peterborough 1630, and of

My Aunt Dayrell and her husband doe now live at Oxford in St Giles parish.

John the only Son of Sir John Sidney by Constance his wife did marry a daughter of Tho: Lyte of Lytes Cary. By Mrs Quorth his first wife had Issue by her, one daughter named Constance, who was marryed to one Farwell of Charlton by Lytes Cary. After this Mr John Cidney went into Virginia where he continues a planter, if yet alive and had Children by an other woman, as my aunt Dayrell his sister told mee. [space] Pembrook Cidney was marryed to Mr Tho. Strowde of Bowlas neer Shepton a rich Clothyer wth whome shee did live happily till her Death. In her mayden-dayes she shee did look after her Mothers Parsonage att Compton-Dundon; I (Tho. Baskervyle) did live there with her 2 or 3 years shee was a woman of good understanding.[44]

The family of Constance (née Huntley) and Thomas Lyte

T̲HE ISSUE OF Tho. Lyte of Lytes Cary by Constance his wife my Grand-Mother. [space] George the Son of George Lyte of Layterton neer Boxwell in Glocestershier is a Lawyer in the Exchequer office, and hath marryed a wife in London, and lives there for the most part; her mayden name I doe not yet know nor whether he hath had any Child by her. [space] Anne his Sister as hee lately told mee, is marryed to one Mr Crompt Wiltshier man. <*inserted in margin:* The 2d wife of George Lyte senior was marry the daughter of Mathew Huntly of Boxwell; he dyed in 81 after the apearance of that great blazing Star.>[45]

But to return. George the Father was a man very pleasant in his conversation haveing Country Jokes att will in his discourse which as hee sent them of would Stir up mirth and laughter in the Company. He was to his Ability a good House-keeper and never without a good vessel of strong Beer which he called his Governour and I have drank at his house in glass bottles excellent beer of two and 3 years old and when he had a humour to be merry, he would put on an Oxford Square Cap and so take up a Cheerying Cupp with his friends. His second wife Mary Huntley (who was his first love) did dye before him and he in her absence having little injoyment of himself did quickly march after.

Bath and Wells 1632, until his death at Walthamstow April 1670, buried there. CCEd.

44 Compton Dundon was a prebend of Wells cathedral. The Parsonage was called the Old Rectory in 2006, largely rebuilt in the early 19th century. VCH Somersetshire 9.

45 The remark about the star hints at TBs interest in astrology.

And much about the same time went off, his intimate friend and Companion Colonel Ivy of Malmsbury Abbey.

Constantine the second son of Thomas Lyte by Constance his 2d wife did marry two wives his first wife was Mrs Pitts of Elme in Sommerseet neer Bath who died without any Issue by him; she came to an untimely end by swallowing a Prune stone which stuck thwart her throat till she dyed.

His 2d wife was one Mrs Leaversuch of Vallis or Vallyes neer Bath, by whome he had also no Issue; he died since his brother George Lyte.

Elizabeth the daughter of Thomas Lyte and Constance his wife had two Husbands, her first husband was Sir Richard Crane a German born and Captaine of Prince Rupert's life Guard 'till he lost his life in the siege of Bristol when besieged, by the Parliament forces. He was shot in the thigh and dy'd of that wound and lyes buried in Bristol Cathedrall, who had two sons by his wife vizt Richard and George but both are dead without any known Issue.

Her 2d Husband was Mr Seymour of Bitton in Gloucester shier neer Bath by whome she had severall children of both sexes whose names I do not know, but I have heard, her Eldest son John is now a Captaine of the Kings Guardes in London. But she and her husband now 1684 are both dead; she was in her mayden dayes an incomparable handsome woman *added in large print letters the following* And George her 2d son by Sir Richard Crane was by report a very lonely man.

He was breed up in the Duke of Sommersets family and dy'd at Charleton in Wiltshiere in the Flower of his Age.

The Huntley family

An account of the family of the Huntleys so far as I know Constance Huntly (my Grandmother[46]) the wife of Captain Nicholas Baskerville had a brother and a sister viz. Matthew Huntley the Lord of Boxwell and Layterton and Mary the wife of William Ivy Esquire of Malmsbury who was owner of the Abby house in that Town. Matthew Huntly married the daughter of Barron Snig, a Barron of the Exchequer and had Issue by her, Matthew, George, Henry, William, who went a Captaine to take Jamaica, and died there, and also Gabriel, his brother, and he had daughters by her, Mary, Alice, Ann:

George the 2nd brother who was heir to his fathers estate married Silvester daughter to Mr Weekes a Councellor of Wells, and had Issue by her, George, Matthew, Weekes, Edmond, Mary, Frances, Susan, Jane and some others;

46 See earlier account of Constance Huntly.

George his eldest som succeeded to his fathers estate and dyed a Batchelor and at present his brother Matthew Huntly is Lord of the Manors of Boxwell and Layterton and hath lately married one Mis Amy Guise who died in Childbed with her Child. Weeks Huntly hath married Mary Codrington the widdow of William Morgan and hath Issue by her a daughter, 1684.

Mary Huntly is married to Mr Alde of Hardwick by Chepsto[47] and hath Issue by her 3 or 4 sons, and a daughter, the other daughters are yet unmarried.

Mary Huntly as before Quoted was married to George Lyte.

Alice Huntly was married but had no Children as we know of.

Ann married Mr Smith a Councellor at Law in London, and had had Issues by him.

A further account of the Huntleys, taken out of a record at Lytes Cary:

John Huntly was born in November 1570

Elizabeth was born the 4th day of February 1574 [1575]

William Huntley was born the 28 of June 1577

Matthew Huntley was born the 26 of January 1580 [1581]

Constance Huntley was born the 13 of January 1583 [1584]

bracketed together and the comment added: These 5 were brothers and sisters. But Mary the wife of William Ivy abovesaid I do not find in this record of Lytes Cary.

Mary Baskerville my mother was born the 6 of January 1602 [1603]

A note added later in brown ink but in the same hand as the previous account of families

Thomas Baskerville had Issue by Marey

the daughter of Edward and Mary Hunney

2 sons

first Thomas Baskerville died and buried att suninwell[48]

second Matthew Thomas Baskerville yeat alive

An account by Hannibal of his birth and baptism

Folio 2 of Oxford, Bodleian Libraries, MS. Rawl. D. 810 is introduced with the statement: 'A transcript of Some writings of Hanniball Baskervile Esqr. as they were found scattered here and there in his manuscripts and Books of Account. And first a Remembrance of some Monuments and Reliques in the Church of St

47 Where TB stayed when investigating Tintern. See Chapter 6.
48 Thomas the Bastard son of Mary Honey was buried 13th April 1685 in Sunningwell. Kingsley, Landed Families.

Dennis and thereabouts in France by Hanniball Baskervyle who went into that country with an English Ambassador in the Reigne of King James.[49] *This has not been transcribed.*

The birth place of Hannibal Baskerville as we found (thus) written by himself in one of his books of accounts.

April the 5 1597 I was born at a Town in Piccardy called St Vallery where was a deadly plague among the French, but it did not infect any of the English Soldiers. I was Christened by one Mr Man the Preacher and I had all the Captains about 32 to be my Godfathers, it being the Custome so of the wars when the Generall hath a son (they say) but two only stood at the Font or great Bason, one was Sir Arthur Savage, the other I can not remember his name; Sir Arthur Chichester was there and other great men that have been since my father, Sir Thomas Baskerville, died of a burning feavour at a Town called Picqueny. I was then 9 weeks old.[50]

> *After this paragraph Thomas Baskerville resumes the account of the family*
> The maiden name of my Fathers Mother was Mary Throckmorton. Her Fathers name was Sir Thomas Throckmorton who lived at a place called Tortworth in Gloucester shier.
>
> She had a brother called Sir William Throckmorton who had an estate at Clower wall in Gloucester shier (which place I went to see in Summer 1684.]
>
> But his son or Grandson Sir Baynam Throckmorton was an ancient Justice of the Peace in these parts being lately dead who left no son but daughters, his estate in Clowerwall is now sold to one Mr Stevens whose son as the report goes here, is to marry one of Sir Baynam's daughters.

The family of Mary Throckmorton and Sir James Scuadamore

THE SECOND HUSBAND of my Fathers mother, was Sir James Scudamore of Homlasey[51] in Hereford shier who had Issue by her, my Lord Scudamore, Sir Barnabas Scudamore and James Scudamore the names of these sons I heard my Father speak of and I have heard him speak of 3 daughters vizt. one

49 The ambassador might have been Henry Peacham, who was engaged as tutor to the sons of Thomas Howard, Earl of Arundel, and to Hannibal Baskerville. 'Introduction', Peacham's Compleat gentleman (1906), ix. Hannibal himself records he went to France in 1617. Bodleian Library, MS Rawl. D. 859 f.6.

50 Hannibal matriculated 1612 at Brasenose College, Oxford. Kingsley, Landed families..

51 Holme Lacy.

married to Sir John Scudamore of Bellingham, in Hereford shier, another to Sir Thomas Ferris who lived at Bow by London, which Sir Thomas Ferris then a prisoner I think in the King's Bench came to see my father (I then being wth him) at his Lodging there at London.

What children they had I know not. The 3rd was married to one Mr Hicford who is yet alive; as Mr Hyde lately told me and he lives at or by North Arson[52] in Oxford shier. But what Children she had or hath now alive I cannot tell.

The Lord Scudamore had a son and a daughter, his son died before him, but was married and left a son, who is now Lord Scudamore anno dmi 1685 and lives at Homlasey two or 3 miles from Hereford Town and hath married the Earl of Exeters daughter.

The daughter of my fathers brother or old Lord Scudamore, was married to Mr Dutton of Sherborne in Oxford shier, they had one Child but it quickly died.

Now what Issue Sir Barnaby Scudamore had, I know not, but his sister who married Sir John Scudamore of Bellingham had two sons, Scollars in Oxford which kinsmen I know.

Sir John[53] the eldest son was of Christ Church and after the restauration of King Charles the second was made Knight of the Bath at his Coronation; my other kinsman who's Christian name I have forgot,[54] was of Alsouls and went into France and died there. What other Children their father had I know not. But he was killed by David Hyde at the Toulsey in Bristol. The occasion as I have heard Thus:

This David Hyde being deputy Governor under Sir Barnaby Scudamore when there he tooke some what in dudgeon from Sir Barnaby and because he could not have his will on him, vow'd to be revenged on the next Scudamore he met, and accordingly meeting this Sir John Scudamore of Bellingham on the Toulsey in Bristol as aforesd, which Gentleman having no accquaintance with David Hyde, now knew nothing of his grudge to Sir Barnab. David by provoking words and his sword first half drawn, forc'd Sir John to draw his sword first out of the scabbard, after which David Hyde quickly drew his, and in their encounter ran Sir John into the eye of which wound he died. David

52 North Aston?
53 John Scudamore (1630-1684), son of Sir John Scudamore of Ballingham in Herefordshire. Student at the Middle Temple 1648.
54 William Scudamore, baptised 1638, brother of John (above), Brasenose College 1656, fellow of All Souls College 1664; Hearne writes that he was told this man was "condemned in France to be broke upon ye wheel for coyning, but the sentence was got off by the interposition of the English Embassador".

Hyde for this fact was tried by a Councill of war but was quitted because Sir John Scudamore drew first.

After the folios concerned with family history, two and a half pages are devoted to moral reflections, for example 'He that oppresseth the innocent shall have an evill end', *displaying Baskerville's frame of mind in his later years. These are not transcribed.*

THREE LETTERS FROM THOMAS BASKERVILLE TO HIS FATHER

Oxford, Bodleian Libraries, MS. Rawl. D. 859 *ff.58, 60 & 61*
This collection of loose papers is said to have been made by Hannibal Baskerville; they have been mounted in a book.

No 45

Good

Father since my last all the account I can give is this that I am at a great uncertainty as ever when my Lord Hatton will imploy mee: when I went last to waite on Mr Clemens (formerly his Gentleman) twas his pleasure scornfully to give mee the Title of Captain and this is all I have yet gotten from them.

The King and queen are still at Tunbridge where Sir George Barker Clarke of the Gren Cloth tooke his bane by drinking the water and is dead. The King to retrench his expences will put his family to board wages. From Ireland wee heard that our loveing frind Dr Hall bishop of Kilalla is dead. At Dublin one Sir William Petty is grown famous for making a Ship with two bottomes, which against the judgement of most men that saw her hath performed a voyage to Holly Head in the Iland of Anglesey (Wales) and is since come safe to Dublin bringing in her amongst other persons of quality the Bishop of Offery who was latly at London. In her returne shee was accompanied by the Offery pacquet boat one of the best sayling Cacthes of Ireland against the wind, but in 4 howers time the Gemini (Castor and Pollux, or new Invention by which names shee commonly is called) against a winde ran her out of sight leaveing the Cacth a stearne.[55] This is al the news for the present I can picke up in the Citty but when time doth furnish me with more I shall not faile to

---

55 TB's Memoir of Tom Hyde contains more about the double-bottomed boat. See Chapter 6 'Miscellaneous Writings'.

Communicate it who am
West[minster] August 11   Yours in obedience
1663   Tho: Baskervile

Down the side of the letter is written 'The King is now come to London'
*On the back is the address in large letters on the originally folded small square of
paper:*

'For his honored father
Mr Hanniball Basker
vile Esq at Mr Wests
in Abingdon.
Berkes Post paid 2d'

No 46

*This letter is slightly torn at the edge. It is written in a print style which is like the
copy of TB's will in this collection of papers.*

Good
Father on Munday was sennight Mr Curtayne the Draper of Abingdon sent mee
to send him 20s which I owed him. And on Twesday my Landlord Stevenson
haveing buisnes in Abingdon and coming on foot I did make bold to come to
Abingdon, and then payd Mr Curtaine. And haveing dyned with Mr Blower
went back to Stanton with my Landlord. Where I am expecting an answer
from my letter I sent by Mr John Hyde to Mr Forbinch, whether to repaire
without Mr Forbinches answer and allowance. I think it neither discretion or
good manners. And so I hope you will excuse me and think so too. Though Sir
if it were well pleasing to you I could willingly stay here where I am seasoned
to the aire and place, for the time I was at Mr Forbinches I was greevously sick.
Mr Blower I doe thanke him proposed my removall to Rowlright to his Cosen
Dixons, but Sir a gentlemans house will not square with my allowance, which
in a farmers house I am well contented with and doe humbly and hartily thank
you for it. I have been here ever since I was at Bayworth last, and could with
you w[illing?] be pleased to enjoyne me to reside in this parish, where being
farr from market townes I am lesse in the reach of expences. And fishing takes
up my sp[are] howers. However I doe willingly and humbly submit to your
pleasure. And desiring your pardon and forgiveness against this good time
approaching your blessing for the time to come I rest

Stanton [Harcourt] Aprill   Your dutifull Son
the 2nd 1664   Thomas Baskerville

No 47

The handwriting of this letter is quite different and might well be a copy as the signature is in the same hand as the letter.

Good

Father I Bless God for it, since my last sharpe cold in may, I have been in a pretty good state of health. Mrs Stephenson had her share un't and her Husband since that has been much afflicted with the same distemper, but is now to our comfort pretty well again. I have had a longing desire these many dayes to present you with some good fish but Perch are so scarce in our waters I do seldome catch any but now Providence having brought a good dish to my Hookes, I have sent them by our neighbour Goody Wesley. Sir I was lately at Bayworth, and would gladly have paid my filliall respects to your person, had I not been conscious of your commands to the contrary; but under favour the cause why I do mention that, is to communicate what I have learned from a Soldier, who did quarter in our town when the King was last at Oxford; for going by the Quarry, where I was glad to see your Plantation prosper so well, I remember your Hops being strong and ranke, were grown so far above the poles, that many did turn down against the earth, now this Soldier being a skillful man, and bred up in those Countreys where Hops are much planted, as he was dressing our Hops did advise us to get the longest Poles we could ; for said he if the strings do overshoot the Poles and grow double, they do seldome bear good Hops : now the want of this knowledge in your woodmen who do cut your Poles much shorter than they need (for they might stripe them to the top sprigs) being likly to bring you some damage doth imbolden me to give you this information that so for the future they may amend that errour. So in hopes you will pardon what is amiss   I rest your dutifull Son
Moridge[56] July 16. 1666.   Tho: Baskervile

THOMAS BASKERVILLE'S WILL

Oxford, Bodleian Libraries, MS. Rawl. D. 859 f.75
This copy of his will, almost certainly written by him but not signed, is amongst the papers bound together in D.859. It was written on a very large piece of paper, the

56 Comments about the garden in Chapter 4 Journey 10 suggest that the Baskervilles owned the house.

lines going horizontally across the width, but is damaged along folds made to fit it in the volume in which it has been bound.

IN THE NAME of God Amen I Thomas Baskervile to save my Estate from sharking people and to gratifie such as depend upon me when my soul shall leave this body to live with Almighty God in the spirit do thus dispose of my estates at Bayworth and Suningwell in the county of Berkes

Item I give and bequeath unto my loving Sonne Matthew Thomas Baskervile and to his children and to the heires Executors Administrators and Asignes of the said children All and every my lands and Tenements with the apurtenances lying and being in Bayworth and Suningwell aforesaid in the county of Berkes. upon condition Nevertheless that hee my said sonn and his children him or them to whom the said lands shall descend shall and do pay or cause to be paid out of the rentes Issues and Profits thereof unto his Mother my loving bedfellow and good wife dame Mary Baskervile as shee has made it apear by bearing me sonns by bringing home my goods when taken from me and by waiting upon me some yeeres during my stay or life in this mortall body the yearly sum of Fifty pounds of lawfull money of England for and during the term of her naturall life by quarterly payments, the first payment thereof to begin and to be made upon the first quarter day that shall happen after my decease and I do hereby charge my said landes and tenements with the payment hereof.

I(t)em I give and bequeath unto Mary Hunny my wive's mother Ten pounds yearly during her natural life to be paid her out of my Estates in Bayworth and Suningwell beginning payment therof the first quarter day after my decease and I do hereby charge my said lands and tenements with the payment hereof.

Item it is my will that the said Mary Huny after my decease do injoy the house and garden wherin she formerly did live rent free during her naturall life.

Item it is my will that my said wife Mary Baskervile if she do outlive her mother the said Mary Huney be paid that Ten pounds yearly which I gave her mother this ten pounds and the aforesaid Fifty pounds making it Sixty pounds to be paid her yeerly during her naturall life the first payment thereof to be made the first quarter day after my decease and I do hereby charge my said lands and Estate with the payment hereof. Item it is my will that my said wife Mary Baskervile, and her mother the said Mary Huney do live in my house at Bayworth during their pleasure [*very thick paper torn at the fold here*] and have the use of such rooms to lodge and dress victualles in, as convenient for their occasions and the use of my goods and Fewel to serve their occasions whilst they stay and live in Bayworth house. But if they are pleased to live in Bayworth, Suningwell or elsewhere I doe allow my said wife Mary Baskervile and her mother the said Mary Hunney 7 loades of Fewell yeerly that is 4 loades of shrowd or block-wood 2 loades of Furle and one load of Ferne. This to be paid them yeerly during their naturall lives and to the longest liver of either of them at such times when 'tis fit to cut Fewell on my estate in Bayworth and Suningwell. But if they do live to far off it will not quit costes to carry it theither then my will is that they be paid by my Heires Executors Admistrators or Assignes the value of it in money.

Item if my wife Mary Baskervile and her mother the said Mary Hunny are minded to dwell in their cottage house in Bayworth then I doe give unto them the ground by their cottage house now rented by Robert Hunny 1694 during their naturall lives and the longest liver of either of them and timber to repaire or new build the house at thier pleasure.

Item I give to them if they do live in the said cottage house and to the longest liver of either of them some goods of mine in Bayworth house for the chamber kitchin and buttry uses And if my said wife Mary Baskervile doe live elsewhere and have occasion for such goods I doe here charge my Heires Executors Administrators and Assignes to let her have one third part of my household goods.

Item I commit the care Education and management of my said sonne Matthew Thomas Baskervile unto my loving wife Mary Baservile and I commit the management of any said sonne's Estate to my said wife till he comes to yeers of disretion. But in case it shall happen my said sonne to dye or depart this life in his maiority or when at age and yeeres of discretion without making a will or leaving any other obligations on my lands to whom God grant a long and healthy life Then I do give and bequeath my said lands and tenements aforesaid in Bayworth and Suningwell unto my loving wife dame Mary Baskervile during her naturall life with this charge that she doe keep Bayworth house in good reparation and the gardens and plantations in such good order as rather to add to it then ?deminish the beauty of them. And for timber I doe allow her to cut down as much as [*over page*] is necessary for the reparation of Bayworth house and the new building of any part thereof. And to order such timber to be cut down as is necessary for the reparation of the Tenants houses. And her cottage house. And such yeerly Rentes as are then paid by my tenants for my lands I do give and bequeath unto my said wife Mary Baskervile during her naturall life. But I doe not allow her to sell any lands nor to make or let any Estates of Coppyholds or Leases in Bayworth nor Suningwell. And after her decease if God be so pleased to dispose of things I do give and bequeath my said lands and Tenements unto William the supposed sonne of my brother William Baskervile and to his Heires Executors Administrators and Assignes. And in case he doth dye without children then I doe give and bequeath my said lands and Tenements in Bayworth and Suningwell unto Mary the supposed daughter of my brother William Baskervile her Heires Executors Administrators and Assignes with this charge that if she hath a sonne who comes to inherit my estate hee write and name himself Thomas Baskervile.

Item it is my will that William Henny and his wife dow injoy my house and garden wherein they now live during their naturall lives paying yeerly for it seven shillings.

Item it is my will that Robert Hunny and his wife doe injoy the house and garden where they now live during their naturall lives paying yeerly six shillings for it. They and their wives behaving themselves with love and duty as becomes good Tenants and kinsfolk of their landlord my son Matthew Thomas Baskervile. And on condition they doe not troble nor molest my said heires him or them on the score of debtes due from me to their father William Hunny. vizt. Legacyes given by their father to the aforesaid William and Robert Hunny.

Item I doe give unto my said wife Mary Baskervile tow Hundred pounds sterling we have in a hole if it be not spent before I die.

Item I give unto my poor kinswoman widow An Crompt now at Caln in Wilts five pounds.

Item I give unto Mrs Stevenson of Mooride Stanton Harcourt Parish such goods of mine as are in her house after my decease. Item I do give unto William my brother William Baskervile's supposed sonn Ten pounds And to Mary his supposed daughter Ten pounds and to Mary his supposed wife Five pounds. this mony to be paid to them in the term of five yeeres after my decease if My Heires do injoy the estate I leave them quietly so many yeeres.

Item I doe give five pounds ten shillings to the poor of Suningwell and the poor of Hinton.

viz. tow pounds ten shillings to the poor of Suningwell and £2 10s od to the poor of Hinton. Item all the rest of my Estate goods and Chattles whatsoever I give unto my said Loving Sonn Matthew Thomas Baskervile whom I pray God to bless and whom I make my sole Executor. As to a good Steward to manage and spend it wisely for his own good and Honor.

For on the Eleventh day of Janiary 1666
A ray of light I saw that day
Enter my heart with heat and joy
Saying these words unto me then
King of Jerusalem

A DESCRIPTION OF SUNNINGWELL AND OF ITS FAVOURED SITUATION FOR FISHING

Oxford, Bodleian Libraries, MS. Rawl. D. 810 ff.13 to 14b
This description precedes Baskerville's observations on Oxford and Oxford colleges and fellows.

IN THE YEAR 1672. An ancient Elm being decayed near St Dunstons Cross, in the upper feild in the parish of Sunningwell. This Elme was cut down and a young Oake planted in the place by the Commands of Thomas Baskervyle then Lord of the manour. This Oake was taken out of his Garden by his House att Bayworth, and might bee then about 20 years old, and now att the present writing hereof, June 18th 1683: This Oake may bee about 31 years growth. This Oake is here ingrosed in this Booke for a memoriall to future posterity, That so they may observe the growth of itt; Because wee hope our Successours, in regard it stands in so eminent a place will not cut itt down: or shrowd itt, but lett it grow for the Comfort and Shade of man and Beast.

There is also sett near itt Some Elms and Pear-Trees beeing a year or two after this Oake was sett.

Wee may here also remember Since wee mention Saint Dunston's Cross, though none of the people now liveing remember any Cross standing there, That in Sunningwell before the late warrs began in 1641 were standing fower Crosses, but without any memoriall of Dedication to any Saint, as I could ever here the Country people Speake of. The places where these Crosses stood are yet known.

By one of these Crosses whose pedestall was neer it now groweth a pear-tree sett there by my honoured Father Hanniball Baskervyle.

An other stood by the pound without the Church-yard. A Third in the Church yard on the northern side of the Church, And the Fowerth att the Towns end in the Lane neer the Green, Which Crosses were thrown down by Sir William Wallers Souldyers (as our people say) not long after The famous Cross of Abbingdon was tumbled down, In which place is now Erected the bravest Markett house att this day in England 1683.

But to proceed. Sunningwell was a place of greater Concern then other Villages hereabout; for in former dayes when Pillgryms were allowed the liberty to ramble, Here they had a House of entertainment, which is now in the possession of the widdow Pinnell. And since I came into this Country, here were some Utensills belonging to the Kitchinn remaining viz. a great Pott Large Spitt and other Things.

Sunningwell took its Name from a dellicate Spring which ariseth, and makes a faire Poole neer the Church. In commemoration of which Blessing, and theyr thanks to God for itt, the People of this Towne with the Priest before them in his Surplice, after they have been att prayers in the Church doe yearly every holy Thirsday goe in procession thither, and read a Gospell.

With reflections on this well the people here will have theyr Joke, and Say

That　　　　　All the Maydes in Sunningwell
　　　　　　　May daunce in an Egg's Shell.

The Names of the Chief Inhabitants now alive in Sunningwell and Bayworth are these Thomas Baskervyle Lord of the Mannor att his House in Bayworth. Henry Jones Minnister lives in the Parsonage house. Charles Holloway a Councellor (whose Father was a Sergeant att Law) hath a good Freehold in Town, on which his Father built a faire House called Bendly Farme, lives in Oxford. Christopher Blower an understanding Lawyer hath a Coppy-hold Here. John Stevenson a Coppy holder etc. *Added in brown ink* <Brookland: Hall greene west Palmer Pinnell Baasley> *and squeezed in down the margin with a mark to insert the names after Baasley* <Sherife Channey Stacy Badcock Brathars Clark Deadman Vinner Robinson Hunney Turner Belcher Cusome Beesley Gillit Cleaseant[?] names of the people in the parish of Sunniwell anno 1691.>

The most eminent Land-marke which the People of Sunningwell, and Bayworth can take notice of is the famous Chochinlo Hill cast upon the Top of Barkeshier downes, right over against Abbingdon and it is a meridian, or Twelve a Clock Line to my house att Bayworth and this is the Beacon Hill for that part of the Country, as wee have another upon a Mount in Barkshier above Ensom Ferry.[57]

Here is to bee noted, That in the way between Bayworth and Sunningwell, is a Fish-pond which hath been three or 4 hundred years a making, and every yeare people at worke in it.

To unfold the Riddle of this discourse, you may know it was thus effected viz. When the famous Abby of Abbingdon was to bee built, of which now so little remaines of its Ruines, that there is scarce one stone left upon another, The builders made Choyce of this Place to digg theyr stones in, and when they had finished that Ediffice and other Fabricks of Consern, as Sunningwell

---

57　Could this be the down above Chilton in Berkshire (SU49990 82695)? Beacon
　　Hill is on the western side of Wytham hill; SP45109 07985.

Tower, Radley Tower the Ocke-bridge etc: were brought to perfection, the people of this Town after this Quarry was neglected, for it is a very hard stone and requires much labour to race [raise?] itt, and few Masons now a dayes will bee perswaded to worke itt, The people of Sunningwell, and Bayworth did yeerly carry out Rubbish, and small stones to mend their high wayes, untill att length in the Reign of Charles the first my Father Hannyball Baskervyle conceiveing it would make a fish-poole, was att the charge of cutting a passage through a Rock, and so brought some Springs out of the Heath to run into itt, and now att this present writeing, 1683, att the Charge of my Father and Selfe, it has in it a vine-yard, Hop-yard, Kitching-garden, and most of the Eatable fruites of this Nation. And in the water of this Quarry, doe breed, and prosper these kinds of Fish - Tench, Carpes, Perch, Roofe and Gudgeon. Here I may also note, that some waters doe naturaly bring forth some sort of Fish, without the helpe of Generation of those of the like Species; for this poole in my Father's dayes after hee had made itt, and turn'd in running, or liveing water, itt brought forth very large mussells, and now again in my Dayes, for itt was dry, and had no fish in it, for above twenty yeares, after I had turn'd the running water in again, and stored it with Fish a second Tyme, itt brought forth mussells, and water-snayles.

It may be ranked among some of the greatest blessings that befall mankinde to have their habitations neer a Hill, Especially such as are of easy ascents, midling heights, with smooth and pleasant ground to ride, or walke on; For there they may enjoy a serene and Healthy aire.[58] And if they be seated in such a Country as our Sunningwell and Wootton-hill, which have brave plaines, or Vales on both sides interlaced with goodly Rivers, as noble and allureing prospects. For here upon our Heath, you may pry, or look into some part of ten Countyes, as I have made itt out by Ocular Experience. Theyr names are as followeth, - first the Hills whereon you stand are in Barkshier - 2dly Through a Glade beyond Wallingford between Barkshier, and Oxford-shier downs you perceive Hamshier; Eastward you see Oxfordshier, Buckingame, Hertford, and Bedford-shier to the Northward, Northampton shier, south-west Wiltshier, and north-west Gloster shier, and beyond Glocestershier, the tops of the mountaines of Monmouthshier; For when I was att Chidworth Beacon in Glocestershier, I could see the mountaines in Monmouthshier and our Wootton Shottover, and Wytam-Hills, and in a very clear aire from Wooton-heath, I have perceived the tops of the Welch-mountaines above the Levell of the Cotswoald Hill.

---

58 TB was alert to good views and his house at Bayworth was on rising ground from where there were extensive views.

Now as to our hills, and the Country in which they stand itt is a peninsula, beeing almost incircled, or girt about with the pleasant Rivers, in which lye Sixteen Country-Townes, most of which are good Mannours, besides the famous Town of Abbingdon. For that neck of Land that lyes between the River Ock and the Temes, is hardly five miles over, so that an Angler for variety and pleasure of that kinde cannot fix his habitation any where else in England in a more delightfull Country than this Peninsula, because the plaines and vales of this Country surrounding those Hills are interlaced with Rivers, and Streames to admiration, for admitt you dwelt at Chiswell Sir Edward Morris his house, and had a minde to goe over your own wat'ry bounds of this peninsula, 3 Miles going will sett you on the Bankes of Charwell, 5 Miles brings you to Emlod or Evenlod by Casington. 5 Miles more to Windrush which streames through Moore and Stan-lake. 3 Miles bring you to the Ock, which breeds the best Eiles, and fower miles more to Milton-stream, where you may finde some fish, and to conclude 6 miles will sett you down on the bankes of Thame beyond Wheatley. Those Journeyes may bee easily gone a foot, if you rise betimes, and you may enjoy the mornings fishing, but a Horse back with a forenoons Journey in the Summer, you may see more and divert a fishing on theyr pleasant Banks in the afternoon, for you may goe to the Kenett by Newberry to the Lodden beyond Redding to Wickham-streame, and to the Ouse att Buckingame, and with a Summers Dayes Travayle, You may see So many with those afore rehears'd, allowing 50 miles to that stretch of way, which men with good Horses doe easily performe in a day, That perhaps they may very near equall for Number all the other Rivers in England, which are above a dayes journey from this place, for in such a dayes journey you see Colnbrooke, Guilford River, Norbery streame by Sir Richard Sty-dolfe's house, which in dry Summers is lost under ground for a Mile or 2, and then comes to light againe, if it bee not a branch of the Guilford, or Wandsor Rivers, But to goe on with their Names, Wandsor River Lucem Streame, bow-River Bainford stream, Walford River, if it bee not a branch of Bowe-river, the New river, the Ouse att Newport-Pannell if that bee not the same att Buckingame, and, Came att Camebridge, Nine at Toster, and Northampton, Stowre att Shipton and Stratford Avon, Strowde water, and Severn below Teuxbury, Christyan Ma-vern Avon which runs to Bathe, and Salisbury Avon which goes into the Sea att Christ Church, Ferfatt River and East Leach Streame, for that which runs from Cubberly Wells to Rentcombe and Cirencester is the Tems, and Crickladd streame which meets the Tems at Cricklad. Att the head of this Streame, a Gentleman of my Name well skilled in the art of Conveying water, Mr Thomas Baskervyle, who now lives with the Lord Ward at Dursley Castell in Staffordshier Hee did propose to the Lord Chancellour Hide a feasibility of uniting the Avon and Tems and so to make good a Navigation for Boates from Bristoll and Bathe up the river till they got into Tems and then down-Streame to Oxford and London.

This Gentleman in 81 Takeing my House in his way from London homeward I fell into discourse with him concerning this thing. Hee told mee there was a possibility of doing itt, and that if ever itt were done there would be such a stock of water in the Dikes that the River Tems Should never want water but bee supplyed from thence for Navigation in the driest Summer.

I have done my Journey a fishing, and shall now give you the Names of such fish, as Scud, and Prime in our neighbouring Rivers which att the first you would think were more than really they bee.

On a time travailing for my pleasure to the Town of Nottingame, where I discoursd my Land lord about the river Trent. Hee told mee it got its Name from 30 mannours lying by itt, and 30 Severall Kindes of Fish breed In it, but when wee went to name them, wee had much adoe to finde them there - I mean eatable Fish,[59] But to return the names of such fish as are bred in the Tems, and the rivers which run into it thereabouts are these

Pike, the fresh-water sharke, Trout, Perch, Carpe Tench the Balsammicke, or healing fish, Chub, Barbell, Roache, Dace, Roof Blay Gudgeon Minno Cull, Loche, Banstekell, Crabsfish the freshwater Lobster, Eyles, and Griggs, if they are two distinct kindes.

Here are also found in these waters Lampurns, which I suppose are young Lampry. Att Stanlake they call them Prides, where I have seen them thrown out with the mudd of the river, with designe to bayte their Eyle-hookes. This kinde of fish I suppose may come up with the fry of young Eyeles but if they stay alwayes here, they doe not thrive, and grow great, like Eyles in our Water.

The Muskell, or fresh-water Oyster may pass here among the rest for an eatable Fish, but with the best dressing of an insippid Taste. Here wee also finde the Neptune or Sea-God of the Rivers exercising his Power on the Land and water. That strange amphibious Creature the Otter, who when his Gutts begin to grumble for meat makes no more adoe, but into the Water hee goes, and presently pulls a great Eyle out of his hole, and haveing landed him, falls to it without grace, eats up the body as far as the navyll, and leaves the Tayle for a hungry Herron.

The water-Rott will have his share of good fish.

Froggs swimm here in their time of gendring, and so doth the loathsome

59 See the journey in Chapter 4, journey 10.

Toade and Evett.
>   And so without fayle
>   I can name no more but the water snayle.

But it's time for me now to leave these waters, and clear my sight again on our Hills, from whence you behold and look down upon the noblest University in Europe, that far fam'd Citty Oxford, beeing sweetly hugg'd in the pleasant arms of those 2 pure Rivers - the Tems and Charwell whose timely floods inrich the meadowes with excellent herbage.

The Baskerville coat of arms.

3
OXFORD

THOMAS BASKERVILLE KNEW Oxford well, and spent time there visiting friends and acquaintances. He was invited to college feasts and explored college and university buildings. He noted that 'my Honoured father Hannibal Baskerville' was of Oriel College, though college records indicate Hannibal matriculated at Brasenose College. Thomas himself did not attend the University; but he claims acqaintance with many men from the various colleges, and conceived of a book on Oxford, the university and the colleges drawing on friends who could supply information.[1] He specifically acknowledged this help, naming the men responsible; many seem to have been young and perhaps earned some money by helping Baskerville. Thomas Stevenson, Baskerville's godson, may have been of particular assistance. The first individual Oxford college history, of Balliol college by Henry Savage, was extensively copied or summarised though in general Savage's accounts of 'Eminent men' are not relevant to the Oxford described by Baskerville, being much concerned with clerical preferments; at the same time their names prompted three of his characteristic lengthy 'diversions'.[2]

One such diversion was suggested by Savage's discussion of the early Lollard John Wycliff (Baskerville seems to have misread the man's name, taking the 'two fs' as an 'es'), leading him to relate his experience of the Levellers who stayed in Bayworth. Baskerville's ebullience led to other interesting if loosely relevant excursions outside the university, suggested by the name or story of a college man, some of which have not previously been published. He visited Farnham because the bishop of Bath and Wells drew an ample income from the market. One diversion prompted by the name of an Oriel gentleman, Christopher Coward, gives an illuminating insight into a village inn. Two

1 The names he quoted can nearly all be verified, thanks to *Alumni Oxoniensis*, BHO Foster.
2 Savage, *Balliofergus*.

Oxford cathedral of Christ Church, the truncated church of the former Priory of St Frideswide, round which Christ Church college was built. (Photo Glyn Jones)

which are quite long are presented separately here in chapter 6 of this book, 'Miscellaneous Writings'.

Baskerville creates a picture of late seventeenth century life. He gives a first-hand account of Oxford at a period shortly after the disruption of the civil wars and commonwealth; he points to the rebuilding of the colleges which was taking place and in writing about Queens College there is an interesting comment on the increase of chimneys and fireplaces. The contrast between the university with the relatively small number of students which Baskerville noted and the university in the twenty-first century is striking, as is the dominance of the church and of the 'gentry'.

A large part of this manuscript where it is of topographical interest or concerned Thomas Baskerville personally has been transcribed here. A small number of omissions can be read in the Oxford Historical Society volume *Collectanea* vol XLVII (1905.)

~~~

A DESCRIPTION OF OXFORD WITH OTHER INCIDENTS

Oxford, Bodleian Libraries, MS. Rawl. D. 810 ff.12 to 89
The manuscript has folio numbers inserted at intervals. The folio number on which each college entry begins has been indicated here. Baskerville seems to have allowed three folios for each college or hall but some contain only brief amounts of text or are blank. The writing is with one exception uniform throughout and is almost without alteration or correction; it is a formal and elaborate hand and it is difficult to discriminate between capital and lower case letters. The English is closer to modern usage than some of Thomas Baskerville's writings. Lists of college principals and fellows have generally not been transcribed but omissions are noted. Only men connected in some way with Baskerville have been identified. Oriel College *is the only heading inserted by Baskerville.*

On the page before the account of Sunningwell in Chapter 2 'Life and Kin' there is a sentence about musicians ('the Musick') at Christ Church (f.12):

THE MUSICK DO now since the Death of Bishop Fell come into Christ-Church and play in long winternights and twelfe Day they are to play at dinner to the Schollers in the Hall where each Scholler of concern do give the musick halfe a crown a peice and after dinner they Retreat to the Common Fyre Room where they play to the Masters of Art till they depart.

f.12b *has an engraving of Richard Allestry and a list of Christ Church Deans*

Following his account of Sunningwell and fishing (ff. 13-14b), Baskerville described looking down upon 'the noblest University in Europe, that far fam'd Citty Oxford, beeing sweetly hugg'd in the pleasant arms of those 2 pure Rivers - the Tems and Charwell whose timely floods inrich the meadowes with excellent herbage.'

Oxford city (f.14b)

As to OXFORD how it got that name. Some say a Queen in Elder dayes being pursued by her Enemies, to save her selfe was forced to ride over a Forde by fryer Bacons studdy on an oxe's back, as shee rode to hasten the ox shee cryed ox on, by which meanes makeing her Escape in memory of this deliverance the place gott the name of Oxon, and Oxford. This story the Oxford Almanack for 79 seems to confirme; for there wee finde a Queen crowned with a Castle rideing on an oxes back in the river by the Citty. The Cittizens doe also give that Beast for their Arms and perhapps it might gett a name when men began to build there from the fine gravelly fords, and pastures by them fitt to fatt and plumpe up those Beasts for the Shambells; but however itt came by itts name, itt is now att this present writing 1683 arrived to great splendor, all the Colledges are now almost finished, and other fresh beautyes are dayly added, an account of which you may have in theyr proper places. As to Oxford, and its Subburbe, St Clement it may contain in Circuit about 4 Miles. It is built (but the houses except those have been mended of late indifferent) upon ground gently riseing from the rivers, and from the Landward to a place called Carfaix, where 4 eminent streeets of this Citty meet where is Erected a very fair Conduit of free-stone. The water which serves itt, is brought thither under the River in leaden pipes from a spring that ariseth in our Hills above Ivy Hincsy, and this is the only Conduitt they have in Town, but for good Wells, whose waters issue from gravelly Ground, Every one who will bee att the Charge to digg them, may have them, but to return some part of the water of this Aquaduct, when they please is converted to fill the Cistern in Christ Church Quadrangell; but as to Carfaix, had there been a faire circling markett place about this Aqueduct, it would have added to Oxford. This and a sumptuous Cathedrall of which a foundation was layd by Cardinal Woolsey, beeing her greatest absent beautyes. Oxford consists of 14 parishes, 18 Colledges and 7 Halls. The names of the parish Churches are St Marys, Carfaix, or St Martins, All-Hallowes, St Aldate, or St Tol's, St Ebbs, St Thomas, St Peters in the East and St Peters in the Bayly, St Michaels, St Magdalens, St Giles, Holly-well, or Holy Cross Church, St Johns which is Merton Colledge Church or Chappell, and St Clement in the Subburbs. To these must bee added St Frydesweeds Church in Christ Church, which was formerly a parish Church, but now the Cathedrall for that diocess in all fifteen Churches besides Colledge Chappells.

The Colledges are thus named, Christ Church, Magdalen, Merton, New Colledge, St Johns, All-Souls, Wadham, Trinity, Baylioll, Exeter, Lincoln, Jesus Colledge, Brazen-Nose, Queens Colledge, Oryell, Corpus-Christy, University Colledge and Pen-brooke Colledge.

Halls, Glocester Hall, New In Hall, Merlynn Hall, St Maryes Hall, St Edmonds Hall, Allband Hall, and Hart Hall.

Every Colledge hath a Chappell or Church belonging to itt, but for the Halls, only 3 have Chappells, viz. Glocester, St Mary & St Edmonds Hall.

Christ Church (f.15)

CH: CH: THE greatest Colledge of any in Oxford had its originall from the Crown, and Miter, a king and Bishopp being the founders, and Godfathers of itt, For Cardinall Woolsey began building of itt in the year 1525 in the place where St: Fridswid's Monastery stood but hee dying, and King Henry the Eight finishing it (or in his Days the Buildings were brought to good perfection) it was some time called Kings Colledge. But because the Cardinall had endow'd it with much riches, The king would neither have it call'd by his, nor the Cardinall's Name, but gave it the name of Ch: Ch: and to encrease the honour of itt, made it a Bishopps Seat in the same year 1546. Hee also joyn'd to it Canterbury College, built by Simon Islyp Arch-Bishop of Canterbury in 1363, and Peck-water Hall which beeing now Quadrangles still retain the same names. It has of latter years been much beautified by Bryan Duppa and Samuell Fell deans, who also built the fine Porch and Stayr-Case to the Hall anno 1630. Nevertheless the Roof of the Northern and part of the Western Squares were not cover'd till after the Restauration of the King, but lay expos'd to the injury of all kinde of weather. But at this present writeing 1683 it is now compleatly finisht, and a noble Tower for great Tom erected over the Gate, the 2nd for exquisite workmanshipp att this day in England, only that of Bow Church in London may bee said to exceed it. A Square in the Quadrangle is also sunk lower to make the Buildings by the walks shew the loftyer, and in the middle of this Square Dr: Gardner a Cannon lately of this house has erected a beautifull aquaduct in form of a Globe in the midst of a large Cistern of Stone lined with Lead to keep the water from soakeing out. Dr Gardner was also at the charge of sinking the Square which now contributes very much to the pleasure and drieth up the walks. Their Library for Studdy and their common fire-room to refresh themselves after meals are both places of good concern. Here is also erected a fair pyle of building nere Ch: Ch: mead in which there are fine Walks, with Elms for shaddow now pretty well grown . . . [sic] Little more can bee said as to the buildings of this ample and royall foundation, because the Church (though well enough beautifyed within with a good Organ in it) is grown old and of small remark, save that itt had in the Windows since I remember rare painted Glass of scripture hystoryes painted by Van Lins a Dutch Man, who also painted the glass-Windowes of my Fathers Chappell of Bayworth, but that was cut in peices, and this of Ch: Ch: taken down not long after the Surrender of Oxford.[3] But the Hall of this Colledge for bigness stoops to none in England, save that at Westmi(n)ster. The kitchen is also a large and well- built Roome, where it may bee worth a strangers sight to stepp down and see that great Grid-Iron drawn on Wheels from place to place as occasion serves. This Colledge contains within its compass 5 Quadrangles, and Mr Jones of Sunningwell once a student of this house, told mee it covers as much Ground as the Citty of Bathe. This is the only Colledge in Town which the Brewers do serve with middle, or small Beer, and therefore, upon that score, their Cellar is of less concern; But to recompense that defect, it makes such as are able keep the better Liquor in their private Roomes; But they have on St Andrew their gaudy Day a cheerfull and free Entertainment to every Schollar of good victualls, and strong Beer, which liquor is given by such Brewers as serve the Coll: and the Bakers make them a present of their Cakes; but persons of Estate, and Quality doe usually on that day bestow Mony on the under Butlers.

The present Dean or Governor of this Colledge is John Fell, now Ld Bishop of Oxford the first person who ever enjoyed those 2 preferments together, who hath at Cudson in the place where a former was burnt down, erected a fair house for the succeeding Bishopps of Oxford. This Bishop, and Samuell Fell, his father, who also contributed towards it, hath lately built a fair Alms-house at Worcester for 8 Men and 2 Women, whose allowance is 2s 6d, with a Chappell to it. In his time, 1681, the famous Tom, now the greatest Bell in England, for it weighs 16,700 pounds, was cast, but it miscarryed 3 times,

3   Van Lins - Abraham van Ling, a Dutchman and glass painter, admitted to Oxford University as a privileged person, 'Artis Peritus' (art expert) on 4 July 1634. BHO Foster. The windows at Bayworth were mentioned without naming the artist. *See* Chapter 2 'Life and Kin'.

twice it wanted mettle to make out the Cannons and a 3d time it burst the mould and ran into the ground, so that poor Keen or King the Woodstock Bel-founder whose ill luck itt was thrice to faile, was halfe besides himselfe, and quite undone, till the Coll: made him amends, at last the 4th time it was cast and brought to perfection by Christopher Hudson a London Bel-founder. The greatness of the Bell, and those failures in its casting, made our poet bestow this song on't-

> Great Tom to Town is lately come
> That long lay in his Mother's Womb
> Although hee bee much older grown
> It will augment unto his Tone.
> Then hang him up, although wee feare him
> That wee at night at 9 may heare him
>   Bome, Bome, Bome.

A Second Song on great Tom in former Days and all the bells of Christ Church which then were 6 but now are 10.

> O The bonny Christ Church Bells
> One, two, three, four, five, six,
> That ring so mighty sweet
> So wonderous great
> And trowle so merrily, merrily.

> O The first and second Bell
> Which every day at four and ten
> Cry come, come, come, come, come
> Come to prayers
> And the verger troops before ye Deane.

> Tingle, tingle, tingle
> Says the little bell att 9
> To call the beerers home
> But the devill a man
> Will leave his Can
> Till hee hears the mighty Tome.

Here are foundation places in Ch: Ch: for 8 Cannons besides the Dean. The present Canons are thus named - Dr: Jane D.D. and Regius professor of Divinity commonly called Dr: of the Chair, and sub-Dean of the house, Dr: Pocock, D.D. and Regius professor Linguarum. Dr: South, D.D. Dr:

Woodroof D.D. Dr: Smith D.D. Dr: Hammond, D.D. and Treasurer of the Coll: Dr: Radcliffe D.D. Dr: Aldrich D.D. and a great composer in musick, Mr Wyatt a student of this Coll: is now anno 83 University Orator, who at the Duke of Yorkes late reception in Oxford saluted his highness with an Eloquent Oration.

In Ch: Ch: are 101 Students, 8 Chaplains, 8 Singing men, 8 Choristers, besides all other orders of Mas(te)r, Bachelors, and under Graduates that are not of the Foundation.

Here is also over against the Coll: an Alms-House with the Kings arms over the Dore, belonging to this Coll. which hath 24 Men in it.

Ch: Ch: is cap(ac)ious, and large enough to entertain and lodge 300 Schollars, and commonly there are so many there when all in Town.

Here are in Ch: Ch: 4 places called faculty places which give liberty to those that have them of studdying what they please, when that the rest of the students are obliged at such a standing to take orders, or leave their places, these are not obliged to live a College life, but may live where they please.

[*large space*]

A List of the names of such Gentlemen Schollars with whome I have had acquaintance bothe before and since the Kings Restauration dead, and yet alive. Imp Samuell Fell the present Bishops Father who dyed att Sunningwell and was buried there, much about the time that King Charles the first was beheaded, who was dean of Ch: Ch: parson of Sunningwell, and parson of Longworth in Berkshiere. Sir John Skidmore made knight of the Bathe, at this Kings Coronation, my Fathers Sister's son, who has an Estate at [space] in Heryford shieir.

Dr: Blandford, first Bishop of Oxford and afterwards of Worcester, dead.

John Fell, the present Bishop of Oxford. Dr: Morley, formerly Dean of Ch: Ch: and now Bishop of Winchester. Dr: Dolben, Cannon of Ch: Ch: Dean of Westmister Bishop of Rochester and now Arch-Bishop of York. Dr: Alistree Cannon of Ch: Ch: and provest of Eaton Defunct. Dr: Jones Student of Ch: Ch: parson of Sunningwell, prebend of Westmister, and St Pauls, and Sub-dean of the Kings Chappell, dead. Mr Washbourn a great Lover and Companion of Dr: Jones who dyed a Bachelor, and made Mr Charles Washbourn son to Dr: Washbourn of Glocester his part Executor, Dr: Dorrell prebend of Winchester Dr Peirce, Bishop of Bathe and Wells. Dr: Hammond, Can: of Christ Church. Mr John Westly now in Ireland, sone to Mr Tho: Westley, minister of St Cuthberts in Wells. Mr Devore his Companion. Mr Killman sometime Curat of Sunningwell, for Dr Fell turned out of his Students place by the parliament Visiters after the surrender of Oxford. Mr Read, parson of Marthum defunct. Mr Low, Bachelor of Musick and organist of the Ch: dead. Mr Speed Canon of Ch: Ch: dead. Mr Robt. Fell, the Bishops Brother dead. Mr William Fell his Brother. Mr Wyatt the present University Orator. Mr Charles Washbourne my loveing Friend and Companion, now Minister of Long Preston in York-shier.[4] Mr William Morgan who was Chaplain to Sir John Harman, that brave Sea-Captn: in the Streights, who beeing wounded to Death in a Sharpe sea-Fight, as I think against the Algerines Mr Morgan told mee, hee held him in his Arms a little before hee dyed of his wounds; after Harmans Death hee was Chaplain to Sir John Narrborough Admiral of our Streights fleet, and came home with him to England and after a years time went for Tangier again. Hee was also Judge advocate to St John Narboroughs fleet. Sir Richard Morgan Knight of the burning Brandy, Mr Tho: Martyn Curat at Sunningwell under Dr: Jones dead. Mr Puleson and Mr Ackworth both Curats of Sunningwell under Dr Jones, Mr Samuell Benson Dr: Bensons son Samuell now parson of Upton Lovell in Wiltshire nere Warmi(n)ster. Mr Tho Willis, Dr: Willis the physytians son. [*in margin* Dr: Willis] Mr Robinson kinsman to Sir John Robinson Leiutenant of the Tower. Mr Robert Pocock Canon Pococks so: Mr Twitty now a Parson in Yorkshier, Mr Tho: Talbott Sir John Talbots son dead. Mr Grub, Mr Graham or Grimes the Lord Prestons Brother hath now a parsonage in Yorkshier. Mr Moystin, Sir Roger Moystins Son at flint Castle in flintshier. Mr Henry Jones son of Dr: Jones Minister of Sunningwell, Tho: Steevenson minister of Drayton in Oxford shier, Mr Richard Corpson minister of Stanton Harcourt, then of Ravensthorp in Northampton shier, and now of Chastleton in Oxford Shier. Charles Herrick, Phillip Bound hath a parsonage in [blank] Charles Allestree, Jacob Allistree, Nathaniell Lacy, Mr Tho: Read Sir Compton Reads oldest son dead; George Popham Collonell Pophams Son. Charles Nixon now parson of [blank] in Worcester shier near Evesham. Joseph Gascoign. Mr Tho: Heylin Dr: Heylyn the Geographers Son, who went a parson to Nevis, and is since safe returned. Mr Isaac Walton a traveller in Italy. John Munday, Dr: Mundaye's Son. Mr Newberry a Londoner. Mr Newport the Lord Newports Son. Mr Bowdler Mrs Jane Fell's Son dead. Mr Norden, Mr Birch Chaplain of Ch: Ch: and lately minister of Abingdon. Mr Hulett once Proctor of the University now travelling. Mr James Mr Rawlins minister

---

4   Charles Washbourne was about 20 years younger than TB; son of Thomas, of Dumbleton, co. Gloucester, matriculated 1667, aged 18, MA 1674; vicar of Long Preston, Yorks, 1677, until his death in 1703. BHO Foster; CCEd. TB travelled with him to Long Preston in 1677. *See* Chapter 4 'Journeys'.

of Culham, Mr Morley the Bishop of Winchesters nephew, Mr Coleman the distracted man one well skill'd in Musick when hee was in his right minde. Mr Gold. Mr Salmon. Mr Stridweeke. The Kings Schollars of Westmister School are elected to bee Students of Ch: Ch: and they are also elected from this School to be Schollars of Trinity Colledge in Cambridge.

Magdalen (f.17)

MAGDALEN COLL: DEDICATED as I suppose to the memory of St: Mary Magdalen is a noble pyle of building whose founder was Wm of Wainflete, Bishop of Winchester, and Chancellor of England in 1458. This Coll: was brought to such perfection that nothing has been added to it in my time, and in some respects it doth exceed all other Colledges, for most of the Fellowes have Convenient Gardens and private Stables each man a part for his own horse. As to the buildings besides private Lodgings which are very good, the Cloyster quadrates a fair quadrangle 60 paces long N. and S.; and 52 E. and west where for decoration on its Battlements are raised in stone figures of various creatures. Here is also a fine Chappell, and a strong Tower with Six very tuneable Bells. The Quire in the Chappell is paved with black and white squares of marble, it has a good organ, and the window over the west-dore is very remarkable for its painted Glass in black and white figures.

Those other adjuncts of beauty and conveniences hereto belonging, is their Bowling Green, delicate walks of their own, of a great lenth by Charwell, and when they please to stirr a little in those of the Phisick Garden and up the Hill towards Hedington.

Dr: Clerk Dr: of Phisick is the present Governour or president of Marling Coll: whose place for profitt is not inferior to any if not the best in Town, and the fellowships of which here bee 40 for income are so reputed. Here are besides the president and fellows, 30 Schollars, or Demyes, 4 Chaplains, or Clerks, 16 Choristers, 2 Schoolmasters, besides all other orders that are not of the foundation. The organist to this Chappell has a convenient house for himself and Family, and a good Sallery yearly to defray such Expenses.

Here is a custome on Mid-summer Day of having a Sermon in the Quadrangle, which is drest on that day with oaken Bows, a Stone pulpitt beeing erected in the wall for that purpose. And again, on May Day at 5 of the Clock in the morning here is a custome for the Clerks and Choristers to Sing on the Tower.

Magdalen is capacious and large enough to entertain and lodge 150 Schollars. Gentlemen of my acquaintance at present 83 in the Colledge are Mr Thomas Bayly, and Mr James Bayly his Brother Dr: Yerbury Mr Nichols. Mr

Vander of hayden now dead, and in former dayes, Mr Brown a great Sympler, now dead also, Mr Joseph Harmour and Mr Baber a man of estate in the west near Bristoll; I fell acquainted with these Gentlemen at Cambridge when I went thither with Mr Baker of All-Souls to see the University.[5]

St Mary Magdalen Hall commonly called Marlyn Hall was built by William of Wainfleete Bishop of Winchester the Founder of the adjoyning Colledge in 1480 only for a grammar School, but both the buildings and number of Students encreasing, First it was called Grammar, but afterward Magdalen Hall. William Levitt D.D. is their present Principle. For Schollars of this Hall: I were once in the Company of Mr Hyde, the Lord Chancellor Hydes Son, who among others was drowned or cast away in the late Voyage or passage of the Duke of York from England towards Scotland. Mr Brockwell another Schollar of my acquaintance att present of this Hall, and Mr Southby Mr John Southby's Son of Abbingdon <Mr Stephens, Mr Good who lives at Broad Chalk six miles beyond Salisbury, an acquaintance of Madam Aubere's in the same town, who once gave me hearty welcome at her house>

The Physic or Botanical Garden (f.18)

A S TO THE Phisick Garden and its Rarityes of that nature since it stands on ground lately purchased from Magdalen Colledge, it may here justly challenge our remembrance, and that you may have a true charracter of its worth and beauty take here an account of't from him that now keeps it. The skilfull and Ingenious Gardener himselfe, my friend Mr Jacob Bobert.

[*double space*]

Among the severall famous structures and curiosities wherewith the flourishing University of Oxford is enriched that of the Publick Physick Garden deserveth not the least place being a matter of great use and Ornament, proveing serviceable not only to all Physitians Apothecaryes and those who are more immediately concerned in the practise of Physick, but to persons of all qualities serving to help the diseased and for the delight and pleasure of those of perfect health conteining therein 3000 severall sorts of plants for the honor of our Nation and Universitie and service of the Common-weale. This noble

---

5 Thomas Baker, son of Andrew of Grafton, Worcestershire; gentleman commoner of Magdalen Hall, matriculated 1670 aged 17, MA from All Souls 1677/8, incorp. at Cambridge 1679, rector of Harrietsham, Kent, 1686, died 1702. BHO Foster; CCEd. *See* Chapter 4 'Journeys'. He was a very young man when he accompanied TB to Norfolk.

thing was the Benefaction of the Right Honourable Henry Earle of Danby, who then lived at his house at Cornebury, who purchasing a most convenient plot of ground of 5 acres of Magdalen-Colledge land thereto adjoyning, being aptly watered with the River Charwell by it gliding, and built thereon a most stately wall of hewen stone 14 foot high with 3 very considerable Gates thereto, one whereof was to the cost of at least 500 pounds which worthy worke was all finished in the yeare 1632. And endowed the same with the Parsonage impropriate of Kirkdale in the County of York to remaine for perpetuitie.

After the walls and gates of this famous garden were built, old Jacob Bobert father to this present Jacob may be said to be the man that first gave life and beauty to this famous place, who by his care and industry replenish'd the walls, with all manner of good fruits our clime would ripen and bedeck the earth with great variety of trees plants and exotick flowers, dayly augmented by the Bootanicks, who bring them hither from the remote Quarters of the world, but to proceed.

This Garden Plot is not exactly square, for the walkes East and West are about 120 of my paces or strides which are more than a yard, But North and South I trod out but 106 and 112 paces with the length of the North-Gate which is extended without the square of the wall. Here is a doore way lately broke through the middle of the South wall, but the Gates spoken of by Mr Bobert are in the East West and Northerne sides, that in the North wall which admits entrance from the City being fairest built; by this Old Jacob some years past set two yew-trees which being formed by his skill are now grown up to be Gigantick bulkey fellows, one holding a Bill th'other a Club on his shoulder which fancy made an Ingenious person strow this Copie of verses on them.

A copy of the verses may be read in Collectanea IV (1905)

Here I may take leave to speake a word or two of old Jacob who now is fled from his Earthly Paradise. As to Country he was by birth a German born in Brunswick that great Mum-Brewhouse of Europe. In his younger dayes as I remember I have heard him say he was sometime a soldier by which imploy and travail he had opportunitie of augmenting his knowledge, for to his native Dutch he added the English Language, and he did understand Latine pretty well. As to fabrick of body he was by nature very well built, (his son in respect of him but a shrimp) tall straite and strong with square shoulders and a head well set upon them. In his latter dayes he delighted to weare a long Beard and once against Whitsontide had a fancy to tagg it with silver, which drew much

Company to the Phisick-Garden. But to save you further trouble view his shadow in this Picture.

The engraving is atached on the page: <D Loggan delineavit   M Burghers sculp: el excu.>
With inscription below the portrait: Thou Germane Prince of Plants, each yeare
to Thee
Thousands of Subjects grant a Subsidie.
Benevolut. 75

Here I may not omit the Remembrance of a worthy person defunct (though not of my acquaintance) and that is Dr Morison a Scotchman who was Botanick Lecturer in Oxford till unhappily brought to his end by a bruise which a coach gave him in London Street Anno 1682 or 3. Some who have heard him, say he was very ingenious and pleasant in his discourse on that subject. But whether there be now any Botanick Lecturer in Oxford I can not tell, but Mr Sherwood of St John's an acquaintance of mine a Lincoln-shier Gent and a Kin to a Lord of that name there, is a great lover of simpling who with Mr Bobert show'd me an Herball set out by Dr Morrison which had the best cuts of Plants that I yet have seen.

Anno 1670. Here was built by the Income of the money given by the Founder a fair Green-house or Conservatory to preserve tender plants and trees from the Injury of hard winter.

New (f.21)

WINCHESTER COLLEDGE COMMONLY cal'd New Colledge was built by William of Wickham Bishop of Winchester and Chancellor of England in 1386 who so fortified it with walls and Turrets that in case of war they may sustaine a seiege and when our present Charles the 2nd made his way from Scotland with his Army as far as Worcester, this Colledge was made choise of to be garrison'd to resist them if they came so far, and one Sir Thomas Draper was to be Governor if I am not mistaken in his name.

As to the structure of this Colledge it has a large Quadrangle, but, the buildings Barn-like till of late Battelments were added to it, but their Chappel which has a good Cloyster adjoyning may pass for the best in Oxford both for bignesse and inward decorations, the floore is paved with very fair squares of black and white marble and their Organ exceeds most instruments of that kinde that I have heard elsewhere. Some new building are now erecting on the East side of this Colledge. And they have in their Garden 4 Curious Knots of

Box in severall quarters, in which are cut, the Kings Armes, the Colledge Arms, tbe Founders Armes and a Diall.

Here is also cast up in this garden, a fair mount and on the top on't to which you ascend by winding walks a diall resembling a bundle of Books.

The present Warden 1684 of New Colledge is Dr Beeson Dr of Divinity who hath here to bear him Company 70 Schollers and fellowes, 18 Chaplains, 3 Clarkes, 16 Quoristers besides all other Orders. <10 Conducts or Chaplins says Mr Hanbury a Conduct there>

Gentlemen as I remember of this College before the King's Restauration my kinsman William Huntley of Boxwell in Glocester shier fellow of this house, who went a Captaine in the Army under Generall Pen and Venables to Hispaniola and from thence to Jamaica where he dyed, and his brother Gabriel Huntley went with him and there ended his dayes.

Since the Restauration Mr Christopher Minshion sometime divinity Beedel of this University who in 1680 (as I think) unfortunatly brake his neck with a fall from his horse as he was riding from Abingdon toward Locking to see Mr Edmond Wiseman and a day or two after Mr Fry a Chirurgion of Oxford going thither as I think to embalm or embowel him by a fall from his horse gat his death. Mr Hanboro now Parson of Letherhead in Surry formerly of this Colledge and acquaintance.

This Colledge is Capacious enough to entertaine and lodge 130 Schollers.

In this Colledge the house of office or Bog-house is a famous pile of building. The dung of it computed by old Jacob Bobert, to be worth a great deal of money, who said this Compost when rotton was an excellent soil to fill deep holes to plant young Vines.

St John's (f.21b)

St John's Colledge on the North side of Oxford pretty near St Giles where among other gentry who live in that street my honor'd unkle Paul Dayrel and dame Barbara his wife my mothers sister have a good house stands in the place of a Hall formerly dedicated to St Bernard which Henry Chiehly[6] Arch-bishop of Canterbury and founder of Al Souls built in 1430 but demolished in the reign of King Henry the 8th in the year 1557. Sir Tho: White sometime Lord Mayor of London founded the present Colledge by the name of St Johns.

I have heard Dr Parrot and some other schollers of that house say, that Sir Thomas White having an intention to build a Colledge, before he built it

6   Henry Chichele archbishop of Canterbury 1414-43.

had a dreame that where he saw 3 Elmes grow upon one root there he should build it.

He first as some tell me found 3 Elmes on a root where Glocester Hall now stands and built there. But afterward, finding 3 more perfectly growing on a root where St Johns now stands, he set about building that Colledge, which Elms now grow in the President's Garden.

Now since the dayes of Sir Tho: White, William Laud and William Juxon were both good Benefactors to it, and both Archbishops of Canterbury in my time.

William Laud (as Mr Robert Baskervile now a fellow of that house, lately told me) built the inner Quadrangle which is a Curious Pile for workmanship and doubtless it cost a great deal of money, and yet my namesake said it cost Archbishop Laud as much more money to treat King Charles the 1st and his Queen when they came to Oxford as the expences of that building. They were treated it seems in the Inner Library and the Schollers of the University presented their Majesty with a play in the Hall I suppose which was Canopy'd over with ivy, and other pleasant Greens, among those Actors, Mr Edward Bosstock made one who for Age might have reacht our dayes, for his eldest brother Mr William Bostock is yet alive in Abingdon, and his youngest sister now Mrs Elizabeth Stevenson yet a vigorous woman.

But to go forward with our description.

Here is in the Library of this house the Efigies of King Charles the 1st drawne by a penman as far as the brest, containing in the haires of his head, face beard and other clothing, the whole booke of Psalmes.

Bishop Laud paid the Penman for this Curiosity.

They have in St Johns a faire Chappel with an Organ in it, a good Hall and pleasant common fire-roome, and very delightfull walkes with out-lets into the Country and new Park-walkes. But here give me leave because I have been at Cambridge to mention St Johns of that University a very noble Pile of building.

For as this has 2 Quadrangles in fair order one behind the other, that Colledge has 3. And it is so contrived that as you enter the Gate of the first Quadrangle you may looke through this and the other 2 Courts and see a brave bridge of stone beyond them which lets you over Came into a good bowling Green, floored walkes and Garden Plots and beyond this the Country is open and Airy and indeed to speake truth here you find the greatest beauty of Cambridge for you see 5 or 6 brave bridges of stone one above the other and Noble Piles of building answerable to them. Some names of the Colleges I remember vizt Trinity above St Johns Clare Hall and Kings Colledge.[7]

7   See Chapter 4 'Journeys' Journey 1 where this phenomenon is described.

But to returne to our buisinesse. The Lordship of Fifild in Berks about six miles distant hath some dependance on St Johns Colledge Mr Francis White the present Possessor thereof being the Founders kinsman. Again such of that name and kindred if Schollers and capable of it are to be chosen Fellowes of this house before such as are not of the Founders kindred and they have the priviledge to be chosen hither from any School in England, or the Kings dominions, which others have not and they have 6 places allowed for them.

Now as touching the Fellows of this house beside the Founder's kindred, they come hither from severall schools vizt from Tunbridge School in Kent 1 scholler, in which place my Friend Mr Stylman at present is there.[8] From Reding two 'tis probable the gift of Archbishop Laud who was born in that Town. Two from Coventry and 2 from Bristoll, of which places from Bristo my namesake Baskervile hath one. The rest for the most part come hither from Merchant Taylor's School in London. And they may if they please, when places are vacant, bring schollers hither from any Colledge in Oxford. But such schollers lose their time before spent in such College or Hall in order toward taking degrees and begin afresh, for which reason few come hither from them who have spent above 3 or 4 yeers in the University.

It is a statute in this house that 12 of the Fellows must Profess the Civil Law and take their Doctors degrees in that science when capable of it, but then they have or take that freedome to move in which sphere they please Law or Divinity, as at present Dr Meaw Dr Morris and others, who are Fellows of this house and tooke their degrees in Civil Law, but yet nevertheless move in the preferments of Divinity.

Here is now 1684 for the President Dr Lewins Dr of Phisick who hath to bear him company 50 Fellowes and schollers besides all other orders.

St Johns Colledge is capacious and large enough to entertain and lodge one hundred schollers.

A list of the names of such Gentlemen Schollers in St Johns with whome I have had some acquaintance.

Dr Meaw the present Bishop of Bath and Wells who now since the death of Bishop Morley in November 84 is nominated by the King to be Bishop of Winchester.[9] A worthy person and great lover of Hospitality, so

8   John Stileman, son of John Stileman vicar of Tonbridge, Kent; matriculated St John's 1674 aged 16, B.D. 1687, died 1733. Also became a rector. BHO Foster.

9   Peter Mew(s) (1619-1706) was the son of Ellis Mew of Purse Candle, Dorset. He matriculated at St John's college in 1637. He was a strong royalist and fought and was wounded in the civil war. He took up arms again for the king in 1685 against the rebels headed by the Duke of Monmouth. President of St John's college 1667-73, vice-chancellor 1669-73. Bishop of Bath and Wells 1673-1684 and of

that as a man may the City Wells and Gentry there about will mourn for his absence, and must needs conclude to his honor be it spoken as Dr Pope at the end of his wish.

> In the morning when sober
> in an evening when mellow
> He is gone and has left not
> behind him his Fellow.

Here before I proceed to mention the names of my other friends in this Colledge a word or two for diversion and information which is this, That the Bishoprick of Bath and Well (*sic*) in former times was one of the best Bishoprickes in England, for but a feaw weeks since it being now 1684 walking into the old Alms-house of Wells to see it, in their Chappel, on the wall I found an Inscription which told me that Nicholas Bubwich was first Bishop of London, 2dly Bishop of Salisbury, 3rdly Bishop of Bath and Well, which Bishop the Founder of this Alms-house for 24 People and a Priest, was Treasurer to King Henry the 4 of England and died The 27 of October 1424 and is buried in the Cathedrall. And I remember my brother Colonel Morgan who is now an inhabitant in that Citie has told me that 21 Mannours has been taken from that Bishoprick but because the removall of Bishop Meaw to Winchester is the occasion of this discourse give me leave to speake a little to that, because that Bishop is their Visitor at St Johns, for I am told by Mr Stylman of that house it is a Custome that at the first coming of the Bishop to that diocese his Tenants are obliedged to present him with 400 pounds. <This Bishoprick may be now worth above 6000 pounds per annum.> At Farnam, this Bishop being Lord of it has a noble seat vizt a brave Castle on a mount overlooking the Town and a Fair Park well stokt with deer adjoyning.

As to Farnam, I was told by some there, for I went thither purposely to see the Town, there is usually sold on their market day which is Thursday 400 loads of wheat, and of other sorts of Grain 400 Loads more. But a great deal of this Corne is brought into store houses on the week dayes for the Town will not hold so many Carts togeither at one time, so that I thinke with allowance this may pass for the greatest market in England. And this yeelds a great Income to the Bishop for he has the tole of all the Corne. From hence they carry the greatest part in wagons to Guiford and Cherse and thence by water toward and to London.[10]

Winchester until his death. BHO Foster; CCEd.

10 Farnham in Surrey; transport via Guilford and Chertsey and thence to the Thames and London.

Here is also a great market for all sorts of Fruit especially Wallnuts, usually sold for 2d a hundred and sent to London. They have one Church in Farnham with a Tower though less, like that at Winchester. The Churchyard abounds with Mallows an excellent Plant for Clisters so that dead bodyes are here found to be good for something, because they breed Mallows to supple the Arses of living People. But enough of this. I proceed to the names of my friends that have been and now are in St Johns.

Doctor Parrot of Fifil in Berks my worthy friend, Dr of Civill Law. Dr Taylor, Dr Morris both of Law, Mr Stowel the Lord Stowel's eldest son of Ham in Summerset. Dr Gibbons Dr of Phisick, my worthy Friend Mr Edmond Wiseman now Captaine of our Troop of Horse in Barks, who now by the marriage of his wife which was Mr Cates onely daughter lives at Lockings neer Sparsel's Court where yet do live my honor'd Friend his father Mr Edmond Wiseman. Mr. John Wiseman son of the old man by a second wife, who now is at Baliol Colledge. My very Loving friend Mr Francis White, too soon taken from us by the small pox fatall to that Family, sometime Esqr Beedel of this Universitie. Mr Charls White his nephew sometime Lord of Fifil, since cut off by the same disease. Mr Francis White another nephew the Present Lord of Fifil. Mr Aldar or Aldworth the son of my antient friend and acquaintance Mrs Mary White (her mayden name) of Fifil who is now married to Mr Mallard a Councellor and lives at Abingdon. Mr Richard Stevenson now Parson of Fulham in Middlesex the brother of my loving friend Mr Thomas Stevenson of Stanton-Harcourt. Mr Ward, Mr Robert Baskerville, Mr Stylman, Mr Sherwood the Botanist, Mr Harper, Mr Davies, Mr Violet, Mr Sawyer <now Minister of St Giles in Oxford> son of Mr Sawyer born at Abingdon and a vintner in London, Mr Palmer dead, and buried in St Giles Church <yard where is an Inscription to his memory on the outside of the wall at the East end of St Giles Church> Mr Morgan sometime Proproctor of the University. Mr Pleydall alias Pledwel now Master of the Free School in Abingdon. Mr Tilsley's both father and son Schollers here, and Ministers at Moor neer Oxford the Father is dead, but the son now minister of St Sepulchers in London. Mr Harding dead. <Mr Hill now Parson of Besesleigh near Abingdon.>

A fellow of this house may injoy a stipend or place worth 100li a yeere, and his Fellowship with it, Provided it be not in the Kings Bookes worth 10li's per annum.

Since this above written, Mr Robert Baskervile came to Bayworth and brought two Schollers of St Johns with him whose names are Mr Connisbie a Hartfordshire man, and Mr Blundell, who said, Bishop Mewe was his Godfather.

An engraving of Bishop Peter Mews bishop of Winchester is inserted here

I am informed by my worthy friend Mr Richard Rod, that when King Charles the first had his residence in Oxford, in the time of our Civil wars The King wanting Cash to pay his soldiers, he was necessitated to send for The Colledge Plate to Coyne money and accordingly had it delivered to him, But St John's Colledge people being loath to loose the memory of their Benefactors, gave the King a summe of money to the value of it, and so it staid with them some time, but the King's urgent occasions for money still pressing him forward he sent to demand it a seecond time, and had it, upon which the King ordered the Rebus of Richard Bayly the then President of St Johns 1644 to be put on the money Coyn'd with the Plate. Mr Rod did help me to half a Crown of this money which hat(h) the Rebus of Rich: Bayly on both sides vizt under the King a horse-back on one side, and under this motto. REL: PRO:LE:ANG:LIB:PAR: The Protestant Religion, The Laws of England, and the proviledge of Parliament.

And under 1644 on the other side.

A copy of the Grace before eating set out in two columns has not been trasncribed.

All Souls (f.25)

ALL SOULS WAS built by Henry Chiehly Archbishop of Canterbury anno domini 1437. Mr Henry Stedman my worthy friend one of that society told me that this Archbishop advising the King in those days to a war with France in which many English were slaine, to Attone for that and aeternise what in him lay their memory, He caused this Colledge to be built and gave it the name of All Souls erecting there a fair Chappell, in which they were to pray for the soules of those deceased gallants, But as a man may say 'twas well for him, he had money to do it.

This account I had from my honor'd Friend Mr Thomas Baker another fellow of that society.[11]

All Soules Colledge founded in the dayes of Henry Chiehley Archbishop of Canterbury falsly said from the denomination of it Collegium omnium animarum fidelium defunctorum, a Colledge of all faithfull souls departed, founded upon that pretended pious in those days account of praying for the souls of all those that were slain in the wars for the recovery of France. The

11 See reference to Mr Thomas Baker above, under Magdalen College.

founder was the Promoter and Chief Instrument in those wars begun by Henry the 5th, carried on and the kingdom vanquished by him and his son Henry the 6th. Crown'd King therein, afterward he was outed that kingdome as also that of England, but he had a design to erect a Colledge before his conquest of France, as we may more largely see in Arthur Duck, fellow of that house, and the writer of Archbishop Chiehley's life. The Colledge consists of a Warden, 40 fellows, 2 Chapplins the rest of young men under four yeers standing and in the quality of servants wth severell others necessary for a family.

The pleasant Jest form'd from their statutes is thus, The fellows must be bene nati, mediocriter docti, et optime vestiti. Well born, well clothed, and meanly learn'd. But not to play to harshly, they are to be Honestis Parentibus nati, mediocriter docti, in plano Cantu, born of honest Parents, indifferently well skill'd in singing necessary for the ancient service of the Mass required, optime vestiti, decently clothed from the garments of the founder commanded to be bought at Bristoll fair, being the best cloth to be had and commanded to be of purple Colour.

All Souls stands in the heart of the City, between Brasenose and this Colledge Archbishop Laud had a design to open the great square, that was, To take away the houses between them as far as the Schools, as you may find in that Bishops diary printed by Mr Prin who was commanded to sease his paper when a prisoner in the Tower. Here is in the Colledge one fair Quadrangle and the onely one that is paved with stone in Town. At the upper end of this Court against the wall is a sumptuous Dial lately set up.

It has a very good Chappel pav'd with black and white Marble and on the wall at the East end since the King's Restauration is painted the Resurrection among the rest old Chiely rising out of his Tombe. But the Colors have now lost much of their beauty, and I beleeve People in these days have not the skill to paint on walls as in former times, for I have seen on the walls in a Church at Bilbo painting retaine its Pristine beauty and doubtless there painted a great many yeers before, and in the Cloyster of Ashridge the Lord Bridgewaters house in Hertfordshier which was a Religious house, you may there see Monkish stories painted on the wall which Colours do yet look pretty fresh. But to proceed here is a fair Hall an excellent Common fire roome and a very good Buttery where the fellows of the house do often treat their friends, and there among other plate you may see Sir William Portman's great guilt Bowl of silver.

They have pretty good walks considering they are now pent up by the City every way.

All Souls besides the present Warden Dr James Dr in Divinitie hath 40 fellows 2 Chaplains 3 Clarks 6 Choiresters besides other orders. Dr Sergeant Dr

Clutterbooke, Drs of Civil Law. Gentlemen of my acquaintance in this Colledge <besides the two Drs aforenamed> were and are Mr Phillip Fel the Bishop's brother, and sub Provost of Eaton Colledge, dead, my Cosen Scudamore, brother to the present Sir John Scudamore of Belingam in Heriford-sheir a Knight of the Bath, he died in France, Mr Clark now a Parson in Shropshier, Mr Baker some time minister of Stanton, Mr Stedman now minister of Stanton Harcourt, Mr Foster, Mr Aldworth now parson of Locking, Mr Orlebant, Mr Pember, Mr Wingford, Mr Snell now one of the Viccars at Bampton, Mr Finch the late Lord Chancellor's son, Mr Gibbs, Mr Osborne, Mr Waldron, Mr Broughton, Mr Web since Mr Stedman's remove now minister of Stanton Harcourt.

Here before I leave this Colledge and the good people in it, I must remember their Mallard night.[12] For the grave Judges have sometime their festivall days, and dance togeither at Sergeants Inn. The Country people will have their Lott-meads, and Parish Feasts. And Schollers must have some times of mirth to meliorate their great sobriety for

There is a time
When wit and wine
Will tickle the pate with pleasure
And make one breath
And vent with ease
The debates o'the mind at leisure.

As touching the first institution of this Ceremony (which is very ancient saith Mr Stedman) I cannot give any account of it, but when they have a mind to keep it, the time is always within a night or two of All Souls, then there are six Electors which nominate the Lord of the Mallard, which Lord is to beare the expences of the Ceremony. When he is chosen he appoints six officers, who march before him with white staves in their hands, and meddalls hanging upon their breasts tied with a large blew ribbond. Upon the meddalls is cut on the one side the Lord of the Mallard with his officers, on the other the mallard

12 According to legend a giant mallard flew out of a drain when workmen were digging the foundations of All Souls in 1437. During the Commonwealth the Mallard song was sung 'after a rude manner about 2 or 3 in the morning, which giving great alarm to the Oliverian soldiery then in Oxon they would have forced the gate open to have appeased ye noise.' The Mallard ceremony lapsed in the eighteenth century but was revived in 1801 and 1901. On 12 January 2001 Donald MacLeod in *The Guardian* reported that the ceremony was again to be revived. A torchlit procession carries the Lord Mallard shoulder high on a chair on a route which takes in the college roofs while he sings the Mallard song and they join in the chorus. The Lord Mallard elected in 2001 was Martin West. The mallard's head on a pole was to be wooden.

as he is carried upon a long Pole. When the Lord is seated in his chair with his officers of state (as above said) before him, they carry him thrice about the Quadrangle and sing this song.

> Griffin Turkey Bustard Capon
> Let other hungry mortalls gape on
> And on their bones with stomacks fall hard
> But let All Souls men have the mallard
> Hough The bloud of King Edward, by the blond of King Edward
> It was a swapping swapping Mallard.

> Stories strange were told I trow
> By Baker, Holinshead, and Stow
> Of Cocks and Bulls and other quere things
> That were done in the Reignes of their kings
> Hough the blood &c.

> Swapping he was from bill to eye
> Swapping he was from wing to thigh
> His swapping toole of generation
> Out swap'd all the winged Nation
> Ho the bloud &c.

> The Romans once admir'd a Gander
> More than they did their Chiefe Commander
> Because it sav'd if some don't foole us
> The P[lace] called from ye head of Tolus
> Ho the bloud &c.

> Then let us sing and dance a Galliard
> To the remembrance of the Mallard
> And as the Mallard does in Poole
> Let's dabble dive and duck in Bowle
> Ho the bloud &c.

The music is included on a separate piece of paper with printed music staves and pasted in.

Written later in the margin in brown ink <The poeth famed Jone Turned

a swan but let them prove ..if they can as for ... tis not that swapping[13]>

The Mallard song being sung by one man, all the rest that are present bearing the Chorus. When that is done they knock at all the middle-Chambers, where most of the Seniors lodge, of whome they demand crowns a piece (I suppose a forfeiture for not assisting at the ceremony) which is readily given, then they go with 20 or 30 Torches (which are allwayes carried before them) upon the Leads of the Colledge where they sing their song as before. This ended, they go into their common rooms, where they make themselves merry with what wine every one has mind to, there being at that time great plenty of all sorts. When they have there sufficiently refresh'd themselves, to conclude all they go into the Buttery where every one has his Tumbler of Canary or other wine. Then he that bore the Mallard chops of his head dropping some of the bloud into every tumbler, which being drunk off, every one disposeth of himselfe as he thinks fit, it being generally day-brake.

This Colledge is Capacious and large enough to Lodge and entertaine 60 Schollers and they come heither from any Colledge in Town, for which reason they have more generall acquaintance in the University then the Schollers of other houses.

This sentence added later not in exactly the same hand-writing <At AlSoules they Enter a Founders Kinsmans [name] in golden letters in their Register Book, and he is immediately Fellow of the House without a years probation.>

List of Fellows (22 names) follows without any personal comments and is not transcribed.

Of this Colledge was Robert Record, a Cambrian by birth, but in what County Mr Anthony a Woods my acquaintance, the Author of *Athenae Oxoniensis*, in all his search could not find, although descended of a Gentile family, who is as famous for Arithmetick, as William Lilie for Grammar, he was the Author of *Records Arithmetick*. About 1525 he first saluted the Oxonian Muses, and in 1531 he was elected Fellow of All Soules Coll: being then Bachelor of Arts, making Phisick his profession, he went to Cambridge where he was honored with the degree of Doctor in that faculty Anno 1545. And honored of all that knew him, for his great knowledge in severall Artes and Sciences. 'Tis said that while he was of All Soules Colledge and afterward, when he retired from Cambridge to this University he publickly taught Arithmetick and the grounds of Mathematickes with the Art of true

13 'Swapping' meaning large.

Accompting. Such as have a mind to read more of him may finde it in the 84 page of *Athenae Oxoniensis*.

Having roome yet leaft in this scantling of paper alotted to the memory of Alsoules, my worthy Benefactors to the Narative of this Colledge must not be forgot how and where they are, viz Mr Baker and Mr Steadman Noble Soules before noted among my acquaintance in this famous Colledge.[14]

Mr. Baker was sometime Curate of Stanton Harcourt under the Bishop of Oxford, and being an Alsoules Schollar had also the stipend allow'd by this Colledge for preaching so many Sermons yearly in Stanton-Harcourt Church, the parsonage being impropriated to that College.[15]

So, his function causing him to spend many nights at Stanton, he was pleased to quarter with me at the house of our honoured friends Mr Thomas Stevenson and his wife Elizabeth, which was the means that begot an Intimate friendship and acquaintance between us. He is an ingenious man, and writ that book intituled *The Head of Wile, or The turnings and windings of the factions*, printed in the reign of Charles the 2d. His parents did live well in Wostershire, but in his youthly yeers having had much Education in Norfolk, I went a Journey with him to those parts as far as Norwhich and Yar-mouth and we were nobly treated by his friends in those parts. He tooke to wife Mary the Daughter of my worthy friend Mr William Porter of Norcoat by Abingdon who was a very ingenious man and had a pleasant vein in poetry. Mr Baker and his wife are both alive 1694 he is now Parson of Harreshame in Kent.

Oriell Colledge (f.28)

ORIELL COLLEDGE, FORMERLY called St Mary Colledge, was founded by King Edward the second whence it was sometimes called Kings Colledge. Adamus de Brome was first Provost and Chiefe Benefactor thereof. Edward the 3d endowed it with a Messuage called Le Oriell, from which the Colledge took its present name. The same Edward the third founded the Hospitall of St Bartholomew belonging to this Colledge. John Frant who in the time of Henry the 8th was Master of the Rolls in Chancery gave four fellowships for the Countys of Somerset, Dorset, Wilton, Devon. John Carpenter sometimes

---

14 A page containing a draft of the description of Thomas Baker is in the collection of papers in Oxford, Bodleian Libraries, MS. Rawl. D. 859, f. 3r. See earlier reference to Thomas Baker under Magdalen College. Henry Stedman, son of Henry of Brechin, gentleman commoner St Alban Hall, matriculated 1674, M.A. from All Souls' Coll. 1680; described as chaplain of All Souls College, Oxford, in 1680, died 1694. (A near contemporary of Thomas Baker). CCEd, BHO Foster.

15 In the late 17th century All Souls College was required to pay £13 6s. 8d. a year from an unspecified bequest for sermons at Stanton Harcourt. VCH Oxon 12.

Provost and afterwards Bishop of Wigorn, gave one fellowship for the diocess of Wigorn, and six exhibitions.[16]

William Smith, founder of Brasen-Nose and sometimes Bishop of Lincoln gave one fellowshippe for the diocess of Lincoln, Richard Dudley fellow of this Colledge and afterwards Chancellor of Salisbury gave a Mannor called Swaynswyck in the County of Somerset for the maintainance of two fellows and six exhibitioners. John Jockman sometimes fellow, gave a Farm house in St Gyles Parish for the Porter.

The Revenues of this Colledge was afterwards increased by the munificence of severall others, the chiefe whereof were Anthony Blencow and John Tolson sometimes Provost in whose times and partly by whose chardge the Colledge then mightily impaired was rebuilt, and graced with so stately and sumptuous a structure, that it is now the only glory and ornament of the University.[17]

Many contributed liberally towards its rebuilding. The chief whereof were these. Antony Blencow Dr of Law and Provost, gave 1300 pounds wherewith the East part of the Colledge was rebuilt. Henricus Ashworth Dr of Physick formerly fellow gave 10li Gulielmus Comb fellow gave 100li, John Tolson, Dr of Divinity and Provost, also John Rause, Nicholaus Brook, John Horne, Daniell Lawford, John Gandy, Richard Owen, John Duncombe, Henry Eccleston, John Warren, Humphrey Lloyd, Richard Winch, William Wyatt, Edward Smallbone <brother to Mr Blower of Sunningwell> James Farren, Robert Say, Richard Saunders, William Washborne formerly fellows, gave 50li a piece, in all 950li. John Tolson Provost gave 1150li, Matthew Lyster Knight formerly fellow gave 30li, William Lewis Dr of Divinity sometime Provost gave 100li, Robert Drewpert formerly fellow Comr. [Commoner] gave 100li, Robert Harley fellow-Comr. gave 20li, Thomas Cave, fellow-Comr. gave 20li, John Parson fellow-Comr. gave 10li, Richard Knightley, fellow-Comr. gave 100li, Robert Arden fellow Comr. gave 50li, Thomas Roe, Thomas Kenrish, Francis Keate, John Southbey, Tho: Adderley, Alexander Pope, Richard Hide, Richard Swayne, Henry Bridgeman, Henry Jackson, fellow Comrs. gave 10li a piece, William Aston Knight of the Garter in the County of Yorke gave 20li, George Crooke knight of the Garter in the County Oxon, gave 10li, Robert Smith Gent. in Com. Oxon, gave 40li towards the rebuilding of the Colledge.

16 Wigorn is from the Latin for Worcester.
17 Anthony Blencow was Provost 1574, John Tolson Provost 1621. BHO Foster.

*The names of the Provosts listed up to Robert Say, elected 1653, died 1691,[18]
'at this time Provost' are not transcribed.*

This Colledge is famous not only for the magnificence of its buildings
but also celebrated upon the account of those famous men therein educated
of whome were Thomas Arundell Arch-Bishop of Canterbury. Richard Praty
Bishop of Chester. John Carpenter Bishop of Wigorn. Gualterus le Hart
Bishop Nordoviensis and afterwards Arch-Bp of York. Reignaldus Peacock
Bishop of Chester. John Halse Bp of Lichfield and Coventry. Thomas Cornish
Bishop Tynensis. [Hugo] Lloyd late fellow of Oriell now Bishop of Bangor.

Of this Colledge (among other noble men) were Sir Walter Raleigh
Knight of the Garter. Sir Francis Kinaston Knight of the Garter, Sir Tho. Row.
Sir Henry Purefoy. Sir Francis Ware. Sir Robert Owen. Sir Richard Wenman.
Sir William Hill.

There belong to the Colledge a Provost and 18 Fellows

Names of the fellows follow without any comments and are not transcribed.

As touching this Bishopric of Tinensis ...

*Baskerville is stimulated to inquire about the meaning of 'Tinensis' and
to go on a journey to Chepstow and up the River Wye in search of Tintern. See
Chapter 6 'Miscellaneous Writings'.*

Gentlemen schollers of my acquaintance in Oriell Colledge were and
are Mr Washbourn, Mr John Stonehouse of Cockroofe now Parson of Radley,
Mr Barrrey the sone of Mr Vincent Barry of Hamton Pile and my friend Mrs
Jane Southby of Abingdon, Mr Thomas Southby's daughter, Mr Williams a
Welchman the Person who gave me this relation of Oriel.[19]

And of this Colledge was my Honoured father Hannibal Baskerville.

This Colledge is Capacious and lardge enough to entertain and lodge
schollers.

18 BHO Foster.
19 Amongst the many members of the university named Williams there are a number
    at Oriel in the seventeenth century. Mr Williams who gave TB the account of
    the college, because of his status, local connection and long period within the
    college was possibly David Williams son of David of Corndean, Winchcombe,
    Gloucestershire, gentleman commoner matriculated 1668 aged 16, BA 1672, MA
    1675 and D.Med.1683. BHO Foster.

Balliol (f.30)

As St Catherine's repute gain'd Churches in England to ye honor of her name as at London and other places, so at Baliol in Oxon she hath a Chappell which bespeakes her story before I treat of the institution of that Colledge so here take it, as I got it from Dr Savage Late Master of that House.

There follows the story of the conversion of the king of Alexandria and the birth of his daughter Catherine, followed by the story of her life.

This Lady wheresoever she dwelt has got the honour of a day in our Callendar devoted to her memory, which is the 25 of November when at night the semsters, spinsters and knitters to Commemorate the freedom she left them do eat Cakes and drink ale in aboundance, if they can get it, her wheel also an Emblem of good housewifery is hung up for signs in most Market towns.

The Chappell in Balliol Colledge called the New Chappell or Saint Catherines, was built in the Reign of King Henry the 8th at the Charge of the House, assisted probably by the contribution of friends, for I find, saith Doctor Savage, that in the 13 year of the Raign Henry the 8 which [was] about Anno 1521 an agreement was made, with a mason of Burford for the finishing of the 3 window(s) thereof on the Quadrangle side. But how long it was before it received its perfection he knows not precisely but still that it was before 1529 is evident by the date of the glazing of the windows, it being then that Lawrence Stubbys gave the East window which is so fair that the founder of Wadham Colledge is said to have offered the Society 200 pounds for it to glaze the East-window of his Chappell as representing in lively Colours and exquisite postures, The Passion, Resurrection and Ascension of Christ. But the Chappell being faire they thought not the window too Gawdy for it.

The South window was at the same time glazed containing the whole story of the martirdom of St Katherine. The next to that was the gift of Dr Wentworth fellow of this house, containing the story of Hezekiah's sicknefs and recovery. That opposite thereunto containing the story of Phillip and the Eunuch was the same year given by Richard Atkins Esq of Glocester Shier, and fellow Commoner of this Colledge, about which time the whole Chappell was lined and adorn'd with joyners work, at the cost of the Colledge and of many Benefactors, one of the greatest whereof was Mr Popham of Littlecot who had been of the house and gave 100 pounds, in memory whereof, his Arms carved or engraven in wood are placed over the screen doors of the Choir.[20]

20 Peter Wentworthe fellow of Balliol, DD 1633, later rector of Great Haseley, Oxon, 1660, died 1661; one Richard Atkyns entered Balliol college aged 14 in 1629. Sir Francis Popham of Littlecote, Wilts. matriculated at Balliol 1588, and became lord

The second best was Mr Boughton Sub-dean of his Majesties Chappell Royall who gave 50li so that now it gives way to none of those of the lesser Colledges for beauty and Proportion.[21] One of the Chappell windows appears to be given by one of the Compton's (a Knight) Sir William Compton of the Ancestors of the now Earl of North-Hamton, both by his name, and Coat of Arms, and probably he gave toward the structure itself for his Charity was great, if it were answerable to his piety, which his Posture with his Ladyes wherein he is represented in the same window, shews to be devout. <1530>

There was as Dr Savage notes in the place formerly where now Balliol College doth stand and neer it these Halls, vizt Hart Hall of which name there have been severall Halls in Oxford one at this day still abiding, Saucer Hall, Margarets Hall, New Balliol Hall, Old Baliol Hall, which stood neer Jackson the stone-cutters house and St Hugh Hall of which for diversion here his story.

This St Hugh was a Bishop of Lincoln in whose diocese Oxford then was. He was born at Grenoble in Burgundy, who upon the importunity of our King Henry the 2d came over and accepted the Priorate of Wittham in Somerset Shhier (sic) <Since the dissolution of Abbeys the Lord Hopton's house who in my time was the King's Generall of the West, Car. 1> And afterward the said See, whose body after his death, which was at London was carried thence to the gates of Lincoln and thence more solemnly to the Cathedrall Church, there vizt upon the shoulders of Two Kings of England and Scotland, and from the Church door to the Choir by a great number of Prelats. About 20 years after he was Cannoniz'd or Sainted by the Pope and anno 1282 his bones were taken out of his coffin and put into a silver Chest 82 years after his first interment. And this was 2 years before Oliver Sutton Bishop of Lincoln confirmed Balliol Colledge. But 'tis probable the Kings of his time would hardly bestow such pains to bear him to Church except it were to be rid of him whose terrible Edict tumbled Rosamond's bones out of her grave at Godstow. It seems as the ballad tells us her crime was too much familiarity with a King, a crime unpardonable, but however, her Chappell has yet the good luck to stand when the very Ruines of the rest of that Religious Fabrick is almost gone. They shew'd me where her Tomb was, when Sir David Walter, a valiant Captain for King Charles 1st was owner of it. But let these severityes passe with their Inventors, since <There is

chief justice and an MP; his son Alexander also was a student at Balliol 1621. The first two windows from the east on the north side show the sickness and recovery of Hezekiah; they were made by Abraham van Linge in 1637 who had painted the glass in Bayworth chapel for Hannibal. Balliol college, 'History of the Chapel.'

21 Harbart Boughton of Hereford, matriculated 1628/9, canon of Hereford. Not recorded as sub-dean of the Chapel Royal. BHO Foster.

scarce a place in heaven or hell where a divel dos not dwell.>

I must again to St Hugh, the venerable esteeme the gentle Craft has still for his memory will not let him dye; so what lately I got in a pamphlet, here you have it.

Several pages are devoted to the story of St Hugh and St Winnifred and a lengthy poem. See Chapter 6 'Miscellaneous Writings'.

f.33 As touching Balliol Colledge which society as to name lived before this structure was built in Old Balliol Hall and New Balliol Hall, which some call Sparrow Hall. John Balliol was its first flounder stiled Baron by Mathew of Westminster the father of Balliol sometime King of Scotes who was his second son. Hugh his elder brother and Dervorguille his mother in whose right he came to lay a successful claim to that Crown being then dead. But to go on our Founder as to his Paternall or own estate was Lord of Bernard Castel in the Bishoprick of Durham, and Fodringay in North-Hamton shier in right of Devorguille his wife (The Castel where Mary Queen of Scots was beheaded). And he was one of those Nobles who assisted Henry the 3d in his warr against Simon Mountfort and the Barrons who in the year 1263 began this work. But as Dr Savage Master of that house doth note being found dead in 1269 little was done in his life time, nor was it likely that he should go about such a peece of work in Oxford then, when the King threatned the Ruine of the University upon the displeasure his Majesty conceived against the Schollers whereof 15000 are said to have departed from Oxford, and most of them to Northamton more anoying the King in the Battel then all the Rebbels besides and the Issue of the said Battell was such if this of North Hamton and Lewis be the same, that the Kings army was defeated and the King Bruis and the said Balliol taken prisoners. But the Northern parts remaining unconquered rose up and recovered all the rest of the land to the King again and set them free.

But to proceed. The Armes or Shield of this Balliol is a field Rubie with an Orle Pearl the simplicity of which Coat is an argument of the venerable Antiquity of the same, which as the Dr notes is yet to be seen tho somewhat defac'd by time, on the inside of the North Aile or wing of that magnificent structure of the said King Henry the 2d, vizt. The Abbey of Westminster the Aile I mean which is extended in length from the Cross-Aile of the said Church to the Belfree westward, by which it seems he was a Benefactor to that building and one of the Heros of that time. But as we before noted, little of this Colledge being built in John Balliols time, Devorgill his Lady Dowager after his death carried on the work and made it fit for schollers to live in which as the Dr notes from Sir Philip Somervile's statutes, a latter Benefactor, that they were at least sixteen which were allowed one poor Servitor to attend them at the Table by the Statutes of Devorgile. To this number of Devorgill's schollers who after were called fellows, Somervile added six schollers under them and one Chaplain beside what Chaplain or Chaplains had been placed there before upon the Charity of other benefactors, which 6 schollers the fellows are to choose, born in places neerest to the sight of the Lands given by him, and they are to be the poorest, the best and greatest Profitients. Later benefactors have added more, vizt. 4 come hither from Scotland, the gift of a late Bishop of Rochester, one from Tiverton in Devonshier, and the Lady Periham gave 1 Fellow and 2 schollers places to this house, with yearly allowance to maintaine them, and Mr Tisdale's gift was like to drop here of the fellowships and 6 schollers places.

But the Cunning Abingdonians by the help of the Charity of Whitwick intertain'd thoughts of building a new Colledge and accordingly effected it. And that nothing might be able to remove them, they made the Earl of Penbrock then Chancellor of the University the Godfather of this new Christened Hall calling it by the name of Penbrooke Colledge. And King James the founder of it who then Reigned. But (ad onera et Costagia) at the Cost and Charges of Tisdale and Whitwick, allowing these onely the privilege of Foster-Fathers. Now this Rejeton (saith the Doctor) had no sooner taken root, then the Master and his Company called the Master and Society of our Colledge into Chancery, for the restitution of 300li of Tisdale's money which had been imploy'd towards the purchase of Lodgings for Tisdale's schollers. Whereunto the Society at first were generally inclined to demur (my Lord Coventry who had been of the Colledge promising a gracious hearing) but in fine it was reserved to my Lord of Canterbury who upon hearing determined that the Colledge was to pay the said 300li to the Master and Society of Penbrooke Colledge, but knowing our Treasury to be emty of such summs his grace paid down 50li presently the other 250li we gave bond for to be paid halfe yearly 'till the whole were satisfied, the which summs as they grew due his grace did likewise pay; which we exprest our thankfullness for by so many severall Epistles, now what part the Prospect of this, and other losses which have befallen this society the Doctor saith, if the starrs had any special influence upon inferior things, we might safely say, that this College hath been subject to unhappy ones, and amongst all its Chronocrators or Dominos Temporum, its hard to Judge whether has had the more malignant Aspect upon it. Viz. The Thievish glance of Mercurie's eye or the firery looks of Mars, for as his History tels us great loses befell them in their revenues in the North by the frequent wars betwixt the English and Scots before the Union which made bad Tenants. And they had likewise great loss by the late dreadfull fire in London. Here give me leave to remember my dear Godson Mr Tho: Stevenson, to soon snatch'd from us in the flower of his days who was a great help to me in these Oxford relations, for he gave me the names of the founders of each Colledge and Hall and the year when they began to build, and the number of schollers in each house at present save Balliol Colledge, which as farr as I can gather from the Doctor's booke, with the Master may be about 34 persons besides Cookes, Butlers and such like people.

The ancient allowance to these Schollers or fellows in Devorguille's time saith our Dr seemes to be 8d per weeke increased by Somervill in case his rent yeelded so much to 11d per weeke, whitch 8d was then as good as a mark now, and 11d as good as 18s 4d, and 12d per weeke intended by Sir William Felton (who gave them the benefice and Mannour of Abboldesley) then as good as 20 shillings, and Sir Richard Baker a late Author notes that in Henry the 8ths days, vizt. 1533 a fatt Ox was sold for 26s and a fat sheep for 3s 4d and Dr Savage found in their Colledge Records that for the building of a barn at Abboldesley Rectory they contracted with one John Harwold a Carpenter for 100s Anno Dmi 1391 which now would cost 100li.

But to pursue our history it appears by the premisis that it was not intended that the schollers of the 1st Foundation should continue in the house any longer than *Quo usque in Artibus Cessaverit* 'till they may be Masters of Art compleat which exposing some to poverty for want of timely maintenance after they had taken that degree The Rigour of this Statute was taken off by the Pope of Rome when Richard Stabbys was Master, about Anno 1520.

An account of the names of other Benefactors to Balliol Colledge as I met with, in Dr Savage's booke.

St Hughes Hall, and Hert Hall were given to this Colledge by Richard Huntington and Walter Horkstow, anno 18 of Edward the 1.

Jeffrey Horkstow and Staynton gave the Site of the Divinity School.

Chimers Hall was given by Hugo de Sancto Yvon and JeffreyHorkstow Land.

Horsemongers Street was given by Gilbert de Pomfrait and Thomas Humbleton, and John Slatter.

Jeffrey Sawcer was another Benefactor of land where the Colledge now stands.

Hugo de Vienna gave lands to this Colledge in St Larence Jury London, Anno 1310.

Hugo de Warkenby and William de Socham gave 4 messuages in Oxford.

Mr Hunsingoure gave land in and about Oxford.

Money given by the Lord Abbot of Reding for the soules of Adam Le Polterer Burgess of Reding, John Burton, John Duke and Julian his wife Benefactors of house and Lands in Oxon to this Colledge.

And George Nevill Bishop of Exon in the days of Edward the 3d and Rich: 2d. John Bel gave a house about Clerken Well, in Philip and Mary's dayes.

And Miss Elizabeth Stevenson Junior lately told me that Mr Snell husband to Mr Coopers wife's sister (which Mr Cooper is now Register of that Archdeaconry of Oxford) gave since the death of Dr Savage 4 places for Scots Schollers being himself born in that Countrey and 10 pounds yeerly to the Register of that Court for ever, to collect the rents for the said schollers for ever.

And since the writing of this gift to 4 Scots schollers, Mr Chilcot, an ingenuous scholler of this house told me of a Renowned Benefactor, one Sir Thomas Wendly a Gentleman of Cambridge shire, of what Town I know not, gave the third part of the Library a Choice collection of very excellent books, being all his owne study, he was formerly fellow Commoner of the same Colledge.

This Colledge of Balliol perhaps lays with some people under some scandal and disreputation by entertaining the Protesting Lords and Associators of Monmouth, Shafsbury, Grey, etc. who gave a great Bowl, the best plate that is to be seene in Oxon, as a testimony of thanks to the Colledge. But all that know the Colledge, must needs know there is not a disafected man in the Colledge.[22]

Gentlemen of my acquaintance in Balliol Colledge have been and are these that follow, Dr Savage now dead, Dr Tocker of Abingdon, dead, Mr Sands the brother of the Lord Sands whose sister was Doctor Savage's wife, Mr Griffin, Mr Dunbar a Scot man, Mr Dickerson, Mr Paine now at present a scholler in this house son of my loving friend Mr Paine Apothecary in Abingdon, the person who lent me the Doctor's Book.

22 The Duke of Monmouth, an illegitimate son of Charles II, led a rebellion, particularly well-supported in the west country, against James II's accession to the throne because he was a Roman Catholic. Ford Grey, 3rd Baron Grey of Werke and 1st earl of Tankerville was a prominent but in the event an ineffective or even treacherous supporter who was not exeeuted as others were after the defeat at Sedgemoor on 6 July 1685. Anthony Ashley Cooper, 1st Earl of Shaftesbury, had tried to secure James II's exclusion from the throne. He also escaped punishment.

[big space]

Here I may not omit the remembrance of a custome they have in Balliol Colledge when they keep an eminent Act Supper which once I saw being invited thither to take part of their good Cheer some yeers before the Kings restauration. And that was in the middest of the Hall in the fire place they had planted an Oak which they would hew a foot square or more, with all his green boughs and leaves flowrishing upright but the bark of the body was taken off. This strange sight it being hard to conceive how they got it into the roome, with the Musick and good Cheer to boot made the entertainment very pleasant.

The next remark I am to speak to before I leave Balliol is to tell you of a firery conflagration that happened as people say before this Colledge, the martyrdome of two of the most eminent Compilers of the Common prayer book, Arch-bishop Cranmore and Bishop Ridley, firy indeed as to that severe sentence and conflagration as to the consumption of their bodyes, but to conclude, let this be the prayers of every good Christian, that God may remove from these Fyrie tops of Sinai to the more comfortable Mount Sion.

Another tragicall action fell out but a few years since in this Colledge. The story is thus. A Taylor named Thomas Hovill a journeyman being usually imploy'd by some schollers of that Colledge living near it, was particularly beloved by one Mr John White a scholler of the said house, and received many kindnesses from him, and upon occasion he would lend him and give him money and cloths. And Hovill being thus intimate with him, knew all his affairs, and that he had by his great care and frugality save up about twenty pounds for to take his Bachelours degree withall. Now Hovill having an intreague as they reported with a maid of the Town, and would have married her, but she not consenting to his desires unless he could procure some money, to make a handsome wedding of it, and to furnish a house and the like, he knew of no possibility of getting such a summe by any direct and lawfull means, And his passion was so firy for the maid that rather than loose her, he would trye any way to gaine her and accordingly the devil who is allways buisiest in such exigencys put into his heart to rob this his friend, of the said summ. To palliate this his designe he came one day just as the bell rang for supper, to the Colledge (haveing a hatched with him) to desire Mr White to write a letter for him. He being a servitor, and so could not conveniently tarry away from the Hall, desired this Hovill to stay in his Chamber 'till supper was ended, and then he would write his letter, and accordingly left him in his Chamber. But Mr White getting some other servitor to supply his place, returned sooner than he was expected, and caught him in the action of breaking open his trunk. Mr White seeing that, runs to him and gives a box on the ear saying to this purpose, you ingratefull dog do you go to rob me one that have been so good a frind to you? Thomas Hovill turning short upon him, with the hatched gave him a blow on the head which made him fall to the ground, and then to prevent a discovery by groaning or the like he most inhumanly mangled his face and head till he was assured that he was dead, and then stole the money with some cloths and linnen and went his way. The next morning one going to see for Mr White on some buisines, coming to his Chamber which was an upper room found the door open and went in where he found his studying gowne spread on the floor and taking it up found the said John White all in his gore.

One thing more in this story which you may think worth the noting is this. This barborus Hovill after he had committed this bloody fact 'tis said, endeavoured to march off, but by a strange impulse was forc'd to go back again before he could get above a mile or two out of Oxon. Upon examination he was sent to Jail and at the Assizes was condemn'd to be hang'd before the Colledg Gate 3 hours in terrorem. And afterwards to be gibbeted on Bullington Green, which accordingly was done. He was filled with terrour of mind 'till his execution, accompanied with interstices of hardnesse and obduracy.

A list with dates of the 'Principals' of Balliol college is not transcribed, followed by 'A list of the names of such Eminent men who have been scholars in Balliol Colledge.' The editor of Collectanea *notes that these are copied from Savage's 'Balliofergus' and in that edition all were omitted, including an account of the Levellers at Bayworth and Burford, which is included here in* Chapter 6 'Miscellaneous Writings', 'Cavalier or Roundhead?'

After the story of the Levellers, Savage and Baskerville's account of the Lollards continues, followed by numerous biographies of 'fellows of this house', also copied from Dr Savage's book, part in another's hand.

Exeter (f.52)

EXETER COLLEDGE AS also Hart Hall were built by Gualter Stapledon Bishop of Exeter and Treasurer of England Anno 1316 who endowed it with maintenance for 12 fellows. And it was first called Stapledon Hall and had the name of Exeter Coll: from Edmond Stafford Bishop also of Exeter who added 2 fellowships to it in 1404. It had more fellowships added to it by other Benefactors. Arthur Bury Dr of Divinity is their present Rector or Governor Anno 1686 in which are now 23 fellows besides other orders. This account my Godson Mr Thomas Stevenson gave me some five or six years before 1686.

But this present year 86: contracting acquaintance with Mr Crabb, a Scholler of Exeter, and one of the University Library Keepers he gave me this further relation.[23]

He saith the Lord Peters gave 8 fellowships, and King Charles the Martyr one, which fellowship given by that King is various at choise for that fellow must be one time a Jersey man, another time a Garnsey man. These with those given by the above named Benefactors number 23 fellowships.

Now besides these fellows they have 2 Exhibitioners and a Bible Clark.

Now the difference (as Mr Crabb saith) between a fellow and an Exhibitioner in this College is thus, The Exhibitioner hath 16li yearly allowance and no Chamber. The fellows have setled Chambers and better means. Now some of these fellows are yeerly chosen to be in offices and have stipends allowed them, which are the Sub-Rector, the Dean and 2 Boursers.

Severall are the Customes of this Colledge, as of others, among which that of the determining Bachelors is most observable, who on the Saturday morning called egg Saturday, viz. the Saturday before Ash-wednesday, These Schoollers are obliged in their formalityes to serve the whole Hall wth Muscadine and eggs, figs, Almonds, and what sorte of wine they please to drink. And when Breckfast is ended, the Dean with the rest of the society of this house, accompany these determining Bachelors to the Schools and there leave them, from whence (after one of the Collectors has entertained them with a speech and received their fees) they go to St Mary's to prayers and so returne to their respective Colledges.

They further have here a Custome after the Solemn exercise of the Schools is ended, on Ashwednesday to treat the Dean and the fellows, Their Aristotles and as many others as they please with variety of wine viands and other accommodations. The Aristotles are those who answere the Dean instead of the declaiming Bachelors.

As to Ædifice here, you find a large and well built Quadrangle, good Chambers, a fair Hall, and a Cellar may vie with the best in Town.

For other ornaments to delight, here is a fine garden, and in't a Box Knot remarkable for having the founders name and the Coll: Armes curiously cut in't and in another a Sun Diall.

They have also a decent Chappel to serve God in, and an Organ lately set up by the present Rector.

---

23 Probably John Crabbe, son of William, of Child-Okeford, Dorset, matriculated Exeter college 1682 aged 16, M.A. 1688; followed his clerical father into the church. His brother Joseph, matriculated Exeter college 1691, B.A. 1695, became a sub-Librarian of the Bodleian. BHO Foster.

The Chappell was built by Dr Hackwell sometime Rector of this Colledge. Now Annually every Consecration day since the Ceremony was performed in the morning, one of the fellows do preach, and at dinner they allow 2 bottles of wine to every 4 fellows, and 1 bottle of wine to 4 of any other order.

This Colledge is Capacious and large enough to entertaine and lodge 120 people (so saith Mr Crabb and Mr Oliver Schollers in't), but my friend Mr Newe the present Butler saith it is capacious enough for 150 people.

This Society consists for the most part of West Country men but the Petroan fellowships as they call them (which are those given by the Lord Peters) any one is in a capacity of standing for them who was borne in any County where his Lordship had any land.

The Gentlemen which I can remember that have been and now are of my acquaintance in this Colledg are these. Mr Crabb and Mr Oliver, the 1st a Dorsetshire man, the 2nd a Devonshire; The Gentleman who gave this relation Mr Morgan son of Mr Morgan in Cranbourn Chase a Rainger there, for the Earle of Shaftsbury.[24] This Morgan told me at his fathers house he had taken his master of Arts Deg: in Oxon, now since dead, I suppose he was of Exeter Colledge both father and son gave me and my brother Col: Morgan now defunct, a very friendly reception, at their house in Cranbourn Chase, and sent a piece of venison after us to Broad Chalk where that worthy Dame Mrs Aubere (since also dead) gave us free entertainment, and this Mr Morgan Senior was a great lover of my brother and would pleasure my brother and Col: Prater with venison when they sent for it. Mr Masters sometime Curate of Stanton Harcourt and now Parson of Bridewell in London, Mr Richard Baskerville the eldest son of Mr Baskerville of Riccason and Winterbourn in Wiltshire. Mr Rodney Fane, since a student of Law in Lyons Inn London.

Mr Newe my loving friend and butler of this Colledge as aforesaid, who had an ingenous son sometimes a Scholler of this House; who went one of the earliest Planters to Carolina whose loss, with his dear father I do much lament as being deprived by his death of further intelligence from those parts.

Yet to make him live what we can in our Memory take here an account of that plantation, as it came in letters from him, before any narrative of that place was put in print.

Baskerville copied three letters here from Thomas Newe in Charlestown

24 For John Crabbe *see previous note*. Benjamin Oliver (Olliver) matriculated Exeter College 1692 aged 17. Henry Morgan, possibly son of Henry matriculated Exeter College 1635/6 aged 15. BHO Foster.

in America.[25] A fourth letter from GL in New Jersey was copied following the comment on geographers below.

It is the humour of Geographers when they have little more to say of a Country to leave an Elephant Renocerot or some other great Creature in the place; so since we have little more to say of this early Colony take here also the Quakers account of New Jersey for diversion a while. Which letter my worthy friend Mr John Hyde did bestow upon me.

Brazenose (f.57)

BRAZENOSE COLLEDGE WAS begun by William Smith Bishop of Lincoln Anno 1513 but dyeing and leaving it unperfect was finished by Sir Richard Suton, 1522.

The number of Fellowships and Scholarships were encreased by these Benefactors, viz John Claymond, Alexander Novell, Jocosa Frankland, and Samuell Radcliff. The present Principle is Thomas Meers Master of Arts, it hath 20 Fellows, 33 Scholars besides other orders.

Corpus Christi (f.59)

CORPUS CHRISTI COLL: was built by Rich: Fox Bishop of Winchester 1516 one of the Privy Councell to Henry the 7th and 8th and privy seal, it hath a President Robert Newling Dr of Divinity, 20 Fellows, 20 Schollars, 2 Chaplens besides other orders.

This Colledge has one fair Quadrangle for entrance from the street and a back Quadrangle with a Chapel and Cloysters: A good Hall, Kitchin, Buttery, Cellar and Common fire-roome.

Gentlemen

with whome I have had acquaintance sometime in this Colledge, were and are, Mr Lanfyre a famous Preacher in Summerset Shire, often at the Cathedrall of St Andrewes Wells, in Bishop Pierces time he was a Minor Praebend of the Church, viz. Vicar of Dinder two miles from Wells. His son was also a fellow of this Coll: in my time and succeeded his father in the same Preferments of Praebend and Vicar of Dinder, both dead.[26]

---

25 The letters from Thomas Newe have been printed in Alexander S. Salley, Jr., ed., *Narratives of Early Carolina, 1650–1708* (New York, 1911), 181–87. The letter from GL from New Jersey does not appear to have been published.

26 Samuel Lanfire, Magdalen Hall, Oxford: prebend of Dinder, Wells Cathedral (1641); Samuel Lanfire, Corpus Christi, Oxford: prebend of Dinder, Wells Cathedral (1665-1672).

Mr Taylor yet resident there who as I remember told me that one Ouldame was a good Benefactor to this Colledge, who has in his Escuchion Three Owls, and they have a Yew tree by the Colledge seldome without 3 Owles,[27] The people it seemes out of respect to their Benefactor taking care to preserve and cherish these Birds.

Mr Davies now Parson of Sandford in Oxford-Shire, who lately did purchase there a good estate of Mr Dunce of Pissie in Berks.[28]

This land was first given by Mrs Isham their Aunt to the younger brother but he dying it fell to the Eldest Brother, these 3 are dead, and were of my acquaintance. Some years before 1693 Mr Dunce stood to be Burguess of Abingdon against Sir John Stonehouse but fayling in the Attempt a few weekes after he died.[29]

Mr Coward

A Summerset man by birth, his Parents had means in Wells and an Estate at East Penard, 4 miles from Wormi(n)ster in St Cuthberts Parish, Wells, where I was borne.

Mr Coward about 10 years since was Parson of Kingston-Seamore in Summerset shier to the West ward of Bristol by the Severn Sea.[30]

Some years before that account, the sea made a breach in a wall which kept out the waves from overflowing these Moores, which was so suddain that although the wall be 2 miles from the Church, on a Sunday when people were at Prayers in the Church they forced to fly for fear of drowning. The summer after the great frost I went to see some friends at Bledon by up hill 6 miles from Kingston Seamore, Mr Thomas Lyte my Kinesman (whose wife was my brothers Daughter) being Parson there, sometime a Schollar at Trinity in Oxon.[31] So by their perswasion we went oversea to St Fagons in Glamorgan Shire to see our old friend Mr Rachboon Parson there.[32] So after a weeks hearty welcome, we had a ship to come back again, and this ship put us ashore by the wall nigh Kingston Seamore and this wall was then rebuilding at the Chardge of Lord Digby a many men were then at worke. The Lordship where the wall

---

27 Either Richard Taylor of Winchester matriculated 1670, or of Salop matriculatd 1672. BHO Foster.

28 Mr Davies has not been identified.

29 Mr Dunch stood against Sir John Stonehouse in the parliamentary election in 1679. HoP.

30 For Christopher Coward *see* Chapter 2 'Family and Kin'.

31 Thomas Lyte, son of Thomas, of Martock, Somerset, gent. Trinity Coll., M.A. 1678, rector of Bleadon, Somerset, 1682. BHO Foster.

32 Thomas Rawbon, plebian, matric 1651. Rector of St Fagan, Glamorgan, 1679-1692 (death). BHO Foster.

stands did belong to another Gentleman whose name I have forgot, but the Charge of Repairation being too great for his Income, Lord Digby undertooke it with that Lordship.

But to returne, it was in August when we landed here, and my Lords Steward was civill and sent one of his workmen to guide us to an Inn in Kingston Seamore. But that which I am to speake to is this. With some a doe we got beds, for we were 4. But after I was a bed I never but once before met with such Tormentors, and that was an Inn by Severnside at Purton Pass, where and here at Kingston Seamore the stings of fleas were so sharp as if so many needles had stuck in my flesh, this paine I did endure till towards day when their bellyes being full there was a Cessation, sure it should seeme, the Sun and Aire from the Severn Sea do make Fleas more venomous here than in other places.

Thus much in remembrance of Kingston Seamore, Mr Cowards Parsonage. I'lle now go back with him to Corpus-Christi wheren in his time of Courting the Muses, he was a lover of Musick, I being then a well wisher to it he gave mee this song which after, I saw printed in Mr Cowley's Book.

> The thirsty Earth soaks up the Rain
> And drinks and gapes for drink again
> The Plants suck in the Earth, and are
> With constant drinking fresh and fair,
> The sea itself which one would think
> Should have but little need to drink
> Drinks Thousand Rivers up
> So fill'd that they o're flow the Cup
> The buisy Sun, and one would guess
> By's drunken firy face no less
> Drinks up the Sea and when h'as done
> The Moon and Stars drink up the Sun
> They drink and dance in their own light
> They drink and Revel all the night
> Nothing in nature's sober found
> But an Eternall health goes round
> Fill up the Bowl then fill it high
> Fill all the glasses there; for why?
> Should every Creature drink but I
> Why man of Moralls tell me why.

So farwell Cowley and his heaths
All heal to him and his good wealth
Clashes and dashes are the fates
Of such as live in troublesome states
Between light, darkness, good, evill,
God keep us all from the Devill
Certain the Devill is not there
Where both sex do use their gear
Popular, and Aristoricall States
Sometime meet troublesome fates
Despotick and Monarchial powers
Scholars and Townsmen feel some showers
Civill & Ecclesiastick Jurisdictions
Have Clashes and Dashes, that breed afflictions
Kings and Parliaments, men and their wives
Have some Clashes while alive
Thus we see how things occur
Between the Termes, Plea and Demur
There is nothing allways quiet found
Because of jarrs are moving round
For Mortalls they have sundry souls
As far distant as the Two Poles
This makes fuieds, fights and fallings
Because they'l dye in their callings
So good and bad are in places
And as to souls, they have their cases
Sometimes better sometimes worse
Much as they please bear the purse
Therefore as Scripture plainly sayes
There is evill sufficient to the day.

Tis a Common saying that sorrows
        are Drye
Therefore Ile wash u'm away with honest
        Tom Hyde's good health
Here is a Carousing Cup, unto the best of men
And when that this is drunk all out, then we'll begin agen
For here is nothing constant in this world to be found
And so drink up your liquor, and let this health go round.

2

Each man his can all in hand and Cup upon the ground
Each man unto his liquor stand, and let this health go round
Then take your Cups and turn them and what you do not drink
Put in your Caps and burn them, whatever you say or think.

*This introduces Baskerville's long Memoir of Tom Hyde's adventures and life,
for which see* Chapter 6 'Miscellaneous Writings'.

The Resurrection of the dead is so great in *Athenae* and *Fasti Oxoniensis*
it might afright the University, the life everlasting was begun.

Therefore to be rid of u'm here upon Earth, they sent u'm all to Heaven
in a fyrye Chariot. Yet in gratitude to Mr Anthony a Wood for his late kind
treat of wine at the Mermaids Tavern Oxon, Ile quot one of the number who
was of this Coll:

*Nicholas Crach or Chrache Kratcher or Kratza fellow of Corpus Christi
1517, the reference in* Athenae Oxoniensis *stated, followed by a list of Presidents,
benefactors, learned writers and eminent men without any personal comments.*

Merton (f.63)

THE FOUNDER OF Merton Colledge was Walter Merton Bishop of
Rochester Anno [blank]. It is governed in Chief by a Warden now called
Sir Thomas Clayton a Dr of Phisick whose income by the Colledge is said to
be worth 600li per annum. The Statutes of this Colledge say, they must never
have above 40 Fellows and never under 16 fellows. This Colledge has had little
or nothing done to it in my dayes, it being brought to perfection before, save
that their Chappell (which is also a Parish Church called St Johns) hath lately
been new beautified at the Charges of one Mr Fisher a fellow of that house
who gave money to do it after his death.

The Schollars of this house have a custome one night in a year when
they have been long and late at disputing to break open their buttery door and
fall to eating such victualls as they can find there.

Gentlemen of this Colledge which I have seen and have had some
acquaintance are Dr White Hall Mr Whitehall his kinesman now Curate of
Stanton-Harcourt, Dr Coward, Mr Hyde, son of my worthy friend Captaine
Hyde of Kingston Lile in Berks, Mr Richard Hyde son of my worthy friend
Mr John Hyde of London borne at Blagrove in Berks.

Lincoln (f65)

L INCOLN COLLEDGE WAS begun by Thomas Flemming Bishop of Lincoln 1430 but he dyeing, Thomas of Beckington Bishop of Bath and Wells added to it, but Thomas of Rotheram Bishop of Lincoln afterwards Bishop of York and Chancelor of England finished it and added 5 fellowships to it in 1475.

Edward Derby Archdeacon of Stow added 3 more in 1534 afterwards John Williams keeper of the great seal and Bishop of Lincoln, afterwards Archbishop of York built the Chappell to it, in 1631. It hath a Rector Tho: Marshall Dr of Divinity; 12 fellows, 2 Chaplains besides other orders.

Queens (f.67)

Q UEENS COLLEDGE WAS built Anno 1340 by Robert Eaglesfield Batchelor in Divinity and Chaplain to Queen Philippa wife of Edward the 3d which Colledg he dedicated to her, and all succeeding Queens. Sir Joseph Williamson added a piece of building to it in 1672. It hath a Provost Timothy Halton Dr of Divinity, 14 Fellows, 7 schollars, 2 Chapplains, 14 poor Children besides other orders.

In this Colledge some tell me, at meals they sit at table or tables in their Hall with backes against the wall or wainscot and their faces looke all one way. The reason why they do so, some say was this. One of their Society being killed by a stab in the back, when eating at a Table in the Hall they do to prevent the like evills sit as I said with their faces all looking forward one way. My worthy friend Dr Hide one of this Society with a good dinner gave me this account of an ancient custome in their Colledge at Christmas.

So take it verbatim as he writ it.

In Queens Colledge on Christmas day at the beginning of dinner is kept an ancient Custome of singing up the Boar's head, which perhaps formerly might be a real Head, but now is a wooden head dress'd with Bayes and Rosemary, and before the mouth, there is put a little burning pitch which flameth, and a little white froth to represent the foaming of the Boar.

The song is sung only by one Person, either the Butler or any body who hath a tolerable good voice, and is strong enough to bear the weight of the Head at his Armes end. But the Chorus is sung by all in the Hall, who have a mind to stretch their voices. But the Taberders or Foundation Batchelors who are Chiefly expected to sing it, do exercise it for above a week before, in the evening altogeither in a Chamber, for which they are allow'd at such times some Beer by the Colledge. And that is the only song which is ever allowed to be sung alowd in the College, it being otherwise an offence to sing lowd. The song consists of 3 stanzas and is accordingly by parts sung at 3 severall stations in the Hall viz. at the entrance, at the middle and at or near to the high Table.

> The Boars Head in hand bear I,
> Bedecked with Bays and Rosemary.
> And I pray you my Masters merry be yee,
> Quot estis in Convivio.
> Caput Apri defero, reddens laudes Domino.

> The Boars Head as I understand,
> Is the bravest dish in all the Land.
> And thus bedecked with a gay Garland,
> Let us servire Cantico.
> Caput Apri defero, reddens Laudes Domino.

> Our Steward hath provided this,
> In memory of the King of Bliss,
> Which on this day to be served is
> In Reginensi Atrio.
> Caput Apri defero, reddens Laudes Domino.

Queens Colledge has one fair Quadrangle, A chapel with some painted glass, a good Hall, Kitchin, Buttery, Cellar and a Common fire roome for the graver people, which convenience as to buildings has been added to the Colleges since my time, for the Common fire places are in the middest of every Hall, But now since this addition of Common fire Rooms in most Colledges the Seniors do retire after meals that the younger people may have freedome to warm their Toes and fingers.

As other Colledges call their people to meales by ringing bells here they do it by blowing a Horne.

As to outlets or walks being now surrounded by other buildings 'tis not much.

Yet they have some Gardens and a Bowling Green.

I am told by my friend Mr John West Shop-keeper in Oxford, that Dr Barlow since Bishop of Lincoln, was a Fellow and then Provost of Queen's Colledge in my time. At his decease (for he dy'd then Bishop of Lincoln) he gave seven waggon loads of Books to Queen College, and they are now at the Charges of that house building a Library to bestow them.

A Gentleman of that name, a great lover of my Father and Mother,

Dean of Wells Anno Dmi 1630 was one of my Godfathers, Mr Thomas Lyte of Lytes Cary Somerset (who took the pains to draw down King James Petigree from Brute) was the other.[33] My Godfather Dean Barlo did dye before I was of yeers to know him, but he left Children. I was acquainted with one of his sons, Major Henry Barlo, a valiant man for King Charles the 1st in those wars. Captain William Morgan and Major Henry Barlo both friends and Commanders under the said King when that party did vanish, did marry two sisters. A third was wife to my uncle George Lyte of Layterton in Glocestershire. Captain Hedges of Wedmore Somerset a Parlamentarian, was their brother who dying without Issue, his estate fell among the sisters, all these are dead, but I'le return to Dean Barlow, one Warburton I think was his successor in the Deanery who being removed or dying, the next Dean of Wells was Raileigh.[34] In his time the warrs being very hot between the Cavaliers and Roundheads (as they then were called) and much blood shed on both sides after the Kings party was forced out of the West Dean Rawleigh was made a Prisoner in Wells and one Penny was there a Marshall or Jaylor, who taking a spleen against the Dean, then under his Custody, gave him a stab of which wound he dy'd he had sons that went to school with me, that time in Wells.

University (f.69)

A s for UNIVERSITY Colledge its Antiquity renders its originall so obscure that we have onely this relation that King Alfred built the great Hall of the University in the year 883 which by the injury of the times was turned to other uses till at last it was redeemed by some fellow students which were maintained by the money that William Dunelm left by his will to the University for that use in 1245. To this Wa(l)ter Skirlaw added 3 fellowships, and Henry Percy Earl of Northumberland 3 more, and Sir Simon Bennet who was himself of this house gave four fellowships and as many Schollars places. It hath a Master Obadiah Walker, Master of Arts, 12 fellows, 10 Schollars besides other orders.

Trinity (f.71)

T RINITY COLLEDGE WAS founded by Thomas Pope Knight, who gave it that name 1556. It hath a President Radolph Bathurst Dr of Phisick and Dean of Wells, 12 Fellows, 12 Scholars with other orders.

33 This is described in his writing about his family connections. See Chapter 2 'Life and Kin'.
34 Baskerville was correct in his suggestion that Warburton was the next Dean (1631-1642), and that Raleigh was Dean (1642-1646, died 10 October 1646) during the years of the wars 'being very hot'. CCEd.

Jesus (f.73)

JESUS COLLEGE WAS founded by Queen Elisabeth 1572 to which there were severall great benefactors, viz Herbert Westfaling Bishop of Hereford, Sir John Walter Chief Baron of the Exchequer, Sr Eubul Thelwell, Thomas Gwin and Francis Mansell formerly Principals. It hath a Principall John Lloyd Dr of Divinity and present Vice-Chancelor, 16 Fellows, 16 Scholars, 8 Exhibitioners with other orders.

Wadham (f.75)

NICHOLAS WADHAM LEFT in his will what was sufficient to build and endow Wadham College 1609 which was very splendidly performed by his wife Dorothy in 1613. It hath a Warden, Gilbert Ironside, 15 Fellows, 15 Schollars, 2 Chaplains besides all other orders.

Pembroke (f.77)

PEMBROOK COLLEGE WAS formerly called Broadgate hall in 1624 to which Thomas Tesdale of Glimton gave money for the maintenance of 7 fellows and 6 Schollars to be chosen out of Abingdon School. And Richard Whitwick Batchelor of Divinity added 3 fellows and 4 Schollars. King James granted it to be a Colledge in 1624 which for the honor of William Herbert Earl of Pembrook, then Chancellor of the University they named it Pembrook Coll: it hath a Master, 10 Fellows, 10 Schollars, with many of other orders.

Gloucester Hall (f.79)

GLOCESTER HALL EITHER had its name from Gilbert Clare Earl of Glocester or from the Glocester Monks who before the destruction of Monasteryes studied here the Arts, in 1283 but however it was, Sir Thomas White founder of St Johns Colledge built up the ruins of this, and dedicated it to the Muses 1560 only changing the name into St John Baptist's Hall, but it rather still retains the first name, the present Principle is Byrom Eaton Dr of Divinity.

Heart Hall (f.81)

HEART HALL WAS founded by Walter Stapledon Bishop of Exeter who also founded Exeter Colledge 1314 the present Principle is John Lanpyre Doct. of Physick an Hystory professor.

St Albans Hall (f.83)

S T ALBANS HALL had not its name so much from the Monastery of St
Albans whose Monks studied here in 1300 as from Robert of St Albans
formerly Governor of that Church. But however it was, its now inhabited by
gownsmen. Thomas Bourchier Dr of Law Principle.

St Edmond Hall (f.85)

S T EDMOND HALL either had its name from one Edmund formerly Master
of it, or of St Edmund Archbishop of Canterbury, it belongs now to Queens
Colledge.

St Mary Hall (f.87)

S T MARY'S HALL either had its name from the neighbouring Church or
from Oriel Colledge, to which it belongs, which was formerly called St
Mary's College Joseph Crowther the present Principle.

Newinn Hall (f.89)

N EWINN HALL WAS formerly called Trilleck Hall 1360 from John Trilleck
Bishop of Hereford and his brother Thomas formerly own'd it but since
falling to New Colledge in 1392 it receiv'd the name of New-Inn Hall. William
Stone Batchelor of Law the present Principle.

*A detailed explanation of Longitude by John Herne follows the Oxford
section.*

*At the reverse end of the folio is an account of the Great Turks declaration
of War against the Emperor of Germany 1683 given to Baskerville by his 'worthy
friend Mr Richard Rodd a Herefordshire man'.*

A Prophecy on the Conjunction of Saturn and Jupiter In the present
year 1682 with some Prophetical predictions of what is likely to ensue in the
year 1684.

4
JOURNEYS IN INDUSTRIOUS ENGLAND

HAD THOMAS BASKERVILLE's travel writings reached the printer, he might have been recognised as the precurser of Daniel Defoe, in his thoroughly down-to-earth, practical observations of the work taking place in different parts of the country, from ploughing through iron working to smuggling.[1] As it was, seventeenth-century collectors fortunately preserved some, though possibly not all, of his manuscripts. 'Among Restoration topographers, Thomas Baskerville remains an obscure figure, but he deserves to be more widely known.'[2] He was not primarily interested in antiquities, though he described some notable examples, but he was interested in the country's economy. He recorded observations of agricultural practices. He noted where there were markets, and the goods generally brought to them. He described ingenious arrangements for pumping water. Mills attracted his attention. He was interested generally in the economics of various trades. Everywhere he went he talked to local people, particularly inn-keepers, and gleaned information, for example, on the price of saffron. It was characteristic of Baskerville that there are interruptions in the accounts of journeys: there is a long list of goods associated with particular places or countries, and another of all the fish he and another could name. Mention of the trade of Ely led to a long account of Stourbridge fair.

The accounts of journeys, however, were also written as if he were compiling a road gazetteer. The smaller places were grouped between one major town and the next. He listed not only towns and villages he passsed through or by, and noted their public buildings, but also he named the owners of prominent houses and the church towers and spires in the view, which

---

1 *The Cambridge History of Travel Writing (2019)* 91 presents travel writing as a literary form, in the 17th century most associated with poetic expression. Daniel Defoe, *A Tour through the Whole Island of Great Britain (1724-6)*.
2 Blair, 'Thomas Baskerville on the upper Thames'.

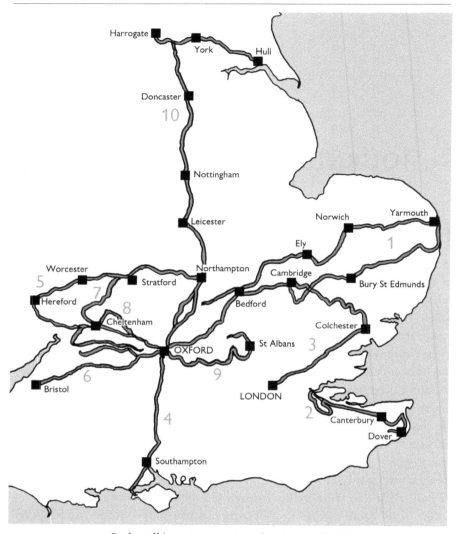

Baskerville's ten journeys in industrious England

would have enabled later travellers to confirm their location; typically he noted some details of the construction of round church towers in Norfolk. He pointed out notable viewpoints for tourists following his route. There are frequent comments on 'sweet' air, especially on hill-tops, a reminder that towns, and especially London, suffered pollution from coal smoke.[3] A travel diary written some twenty years after Baskerville's writings described a tour to the north of England by the two sons of William Blathwayte of Dyrham Park,

---

3   Celia Fiennes similarly commented on 'Banstead Downs where is good aire'. *The Illustrated Journeys of Celia Fiennes* ed Christopher Morris (1982) 231.

together with their tutor; they concentrated on visiting churches and houses like Audley End and the Cambridge colleges, but took no obvious interest in matters economic or practical. Baskerville, too, had visited some of these attractions, showing a recognised tourist trail, but the interest of his accounts of journeys is much wider.[4]

Baskerville anticipated the trend in travel writing, which expanded considerably in harmony with the amount of travel in the mid- and later-eighteenth century; diaries were often compiled to be passed round family and friends. Esther Moir listed only a small number in print before Baskerville was setting down his experiences, and she included books such as Lambarde's *Perambulation of Kent* (1576), which is a local history about his own county rather than a travel diary; the Historical Manuscripts Commission transcript of Baskerville's prose travel writings was on her list.[5] Her list of eighteenth and nineteenth century travel writing was a great deal longer, much of it not published until years after it was written, or still in Archive Offices. A survey by the Association of County Archivists in 1989 identified 608 unpublished travel diaries at that date, by 369 writers; only five were written in the seventeenth century, between 1700 and 1750 there were 20, but after mid-eighteenth century the number was in the hundreds.

The publications of John Taylor were in Moir's list of seventeenth-century travel writing. Baskerville was no doubt aware of Taylor's works. Taylor had published his writing as he went along, with a first collected edition in 1630, while he added more printed works as he continued to travel;[6] he died in 1653. Baskerville perhaps tried to emulate Taylor in describing a journey in verse, the subject of Chapter 5, but overall his writing was more pithy and practical. He nowhere mentions Taylor, nor Leland nor Camden, but their topographical writings may have informed his.

His journeys were for his personal entertainment and the satisfaction of his curiosity. He went to Farnham because he noticed the considerable income generated by the market which enriched the Bishop of Bath and Wells. Once only did he state 'On a time travailing for my pleasure to the Town of Nottingame'.[7] He occasionally uses the word 'travail' for journey, and as Moir points out, travail and travel were originally the same, implying trouble

---

4 *The Observant Traveller* (HMSO 1989), x-xi; 'Journal of tour of the young Blathwayts 1703', Gloucestershire Archives, D1799/F213 and SB3.35GS (translated from the French by Nora Hardwick (F. Bailey & Son Dursley, 1977)).

5 Moir, *The Discovery of Britain* (1964) 159-178.

6 Taylor, *Travels and Travelling* (2020).

7 Chapter 2 'Life and Kin', 'Sunningwell'.

and discomfort, but despite some hardships, he appears to have thoroughly enjoyed his journeys and found much generous hospitality on the way.[8] The journeys were on horseback, and there is frequent reference to riding to the next place, and occasionally to putting up the horses at an inn. The road from Sudeley down the hill was very difficult for horses because of the loose stones, but at other times he rode over 'fine sandy down'. Very occasionally he mentions enjoying walking; there is no indication of a coach, and indeed on one occasion a host provided a coach to take him back to his lodgings.

It is striking that Baskerville was sometimes accommodated in private houses, even in one instance having met the gentleman who was his host only a short time before when playing bowls. He was well-informed about the current owners of the large houses he passed. It was accepted that a guest might arrive unannounced, and might be given hospitality for a week.[9] The large houses of the gentry were in effect small private hotels. The openness to receiving guests had been commented on a hundred years earlier by William Harrison, although the acceptable length of a stay in a townsman or Londoner's house was said to be no more than four days. At sixteenth century Syston Court in Gloucestershire, the arrangement of 'lodgings' for guests in wings either side of the courtyard still exists.[10] Baskerville more often stayed in local inns, and reveals the importance and status of an innkeeper, commenting on the good ones and so assisting someone following in his tracks to find good lodgings. He was not always lucky, as his experince in Kingston Seymour illustrates.[11] He appears to have been robust and cheerful in all situations. Wine, ale and beer are frequently the subject of favourable comment and he clearly enjoyed a game of bowls, commenting on where he found a bowling green.

It seems likely that Baskerville had some maps to guide him in the area of Bayworth. Did he use Saxton's or Speed's maps? Had he seen Ogilby's atlas of road maps?[12] The latter was published in 1675, too late for some of the journeys he describes, and it was much too large a volume to be taken

---

8 Moir, *The Discovery of Britain* (1964), xiii.

9 'If the freends also of the wealthier sort come to their houses from farre, they are commonlie so welcome till they depart, as uppon the first daie of their comming'. *Harrison's Description of England* (1877), 152-3.

10 Syston is near Pucklechurch where TB was accommodated for some days. See Section 7 below.

11 Chaper 3, 'Oxford' page 27.

12 Christopher Saxton, *Atlas of the Counties of England and Wales* published in 1579; John Speed, *The Theatre of the Empire of Great Britain* published 1611, 1616, 1623; *Ogilby's Road Maps of England and Wales 1675 from Ogilby's Britannia* (Osprey Publications Ltd 1971).

on horseback. The occasional reference to a place being 'underneath' a more prominent town does imply that he had a map with East at the top; if north were at the top of the page, 'beneath' should have been 'to the left' or west. The convention of orienting maps with north at the top was not established until the following century.[13] Baskerville was well aware of direction, frequently noting that he was travelling eastward and so on, so the obvious reason for odd indications of direction is a map. The roads he travelled were sometimes Roman roads still in use and some routes were close to modern main roads; on other occasions he travelled cross-country, and sometimes had to follow a circuitous route to reach the destination he was aiming for.

Rivers were much more important to the traveller in the seventeenth century than they are to the traveller in the twenty-first. Baskerville noted small streams and where they flowed into larger streams, and whether the rivers were good for fish. Rivers were also markers for the routes; in the fen country he observed how the roads follow the river banks, and he rode beside the Medway between Maidstone and Rochester. In Tewkesbury he noted the three rivers and the effect of floods. Bridges were very apparent to the seventeenth-century traveller, together with their sometimes lengthy causeways; Baskerville was particularly interested in their design, commenting on the flow of a river under a bridge, and he made detailed surveys of bridges on the Thames, set out at the end of this chapter. He was fascinated by Chepstow bridge.

He did not travel alone, though there is no more than an occasional reference to the men who accompanied him; on one occasion it seems there was a general joining up with others travelling the same road. When he went to Coberley to buy horses from Mrs Castleman, he said there were seven in the party as well as horses, and so they declined to stay with her. This party got lost in the fog on the Cotswolds. When he went north, he had Mr Washborne for company on the outward journey; his man, Mr Griffiths, accompanied him to St Albans and Mr Baker acted as his guide when they went to Norfolk.[14] He invariably writes 'we' in his accounts. He does not say anything about travelling with baggage, or a servant, but could have had a pack horse to carry luggage, and almost certainly travelled with a man-servant to aid him. Like Don Quixote, he had a Sancho Panza.

The manuscript in which Thomas Baskerville described in prose his travels through England is the British Library, MS Add. 70523. The Historical Manuscripts Commission presented it in the order as in the manuscript.[15] It

13 Black, *Maps and History* (1997) 15.
14 See biographies of Mr Washborne and Mr Baker, Chapter 3 'Oxford'.
15 *See* Chapter 1 'Introduction'.

appears that Baskerville did not write his journeys up in chronological order, nor did he date his journeys, but some dates were given within the texts, and a date can be ascribed to others because of a mention of a particular event or person. The journey to Southampton, for example, was shortly after the execution of Charles I. He travelled to Colchester in 1661 or 1662, staying with Charles Forbinch, the rector. He gives the date of 1673 for his journey to Northampton and as he notes, a great fire some years after, in 1675, prompted him to go there again; he wrote up this journey in the early 1680s, so he was able to add interesting details about the fire. Other accounts of journeys may also incorporate information from more than one occasion, as well as details he could add at the time he was writing. His journey to the north can be dated because Baskerville travelled with Mr Washborne,[16] who was inducted in York into his living of Long Preston by the Archbishop in 1677, and he and Baskerville then proceeded onward together, before leaving Mr Washborne in his Vicarage; however, Baskerville also comments misleadingly on an organ in Nottingham church in 1675, referring to the date of installation not to his visit there. Riding through the Fens on his way to Norwich, he noted the extreme heat and drought 'in May 1681'.

This manuscript is not a neat copy like the Rawlinson volume. It gives the impression of drafts written up in sections over a period of a year or two, which he might have intended to copy up neatly into a larger folio volume. Throughout there are a number of corrections, and as indicated in the Introduction only significant additions are placed between brackets. The manuscript is particularly full of odd place-name spellings; Baskerville often relied on being told a name by a local person and accordingly wrote down a phonetic spelling. Place-names were by no means standardised until the early nineteenth century when the Ordnance Survey made a concerted effort to establish the most acceptable spelling; the hope then was that 'wherever possible the name should be endorsed by written evidence' as 'when taken down by word of mouth, errors are very liable to occur.' The principle established was that 'Ordnance Survey names should follow those in common use by the residents of an area, even if these were etymologically incorrect or suspect'.[17] Printed names on maps which Baskerville might have consulted were not all uniform or as later established by the Ordnance Survey. Nearly all his place-names have been identified and their modern spelling indicated.

It is interesting that the first journey in the manuscript, to Norwich in 1681, was almost his last; there is an account of one more short journey the

16 Washbourne in other sources.
17 Owen and Pilbeam, *Ordnance Survey Map Makers (1992)*, 75.

following year. He had a knowledgeable guide on his tour to Norfolk, and the places and scenes were clearly fresh in mind. The density of settlement is reflected in the nunber of places Baskerville named as he rode through Suffolk and Norfolk. The words tumble out breathlessly. It could even be that this account was written day by day during the tour: there are blotches on some pages and the handwriting is not carefully formed. It perhaps inspired him in the next two years to write up his other journeys.

~~~

British Library, MS Add. 70523

The folios in this manuscript are not numbered; there are 110 pages of text. The manuscript appears to consist of a set of drafts written at different times, some possibly while on one of the journeys. The frequent use of a new line for each sentence has been reproduced. The names of Inns are italicised by the editor.

JOURNEY 1
TO NORWICH FROM OXFORD VIA BEDFORD, CAMBRIDGE, BURY ST EDMONDS AND YARMOUTH

The journey can be dated because of the remark about the dry weather in May 1681

THE NAMES OF the Townes from Oxon, to Cambridge and other places as wee went from thence to Yarmouth and Norwich - Tame ten miles from Oxon, in the waie from thence to Alesbury wee saw these countrey villages, viz: Long Crandon, Haddon, Winchenell, where the Lord Wharton's eldest son has a faire house on the top of the hill.

Ethrop is next, where the Lord of Canarvan hath a house, whose surname is Dormer, -

Stone, another countrey parish.

Hartwell, where Sir Thomas Lee has a faire house[18] -

---

18 Oxford, Thame, Aylesbury, Long Crendon, Haddenham, Winchendon, Eythrope, Stone, Hartwell. Upper Winchendon belonged to the Wharton family from 1623; Charles Dormer Earl of Carnarvon died 1709. Sir Thomas Lee 1st baronet (1635-1691), MP 1660-1685 & 1689-1691; Hartwell is a Jacobean and Georgian house listed Grade I. HoP; Historic England.

Alesbury, a great markett Towne where is some times kept the assize for Buckingham shire, situated on a pleasant hill, over looking the vale which has its name from thence. In it ar many faire Inns to entertaine travellers, of which the *White Hart* is Cheif, famous for a large roome, overlooking a fine garden.

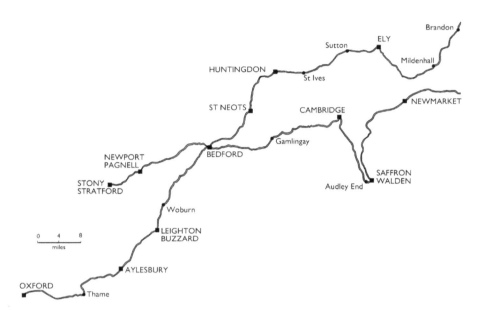

From Alesbury to Layton Buzard another markett towne in the road to Cambridge, is accountted 7 miles these parishes lie in the waie or in sight thereof, viz: Berton Ascott park and house, which is the Lord Canorvans, Hethern reach, where Mr Ironside has a good house.[19]

Then Layton, a small markett towne with one church and a small river in the county of Bedford -

Hence to Wooboorne 4 miles, here was antiently a Abbey called Wooborne Abbey but now the Earle of Bedford hath in place of it, a large house with a parke, fish ponds, and a warren adjoyning to it[20]-

From Wooborne in the waie towards Bedford about ten miles off wee had sight of tall steeple in a Towne called Handslip, and on the hill above Marston a fair prospect over the vale to Bedford.[21]

Bedford is a great Towne situated on the river Ouse, it has in it 5 churches, and the ruines of an old Castle, containing within it, a fine bowling-

19 Ascott Park (Wing), Heath & Reach.
20 Leighton Buzzard, Woburn
21 Hanslope, Marston, Bedford.

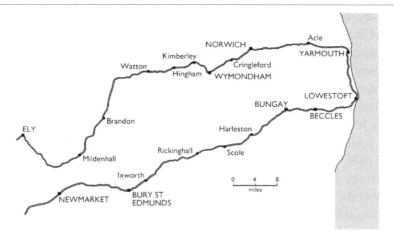

green, Mr Lowns, the master of the *Swan* where we lay, looks to it, this Inn is the best in Bedford and is built by the Rivers side att the Bridge foot, having a passage through the back side to the bowling green, where we found very good company, and dranck excellent bottled ale and wine.

From Bedford, to Cambridge is accounted 20 miles. These villages lie in the waie, viz: Penlake next Willington where Mr Gostick has a house and parke,[22] then Muggeranger where wee saw St Neotes about 4 miles off, vulgarly called St Needs a market Tow(n)e where boats come from Linn with Coales and other lading.[23] This Towne is about 8 miles from Bedford, and the river Ouse is navigable for boates of burden no farther than this Towne.

Passing over a fine sandy downe wee came to a through fare town called Gamgay, where nothing is remarkable but a new Almes house a mile from this place, people told mee of a great markett Towne called Potten famous for corn.[24] From Gamgay wee went to Taft and then to Comberton 3 mile from Cambridge.

A mile beyond Comberton wee had a fair prospect of the university and Kings college Chappell.[25]

---

22 Sir John Gostwick probably built Willington Manor House after he acquired it in 1529. The family remained there until 1731. Bedford Archives https://bedsarchives.bedford.gov.uk/CommunityHistories.

23 Fenlake next Willington, Moggerhanger, St Neots, King's Lynn.

24 Sir John Jacob's Almhouses in Gamlingay, Suffolk, built 1664 for 'the poor widows of good character resident in the village of Gamlingay'. https://housingcare.org.

25 Gamlingay, Potton, Toft, Comberton.

Cambridge is a great Towne with 14 parish churches in it, besides Kings College Chapell and other College chapells, people there told mee the beauty of it consists most in the scituation of the colleges on the banck of the river of which there are 5 that have fair Bridges over to delicate walkes, bowling greens and gardens on the other side viz St Johns College, Trinity college, Trinity Hall, Clare hall, and King's College -

St Johns College is famous for 3 curious quadrangles with the Gates built, in such exact order, that you may see through all 3 to the bridge that goes over the river -

Trinity College is little less than Christ Ch: in Oxon having a fair Conduit in the first quadrangle or front of the College towards the Towne, and by the river side a very stately library is now a building and almost finished,[26]

The walls of Clare Hall is exquisite for workmanshipp, and Kings College Chapell is the wonder of England for a gallant structure.

The mode of College building in this towne in these days is brick cased with free stone, the brick is brought from the Ile of Ely, and the stone from Peterburough up the river, Came, by water and so is their fuell of turf and cole. They have here pleasure boates on the river as att Oxon - which go downe streame to Ely, distant 10 miles by land from Cambridge, but more by water and Linn, the sea port towne to this river and others is accounted sixty miles from Cambridge[27]

They have a better faishon for undergraduates capps in Cambridge to keep off the sun then wee att Oxon, and the tuffs of silke on the Masters capps is 4 or 5 inches long.

The people of the town ar very civill to strangers and the Schollers as kind to their acquaintance that come from Oxon, as wee found by experience, being treated with wine and other good things by them.

Mr Collingson then proctour in May (81) Mr Martin a Beadell, Mr Thornbourough, the Lord Chancellour Finch his 2 sons, were persons who obliged us with their kind favours.[28]

Wee lay att the *Angell* a good Inn for beer and mumme, Mr Peck now master of it, and the *Rose Inn* Taverne joyns to it, where Mr Fage a gentile man

26 It was not completed until 1695.
27 Ely, Peterborough.
28 TB enjoyed a high social status: Heneage Finch, 1st earl of Nottingham (1621-1682), lord chancellor of England (1675–82); https://www.britannica.com/biography/Heneage-Finch-1st-Earl-of-Nottingham. Obadiah Collinson, proctor 1680-81. ACAD.

was then Master. They have generally very good Claret and ar well served with sea Fish, but the Barbell is not in the river Came -

From Cambridge to Audley Inn is accounted 10 miles, these parishes lie in the waie, thether viz 1st Trumpington 2ndly Selfoord 3rd Stablefoord then Sarson where one Mr Hudlestone has a house,[29] Chesterford, here the countrey is so pleasant and parish townes so thick, that one may tell 9 towers the farthest not above 2 miles off as wee ride between Stapleford and Sarson[30] -

Audley Inn is a great and sumctuous house inferior to none in England, for biggness, built as I suppose by a Duke of Suffolke, but now belonging to the King, and the present Earle of Suffolke for his life, 'tis seated on a small river, containing within a square of buildings, a large quadrangle having a fair park and sumptuous fish ponds adjoining.

Tis adorned within with many fair Roomes divers of them richly hung with Arras, with many rare pictures and Chimney pieces in most roomes, of well polished marble of varied collours. And in that most noble gallery is the best sealing for plaister work as ever I saw, having many various figures of birds, beast, flowers, and fishes, trees, and men.

Wee rod from hence through the park, to Saffron Waldron, a fine markett Towne, about halfe a mile off; governed instead of a Mayor by a Treasurer, and 2 Justices and Aldermen;[31] it has in it very fine church and a Tower of exquisite workmanshipp one Mr Norton a very respectfull gentleman, being their parson, with whome wee fell acquainted att a very good bowling green without the town.[32]

Wee lay att the *Bell* and had very good bottle'd Ale, Mr Mayor being then master of the Inn. This town lies in the county of Essex.

From this town we went to New Markett which is accounted 15 miles, townes in the way thither are little and great Chestoford, Bournbridge,[33] in the

---

29 Henry Huddleston owned Sawston Hall from 1665 but mainly lived in London and his daughter and her husband occupied the house. The family were royalists and Roman Catholics. https://cudl.lib.cam.ac.uk/view/MS-VIEWS-RELHAN-00285/1

30 Audley End, Trumpington, Shelford, Stapleford, Sawston, Chesterford.

31 Saffron Walden.

32 Edward Norton, vicar of Saffron Walden 1674-1712, also prebendary of St Paul's Cathedral 1679-1712. CCEd.

33 Great & Little Chesterford, Bourn Bridge, Newmarket. Bourn Bridge, Babraham, carried the Icknield Way over the Granta river. https://en.wikipedia.org/wiki/Babraham#History

fields and grounds about these townes is much saffron planted.

They usually take upp the heads or roots <once in 3 yeres[34]>, about midsummer, of the saffron to dung and dress the ground and then sett them againe to bear a crop of flowers in autumn, <which are few the first yere> but the value of that commodity is much fall'n over what it was <A bushel of saffron heads is now got for 1s 6d and sometimes 1s and saffron about £1 5s. the pound.>

New Markett is a poore through fare Towne, with 2 small churches, having little else remarkable in it save, the Kings house lately built to entertain him when he comes thither to hunting and raceing[35] but inviorned on all sides with a rare downy open countrey.

This Town lies in Cambridge shire about 10 miles from Cambridge, and 10 miles from St Edmondsbury,[36] and about 16 or 18 miles from the Citty of Ely.

The waie as we went to St Edmondsbury being a downy open countrey, we only went through Kentford.

St Edmondsbury is a very buityfull Inland Towne full of rich shopps, and tradesmen, the streets spacious and the houses well built, governed by a Bayliff and 12 Aldermen, for publick buildings most remarkable, here is, the ruins of a large Abbey with the largest portche as yet standing I have seen yet to any house in England; nere unto it ar 2 great Churches, so nere one the other as they seem to bee in one church yeard, there is also a fair markett hous, with some lesser houses for the sale of things -

Here is also a free schoole one Mr Leeds now master, and because Gentrey do much frequent this Towne, they say here ar five physitians for which reason the Appothecarys shopps ar large and full of good druggs, and the milleners shopps as full of variety of rich weares.

Wee lay att the *Bull*, Mr Payne now master of it nere unto which is a fine bowling green this Towne is in the county of Suffolke and has a small stream of water running by it.

34 The additions about saffron are in the same distinctive, formal handwriting as on some later pages. Saffron was widely grown on the sandy soils of South Cambridgeshire. https://www.cam.ac.uk/stories/saffron

35 James I built the first house in Newmarket, but it was partly demolished during the civil wars. Charles II had a larger house designed by a local architect, William Samwell. A small part survives, now the National Museum of Horseracing. https://www.royalpalaces.com/palaces/newmarket

36 Bury St Edmonds.

From St Edmondsbury wee rode to the famous *Scole Inn*, whose signe post as my Land-Lord told me cost 500 pound the making its accounted between bury and Scole 15 miles.

These countrey Townes lie in the waie, viz: Ikesworth, Stanton, Dilingale, Budesdale, wher Sir John Castleton has a hous.[37]

The Inn att Scole is Large and well built, with <fair dining room> and a Balconey to it, to Look on that sumptuous signe post.[38]

The signe post haveing most of the Effigies cutt in full proportion is contrived with these poeticall fancies, for supporters to the post, on the further side of the waie there is Cerberus or a large dogg with 3 heads on one side, and Charon with a boate rowing an old woman with a letter in her hand, on the other side - The other figures ar Saturn with a child in his armes eating it upp, Diana with a Moon Crescent on her head, Acteon with his hounds eating him, and the Effigies of his huntsmen here are also cutt in wood the Effigies of Justice, prudence, Temperance, and Fortitude, Neptune, the sea god with his scepter or Trident, and for a weather Cock a man taking the altitude with a quadrant, moreover this sign post is adorned with 2 figures of Lions, 2 of harts, the one painted on a board the other cutt in wood in full proportion of it, 10 Escutheons 2 figures of Angells Bacchus the God of wine and a whales head spueing out Jonas, with other figures and flourishes, and adjoining to the house is a faire garden wee found good wine and beer and one Mr Patten now lives there, and after the first setting of it upp there was a great resort of company came to see it.

About 2 miles from Scole and a mile out of the road on the right hand, between Scole and Bury, lies Dis a markett Towne on Norffolke side of the river Waveney[39]

From Scole to Harlesone is accounted 5 miles the waie lies by the river side which sett with parishes in the road these viz: Billinford, Thorpe,

---

37 Ixworth, Stanton, Rickinghall, Botesdale. Sir John Castleton 3rd baronet, of Stuston, has an opulent memorial in the church.
38 The sign of the Scole Inn, named the *White Hart*, was designed to attract visitors. It was like a proscenium arch over the road. Inn and sign were erected by John Peck, a Norwich wool merchant, in 1655. The cost is given by Waveney Archaeology as £1057. It did not make the inn a financial success and it was taken down in the later eighteenth century. http://waveneyarchaeology.org/wp-content/uploads/2016/11/19-Scole-Inn.pdf
39 Diss.

Thomas Baskerville commented on the round towers he saw on some Norfolk churches and commented on the bell towers on top of some. Many, like Hales, Acle, Moulton and Surlingham still exist (clockwise from top left).

Broadwash, Needham then Harleston,[40] a tolerable good markett Towne, where wee lay att the *Swan*, one Mr Disermew Master,[41] here is an ingenious gardner one Ludlar, late come to Towne who is contriveing a dainty garden-

5 miles further in the road towards Norwich lies Bungay, another markett towne as bigg as Harlestone, and here also the countrey townes stand thik on the river Waveney, till you come to Beckles[42] 5 miles beyond Bungay, in these parts many towers ar built round, some round from bottom to topp and some 2 third parts round from the foundation upward the rest round in 8 squares to the topp of the Tower.

The matterialls for walls to churches and towers, in these parts of Norffolke and Suffolke, ar flint and freestone, the round towers have usually two or 3 Bells the square Towers have very good rings, and ar curiously wrought with flint and free-stone especially one between Bungay and Beckles, being lately built by Norwich workemen.[43]

Att a place called Flixton in Suffolke, wee being then in our waie of Norfolke side of the river, wee saw Mr Tetboroughs[44] hous.

From Bury to Beckles, this countrey affords good and well Tasted beer and ale both in Barells and botles, and here in the waie between Bungay and Beckles I had first sight of a man att plough with 2 horses, for they seldome goes with more att any time in these parts, he held the plough and drove the horses himselfe, he had but one handle to his plough and had 3 things to do with 2 hands viz: to hold his plough, to hold his whipp, and to reyyne his horses with little cords that reached to the handle of his plough, all this he did with great dexterity, turning very nimbley att the land's end.

The women also in this countrey I saw go spinning up and downe the waie as I went with a rock and distaffe in their hands - so that if a comparison were to bee made between the ploughmen and the good wives of these parts, their life were more pleasant for they can go with their worke to good company and the poore ploughman must do his worke alone.

---

40 Billingford, Thorpe Abbots, Brockdish?, Needham, Harleston.
41 One Daniel Disermew is named on the Norwich subscription list for the regaining of Newcastle in 1643. *Norfolk Archaeology* 18(2) (2012), 153.
42 Bungay, Beccles.
43 The round towers of Norfolk and Suffolk drew TB's attention and were accurately described. The Round Tower Churches Society says there are 124 in Norfolk and 38 in Suffolk. https://www.roundtowers.org.uk
44 Flixton. TB is probably referring to Flixton Hall, built in 1615 by John Tasburgh; it was the former site of Flixton Abbey. https://heritage.suffolk.gov.uk/media/pdfs/flixton.pdf

In the Fields of Norffolke, Suffolke, and Cambridgeshire, as wee rodd along, wee saw people baiting their beast att the ends, and between corne lands, and commonly a man or a woman had 5 or 6 beast with cords tyed to their horns in their hands att once.

Beckles is a fair well built towne in Suffolke seated, on a pleasant hill, overlooking to the eastwarde a large common belonging to the towne containing by estimation 1700 acres or more, and to the westward on the other side the river Waveney (the town on this side extending to the river side) are large commons belonging to other countrey townes.[45]

It hath a large markett place with fair streets and divers well built Inns belonging to it as also a great and well built church on the brough of the hill, besides markett houses and shambles for butchers and such like places there being so large commons (as I formerly said) belonging to this towne. They ar governed instead of Bailiffs and mayor, by the grass Stewards, and the proffitts that occure by the common is the cause as some told me of much poore people in this towne, for customes permitting them if they are able to rent a house of so much per annum, to enjoy the proffitts of the common so when their stock failes and poverty comes upon them, then they comes (sic) to the parishes charge.

We lay at the *Kings head*, Mr Lambkin being master then of the Inn, and wee were merry with good clarett with one Captaine Plater of this towne, and one Mr Watts of Elsingham a towne about 3 miles off, an acquaintance of Mr Bakers my Companion in this jorney.[46]

From this town we rodd to Lostaft,[47] a markett Towne 7 miles from Becles in the Ile o Lovingland by the sea side[48]

In the waie wee mett with these villages viz: Worlingham, Barnaby, and then Mettford brige where we entered the Ile of Lovingland[49]

This brige is a damm of earth between 10 and 20 yards broad secured,

---

45 TB noted commons without making reference to their reduction in area through enclosures. His suggestion that commons brought poor to a parish continued to be a frequent complaint. Everitt, 'Common Land', *The English Rural Landscape* (2000), 232-3. Beccles common or fen and marsh is still 1,400 acres. https://heritage.suffolk.gov.uk/media/pdfs/beccles.pdf

46 TB referred to Mr Baker accompanying him on this journey in his account of Oxford. See Chapter 3 'Oxford'. 'Elsingham' was probably South Elmham.

47 Lowestoft.

48 Lothingland.

49 Worlingham, Barnby, Mutfordbridge, Isle of Lothingland.

on the right hand sea ward with piles of wood to breake the fury of the waves.

And on the left hand runs the fresh water river of Waveney, which I did then observe to bee lower than the salt water, so that if the sea should break through the banck, it would overflow a great deale of the marsh countrey, by the river and about a mile from this banck Lostaft is seated, on a plesant brough of the hill, overlooking the sea, pretty well built, haveing in it many large houses to dry herrings

Here is no Castle for defence, but wee saw a fair Church, Tower, and Steeple, att the entrance of the towne, and one church more in the towne. Here wee dined, and had fish incomparably well drest, with excellent good clarrett and beer but the signe of the house and the name of our Landlord and landladie who drest the fish I have forgotten.

From this pleasant Towne for situation wee road along by 2 watch or light houses one for candle and in the other a great fire made with cole.

For in the sea hereabouts ar dangerous shelves of sand, so every night especially darke nights they keep lights and fire to give shipps warning of those dangerous places.

After we had road some 2 miles on the sea shore wee came to a tall post with inscription on it to signife that so farr the bounds of Yarmouth did reach.

After wee had rodd six miles some part by the sea the rest on the brough of a hill a little above the shore it affording a delicate prospect both to landward and also to seaward by the reason of a many shipps that then came saileing by and also of the Towne att a distance and shipps that rodd there, wee came att length to Gulston[50] the suburbs or begining of this famous towne of Yarmouth, that part of the towne being in the Ile of Lovingland and here att the begining of the Towne is the mouth of the river Yar and Waveney, or entrance into the haven, and hard by stands a strong built fort well planted with guns.

Yarmouth

TRAVELLING ABOUT A mile through this towne replenished with Inns and ale houses for the entertainment of seamen and also a place to bowle in on the greens of the shore[51] wee came att length to a well built bridg over the river Yar and Waveney, with a drawe bridge in the midle and weighty chains of iron crossing each side to save passengers from falling in, and also to draw up the bridge when occasion requires.

These rivers unites not far above the bridge or here about a bow

50 Gorlestone, Yarmouth.
51 Some ink blotches on the last 4 lines of the page.

shott over on which the Bayliffs of this towne in their pleasure barges once a yeare being attended with musick much good company and cheer go in procession to asertt their boundes and Franchises and where the rivers meet the Bayliffs part company the one part sailing up Yar the other Waveney, but to proceed, haveing as I rodd along told 102 shipps riding in this river (and some Gentlemen of Yarmouth told mee they had 600 saile belonging to their Towne) wee went out of the Ile of Lovingland over the bridge into Yarmouth in the county of Norffolke, the best built and best contrived of any towne or Citty, I have seen in England.

The Matterials for the most part brick and excellent hewed stone, brought from the Iles of portland and purbeck it hath a gallant Key stretching along by the river of great breadth and length, and as fair a markett place for breadth and length.

And between these 2 eminent places there ar fair and large streets for coaches and carts to pass too and fro' att pleasure so are their narrow streets contrived on purpose, answering to all parts of the Key to carrey goods from their shipps to any part of the towne which is performed usually by a horse and a man, with little low carts no higher than the carrage of a Gun and of these there ar many in this towne who gaine a good lively hood by it.

For other publick buildings in the towne there is in the markett place 2 round markett houses att good distance one from the other covered with lead, and they have both fair Dyalls on the topps there is also on one side of the markett place a Bordwell house,[52] and att the end of the markett place before the chief Church of the towne a large building for the townesmen to meet about their affairs.

And behind this building which stands as a Gate house, is the Church yard and Church, the church is large and hath many gallereys for the reception of people, and a chancell the fairest for breadth and length that I have seen to any church, and on this church a leaden Steeple of no great curiosity for workmanshipp.

Here is in the town also a large roome above stairs, which they call the Dutch church, and thither the people goe every afternoon to heare prayers; <where their fine women may be seen.>

All parts to landward of this towne is fortified with a strong brick wall with forts to plant Guns, and Gates att convenient places to go out. Out of one we went to a fair garden where was good fruits and liquour for the entertainment

---

52 Probably a Bridewell house i.e. a prison or house of correction.

of persons that go thither.

The cheife trade of this towne is Herring catching and smoking, so that they ar brought from many parts hither to markett which in the season employs many hands to gutt, salt, and dry them - for which purpose they have square roomes built from the foundation to the roofe of brick, being covered with Slatt in which they hang their ranges of herrings in stories on(e) above the other on sticks as chandlers do candles.

To dry them they make fires with great billet on the floor in severall places of the roome which with the heat and smoak the doors and windows being shutt close, effects the buisness. They require about 3 weeks time to dry for ordnary sale, but a month or more, to send as farr as the streights.

This towne as some persons of quality told mee is now over built or too numerous in shipping so that they ar now att a loss for want of trade. The people of the town though I have heard some say to the contrary as to strangers was very civill to us we were kindly treated by Captaine England and Mr John Egland (*sic*) his brother att their house who after diner went abroad with us to the places of good liquour in the towne, by which meanes wee gained the acquaintance of Mr Huntington, Mr Simmonds Mr Good Mr Reynolds, and divers other worthy Gentlemen.

Wee lay att the Signe of the *Feathers* a very good Inn one Mr Craske being master.

As we rod along by the river side to Yarmouth wee saw an Engine in the river to take upp mudd in shallow places as the people told mee.

From Yarmouth to Norwich is accounted 16 miles in the waie thither wee went over a river on this side a place call'd Okley, where wee saw much Alexander or Elessander grow wilde.[53] For the rest of the waie it being allmost night wee took notice of but few townes till wee came to Norwich which wee obscurely saw from the brough of a hill a mile above the Towne.

Norwich

As to Norwich it is a great Citty and full of people, I cannot say which is the bigger Bristoll or Norwich but of the 2 I think Norwich.

It hath 34 some say 35 churches and those for the most part not small but large and well built of Free Stone and Flint, I told as I stood upon the castle yard my self 28 towers; of these Christ church the Cathedrall is cheif,

---

53 Acle, Norwich. Alexanders are Mediterranean herbs much used in the 17th century; the flower buds, the leaves and the roots all had culinary uses. Willes, *The Domestic Herbal* (2020), 113.

situate in the lower parts of the towne not far from the river; it hath a tall spire or steeple in the middle and 2 small spires att the west end front with thick bulkey pillors in the body of the church like those of Wells in sommersett, and so is the cloyster adjoining containing like that, a church yard within it. The Bishop hath now a large antient house hard by the church, but by the ruins which Mr Burton the Schoole master shewed us it hath bin much bigger.

Dr. Raynolds the late Byshop of this Diocess hath built to the now standing part of the hous, a very fine Chappell, and as I remember lies buried in it.

Byshop Sparrow late of Excester is now the present Byshop of that diocess.[54]

The Doctours and prebends houses they lies (sic) here and there scattering about the church and att the entrance in of the Gate from the Citty to the church, is a fair Schoole hous and a house for the Schoole Master and schollers to lodge in which Mr Burton the Schoole master told me had formerly in it before the dissolution of Abbeys, 4 religious men, preachers, who had good lands belonging to their place.

Here is also not farr from the church (formerly some Abbey or religious house) a good Almes house whose first founder was Edward the 6th, to this hospitall Dr. Smith an honest prebend of this church brought us, and shewed us the Roomes of the house viz: 2 long large roomes below stairs for men and women, and 2 long large roomes above stairs for men and women thick sett with small beds and little partitions on both sides the roomes for their lodging, where these antient people wearied with the toyles and care of their forepast life, find a comfortable subsistence. And they have a Chappell and prayers constantly read to them every day. From this place Dr Smith and Mr Burton lead us to shew us the rarities of a flint wall of the Bridwell house; this wall being made of 4 square pieces of flintt, each Square about 3 or 4 inches, and so smoothly sett and so closely joynted together in exact ranges, that one would admire considring the brittleness of that kind of stone, how it could possibly bee effected.

This Citty is is (sic) encompassed with an antient flint wall with Towers att convenient distance for defence, and Gates for entrance. And this wall is of such extent that within the compass of the citty ar many gardens Orchards and inclosures, so that a man may boldly say it hath the greatest inclosure of any

54 Bishops: Edward Reynolds 1661-1676; Anthony Sparrow D.D. 1676-1685. CCEd.

towne in England.

There are also on the other side the river some forts or Towers of stone where they may cross the river with chaines of Iron to hinder the passage of boates.

Here also remaines the ruins of a very stately Castle, built on the top of an eminent hill in the middest of the towne, overtoping all the rest of the Citty. And to this castele surrounded with deep dikes, there is an entrance by one bridge haveing only one great and entire arch under it, of such a vast breadth and height that it surpasses any of the bridges in Yorkshire over the river Wharfe or elsewhere.

Here as in many other Cittys in England the Assizes is kept and the jayle for County prisners.

A little way from this Castle on the opposite side of a hill, is the chief markett place of this Citty: and this being the only place where all things ar brought to be sold, for the food of this great Citty, they not as in London allowing marketts in severall places, make it vastly full of provisions especially on Saturdayes, where, I saw the greatest shambles for butchers meat I had ever yet seen. And the like also for poultrey and dayrey meats, which Dayry people also bring many quarter of veale with theyr butter and cheese. And I believe also in their seasons pork and hogg meates.

These people fill a Square of ground on the side of a hill, twice as big as Abington markett place, they setting their goods in ranges as nere as may bee one above another, only allowing roome for single persons to pass betweene and above these; the butchers have their shambles and such kind of people as sell fish: of which there was plenty <of such kindes> as the seas here abouts afford viz: crabs, Flounder, mackerll, very cheap, but Lobster for sea fish and pike or Jack for river fish were deare enough.

They asked mee for one pike under 2 foot 2 shilling 6 pence, and for a pott of pickled Oysters they would have a shilling.

Here I saw excellent Oatmeale which being curiously hulled looked like French barley with great store of Ginger bread and other edible things.

And for graine in the corne markett which is on the other side the markett hous as large for space of ground as thatt on which the dayry people stand.

I saw wheat, rye, oates, malt, ground and not grou(n)d, French wheat, and but little barley, because the season for malting was over.

Their cheif markett hous stands in the midst of this great markett place now very full of people and provisions, being circular or round in form, having chaind to the severall pillars thereof, bushells pecks scales, and other things for the measuring and weighing of such goods as are brought to the markett.

And over against this declivity where the markett people stand, is a fair walk before the prime Inns, and houses of the markett place called the gentlemens walk or walking place which is kept free for that purpose, from the encumberance of stalls, Tradesmen and their goods; about the midle of this walk is the signe of the *King's Head* where wee lay, Mrs. Berne a widdow then Landlady who keeps a good ordnery on Saturdays for 12 pence meate, where we dined in the company of many Gentlemen, the names of those I remember and was most intimate with, were, Captaine Springhall of Reedham Mr Elwin Mr Wharton, Gentlemen of Yarmouth.

Here is also in the compass of this markett place a fair Towne Hall where the Mayor and his Brethren with the livery men of this Citty keep a great feast, presenting the Ladies that come thither with march panes to carry away.

They have also fine shows in the streets in some measure like that of the Lord mayors day of London.

And as Mr Burton told mee one of the eminent Schollars of his School, dos usually make an elegant speech, to the Mayor and his brethren as they pass by richly clad in their scarlett robes.

The cheifest trade of this famous Towne mostly consists, in making stuffs, and worsted stockings, they in these sorts of manyfactures excelling all other places.

As to the river it is not so broad as Thames below Oxon, yet the boates that trade between this and Yarmouth usually carrie between 20 and 30 tuns.

Taking a boate for pleasure to view this Citty by water, the boatman brought us to a fair garden belonging to the Duke of Norfolke, handsome staires leading to the water, by which we ascended into the garden, and saw a good bowling green and many fine walkes, the gardnier now keeping good liquours and fruits to entertaine such as come there to see it.

From this garden for the rest of the Citty downe stream, and about a furlong upp stream there ar no houses built on the other side the river to hinder that prospect into the countrey. But after as wee went further up the stream the Citty is built on both sides the river, here being divers parishes and a tollerable bigg town for houses on the right hand side.

In this passage where the Citty incloses both sides of the river wee rowed under 5 or 6 bridges, and then landed att the Duke of Norfolke his pallace a sumptuous new built house not yet finished within, but seated in a dung hole place, though it has cost the Duke already 30 thousand pound in building, as the Gentleman that shewed it, told us, for it hath but little roome for gardens and is pent up on all sides both on this and that side the river, with tradesmen and dyers houses who fowle the watter by their constant washing and cleansing their cloath, whereas had it bin built, ajoining to the aforesaid garden, it had stood in a delicate place.[55]

Above this hous there ar more bridges <upon the river> which I cannot give account of.

Here is in this citty an order the like is no where else to be found in any towne in England, and that is, the butchers ar obliged to sell the meat they kill the fore past part of the week by Thursday night, for on a Friday night speaking to our Landladie for a joynt of mutton to be roasted for our suppers she told us it was not to be had.

And this they do to oblige the Fishermen to bring plenty of fish from the sea as also to make good the sale of that kind of food, so that as some gentlemen of Yarmouth told me they many times there for that reason, have but bare or scant marketts of fish.

The return via Ely, Huntingdon and Bedford

ON OUR WAIE homeward we went to a markett towne called Windmonham, about 6 miles from Norwich, in the waie thither we mett with these countrey parishes viz: Eaton, Crinkleford, Hithersett and so through a long common, to the aforesaid towne,[56] where Mr Baker had an acquaintance one Mr Clark schoole master there, who treated us kindly att his house. He said there was an Abbey formerly in this towne but the ruins are now almost lost.

This Gentleman brought us upon the road as far as an eminent Gentlemans hous one Sir Thomas Woodhous who was but lately dead and some roomes being hung with mourning and escutcheons.[57]

---

55 The Duke's Palace was built in 1561 and underwent a second build stage in 1672. The main building was demolished in 1711 but the associated bowling alley survived until the 1960s; the site is now the Post Office exchange and offices. https://www.heritage.norfolk.gov.uk
56 Wymondham, Eaton, Cringleford, Hethersett.
57 Sir Thomas Wodehouse knighted 1666, and died of the small pox at Kimberley, 1671. His wife, Anne, survived him and married two more times. BHO Blomefield 2. However, Sir Philip Woodhouse died in 1681 and his wife Lady Wodehouse in 1684, suggesting TB remembered the wrong name. HoP.

Here wee were kindly treated att diner by the widdowe Ladie and Mr Woodhouse her 2nd son, now a Cornett of horse in my Lord of Oxfords Regiment.

This worthy Gentleman brought us from this hous to Mr Payns house, another Gentleman of Mr Bakers acquaintance, where we lay that night and were friendly treated, and next morning he went with us to one Mr Cowpers hous about a mile from Hingham another markett town in Norffolke, to showe us that famous tree which Mr Evelyn as he had an account from Dr Brown mentions in his discourse of forest trees.[58]

This Famous Lime tree for bulck, height, and goodly spreading limbs, surpasses all other trees I have yet seen in England, so that it seems to appear rather a wood than one tree in the air;

Mr Payne first and after myself did pace it and found it to be 16 of our paces in compass.

From hence Mr Payne had us to a famous Meere in the Ladie Woodhous's Lordshipp full of excellent clear water and replenished with good jack pearch and other fresh water fish some of which wee tasted both att Mr Payns and the aforesaid Ladies hous.

In the waie from Hingham to Watton another markett town 5 miles further in our Road, we went by more of these meeres, of which there are many more in these parts as Mr Baker told mee.

Watton is a small towne, lately burnt, but now rebuilt in which there is little remarkable save a fine new bowling green att the *George* Inn where we dined, Mrs Jeames is the Landladie's name. <Mr Leigh a Master of Arts in Cambridge>

From Watton we rod to Bran, a through fare towne 5 miles below Thatford on a river, navigable from Lin to both townes.

The waie 9 miles distant from Watton is over a fine downy countrey and so it continues from Bran to Brandon surrounding the Fens till we came to Milden Hall some 7 or 8 miles distant from Bran situate on the edge of the Fens, by a river navigable to Lin, accounted 30 miles from this place.[59]

---

58 The first edition of John Evelyn's book, *Sylva or A Discourse of Forest-Trees and the Propagation of Timber* was published in 1664. He had only just received from Sir Thomas Browne a description of a lime tree near Norwich eight yards and a half round, named after its native village of Depeham.

59 Bran is difficult to identify; it might be Barnham on the Little Ouse. Brandon, Mildenhall. The Little Ouse flows from Thetford to King's Lynn.

Here is a larg church in the towne and a well built house of the Lords of the mannour whose name I've forgott. Mr Maxe was the master of the hous his name where we lay.

The Citty of Ely is accounted 12 miles from this towne, although to the prospect of the eye it seems not to be so farr.

Wee went the banck waie through the depth and levell of the Fenns to this towne a great part of the waie being by the rivers side, it being now in May 1681 after a dry winter and scorching dry spring the effects of the late comett or else it had hardly bin possible so early, and as dry as it was we could hardly gett over the rotten bridge with our horses, being glad to alight for fear they should brecke through and stick in the rotten boggs under them, but they have another waie to go thether in the winter but some thing farther about; but to proceed.

This level or countrey from Milden Hall to Ely being nothing but turffe or peate and the by its insufferable and heate, and dryth having exhausted all the moisture out of the ditches, it was so suffocating hott by meanes of the Brimstone or sulfery vapours, we could hardly breath or endure it, so that I veryly thinke 'twas possible to have sett the countrey on fire the earth was then so dry.

As we rod along this banck we saw here and there some poor Cottages and wretched farmes where some poor souls with their thatch .?. att a hard fate, do weather out a winter to look after the cattle that feed here -

But doubtless here is incomparable fowling to make those amends that will undertake that pleasant toyl, for the red shanks and other birds were very tame and not afraid of us.

Here is also good snaring of jacks for wee saw abundance for 2 miles riding in the ditches on this side the towne of Ely.

Att 9 miles distance from Mildenhall this banck winding about the river and not made in a direct line towards Ely, wee came att length to a place where this and another river mett, here on an old high wodden bridge, wee went over Mildenhall river, where were 2 or 3 ale houses for boate men to refresh themselves and about a bow shott below this bridge the 2 rivers mett viz: that of Came and Ouse united below Cambridge, and this of Mildenhall.[60]

From these ale-hous's 'tis accounted 3 or 4 miles to Ely.

60 Some alterations and not clear quite what TB intended. He crossed out 'I can not tell whether Ouse or any part of it joynes with Came before it comes to Ely'.

The waie thither as before lying on a banck of Earth, with enclosures on both sides as most of the Fenns between Ely and Milden Hall are save what they allow att large for the waie it self.

Where here and there poore men that have no land do digg peet or turff for fuell to burn

In this passage between the ale-hous's and Ely bridge it was wee saw so many Jacks, suning in the ditches, between the high waie and the Enclosur's.

At the bridge which lies about half a mile below the town wee came into the winter waie or grand road which comes from London and the countrey adjacent to Ely.

On this bridge it being now the time of washing sheep, was sheep to bee washed. The bridge on which they stood was high it may be 10 or 12 yards above the water and from hence they were tumbled into the river within the compass of a frame of fir poles to keep them from swimming awaie till such time as they were cleansed by the washer -

The men as I suppose stood on a boate sunk in the water middle high for the water was deep where the sheep fell, and which being throughly washed they lifted them over the frame and so they swam ashore.

The Cathedrall and markett place of the Citty of Ely is on the plaine of a hill, but one street extends down the hill almost to the bridge.

The buildings of the town are very indifferent. but the structure of the Cathedrall being different from most I had seen before is very noble and statly to look on.

For over the Quire there is a large round or Lanthorn full of lights or windows, mounting perhaps 20 yards above the body of the church, this with the 2 towers att the west end makes it appear to such as travell on the Downs beyond New Markett like a great man on horseback.

The inside of it is very well repaird for the body is lately paved with large squares of new freestone the vaulting beautified and the lanthorn or round over the Quire well painted. And the East end above the Quire is a very noble and spacious building surpassing any I have seen in other Cathedrall Churches.

Here is one small church more in the town and little else to bee said more of the other buildings.

The great trade of this town and countrey here about is making of bricks and earthen ware for which purpose they have excellent sorts of earth.

For being my self att Sturbridge[61] fair the september after this jorney it was methought a goodly sight to see the vast quantitiys of earthern ware there spread on the turff of all sorts to be sold, brought out of these parts.

The place where this fair is kept is in the fields a mile without Cambridge, between Barnwell and Chester towne [62] which is on the other side the river where the fair is kept. And Mr Butler of Barnwell a very civill Gentleman in whose stable wee left our horses, is now Lord of the mannour where they keep the fair.

Some Say it had is name from a pedlar coming hither to sell his wares who when suspiscious persons came nere him in the night time, would usually call out and encourage his bitch to bee watchfull and cry Stur bitch. But however it gott its name 'tis now the greatest martt or fair wee have in England.

For here you shall see large Streets and Shopps full of all the variety of wares that ar to bee sold in London. <And great quantities of iron brought from several parts of the Nation and elsewhere. The wooll fair there to which they come from all parts of England at that time to be furnished is no less considerable.>
      Here you shall see Cartts loaden with Oysters,
      here you shall see great heaps of salt fish
      and here you shall see on the bancks side vast heaps of cole, to be sold, and the river thick sett with boats for a mile or more in length with all sorts of provisions.
      And to conclude from the fair to Cambridge, and from Cambridge, to the fair, the waies ar as full with Coaches as att London. <During the fair time a streett as it were of booths fraught with chese of all sorts from all parts of our own Nation, and from Holland and other countreys.>

Now for the decision of all differences that may arise between Chapmen and others the Mayor of Cambridge and his brethren do keep a court of 'pypoudres' and dayly com thither a horseback in their Scarlett robes attended by their officers to a house or court built for that purpose.
      The concours of this fair as also of such another kept in the sommer for a fortnights time in Barnwell must doubtless contribute very great riches to Cambridge for then the town is so full you can hardly gett a lodging.
      And to put a period to this discours the Farmers of Sturbridge field ar allso enriched by it. For besides the great rates that ar given where shops and

61 Stourbridge.
62 Barnwell, Chesterton.

victualling houses do stand, the soyle is greatly enriched with Oyster shells and other muck.

For when people eat Oysters they tumble the shells under the table without more ado in all victualling bowers and there they remain till the time of tillage.

From Ely to Huntingdon is accounted 14 miles, the names of such towns in the waie as I remember were first Sutton on the brough of the Fenn.

Then desending down a hill wee came to a gate wher we paid a penny a horse for passage this waie being on sufferance through another mans ground and not the common road as they told us and here is a house where they sell ale.

Being past this Gate wee road on the banck of the other branch of the river Ouse.

For the river Ouse parting either above or below St Iwes[63] makes this countrey an Iland.

On this Stream we saw many Swans and signetts as we rodd towards Erift,[64] going over 2 bridges ere wee came to the town.

This is a through fare place with some Inns in it for entertainment and three miles further lies St Iwes a fair markett town on the aforesaid river.

And this town is about eleven miles from Ely as I think in Cambridgeshire.

And 3 miles further on the road lies Hun(t)ingdon the chief town in Huntingdon Shire, and situate also on the river Ouse.

The Countrey between St Ives and Huntingdon is well planted for we told 14 or 16 towers or steeples in vew of the eye att one station and none of them very far of yet those of Huntingdon were obscured from our sight by trees, and the town not then above two miles from us.

Huntingdon hath 3 churches in it and is an old built towne. Wee lay att the *Chequer* a very good Inn for entertainment Mr Foulk and his wife Gentile peoples being the present hous keepers.

Next morning wee rod to St Neotes or St. Needs some 5 miles further in the road to Bedford, the countrey parishes between in the road is Finchingbrook where the Lord Sandwich hath a fair hous next is Breirton and then by Buckden where the Bishop of Lincoln hath a fair hous and so through Deddrington to St Needs a good markett town and thus farr the river is navigable for boates of

---

63 St Ives.
64 Earith.

burden from Linn, and no higher.[65]

For such goods as are brought hither by watter ar carried by land to Bedford which is accounted 7 miles.

There wee baited att one Mr Cooks house an honest travelling Cook to Smirna and Constantinople in company and servant to Sir Henry Hide when he was trapand to England and beheaded.

From hence wee went to great Barford[66] which is 4 miles from St Needs and so to Bedford.

From Bedford wee went to Newport Pagnell which may bee some 7 or 9 miles distant. These villages lie in the waie viz: Broome hall, Chicherly.[67]

Newport pannell is very pleasantly seated on the brough of a hill overlooking the river Ouse and the verdant meadows by it.

It hath one church and 2 great new built Inns besids many others.

We lay att the *Swan* one of the new Inns Mr Chambers being master of it

Next morning we road to Stony Stratford which is 5 or 6 miles from Newport Pannell 6 miles from Buckingham and 22 miles from Oxon.

In the road between Newport and Stratford lives 3 Gentlemen who have their parks one in sight of another viz: Sir Thomas Longfield of <Wolverton says Mr Hanbore> Stoneton, Esq Whiteron, and Sir John Thompson of Hersom.[68]

Stony Stratford is a town of very ordnary building and hath 2 small churches in it.

Added in a different hand, like the following several pages.

Hemingford Abbots betwixt Huntington and St Ives. There lives my loving friend Mr Hanbury, sometime one of the Conducts of New College Oxon of which there are [unfinished]

65 Hinchinbrooke House, Brampton, Buckden, Diddington, St Neots.
66 Great Barford.
67 Broom Hall (Broom), Chicheley.
68 Old Wolverton (Sir John Longville, died 1685; 'Baskerville the topographer noted the park at Old Wolverton in 1681'. Stantonbury (Sir John Wittewrong, died 1693), Haversham (Sir John Thompson died 1710). [All part of Milton Keynes] VCH (Bucks) 4.

An alternative route to Oxford from Cambridge via Royston, Baldock and Dunstable

The first half page is in a different hand to the previous pages, with elaborate capital letters. It starts on a right-hand page with a heading.

From Cambridge
to go to Oxford or Abing
don in the winter time the
Hill Countrey way
is best

From Cambridge wee went to Melsom and so to Royston a faire town with a great market for corne in the Rode from thence to London.[69]

Here we went out of London Rode thwarting the fields under the browes of the hills in Hartford Shire to a Town called Baldoak,[70] in the way thither we saw a hare warren lately made and railed in by the present Earle of Salisbury. This town is so called from the scarcity of oaks my Landlord told me there is now but one in the Parish. He also told me by meanes of the Hare Warren there being holes to let the Hares through the Rayles they are now very plentifull in the fields hereabout.

From hence we went to Dunstable and in the way thither we saw a high round Hill cut of from the main ridge of mountaines which are in Hartford shire. This Hill may be seen upon our Rye Hill in Sunningwell and Bayworth.[71]

The hand writing here reverts to a more cursive style.

Dunstable is a pretty good market Town in Hartford shire. It hath a faire church in it and the ruines of an Abbey or a religious House situate in a plain under the Hills having large fields about it where in the season they catch good larkes which have the greatest esteem for birds of that kinde in London. And some people of this town are here very curious in making Straw Hats and other workes of that nature.

From Dunstable you may go to Tring and through Alesbury or else leaving

---

69 Meldreth or Melbourn? Royston.
70 Baldock. Was the hare warren at Clothall, where the earl of Salisbury had an estate and occupied the principal residence in Clothall named Quickswood or Quicksett, in the 17th century? VCH (Herts) 3.
71 Is this Warden Hill?

Alesbury a mile or more on the right hand go to Tame[72] and so to Oxford.

Lists of notable local specialities

Two facing pages contain these lists. The second has a heading 'An Account of some remarkable things in a jorney between London and Dover' which is repeated at the start of a later page where it is relevant to the journey that followed. The list is not easy to read: the first side is in the rather elaborate hand, the second less well written.

A Dunstable Lark   <and straw hats>
<St Albans straw Tankards and pots >
An Essex Calfe
A Chedar Cheese
A Warfleet Oyster
Hereford Shier Cyder
Darby Ale
An Ock Ele   <The river Ock by Abingdon>
A march Hare
Witney Blankets
A Flanders mare
A Lancashire Las
And Ham-shier Hunney
is currant goods for every mans money
Stroud Water Reds
Burford Saddels
Banbury Cakes
and Ducth Cradels
<Indian pancakes>
French Spaniels
Barbary Horses <Arabian cammels>
Cannary Sack and Bristow Sherry
will make a Sadmans heart to be merrey
Bilbo Blades and Spanish Wool
Spanish Tobacco
Cyprus Cats
Dorset shier yewes for the early lambes
And Warwick shier breeds most excellent Rams
Castile Hemp.

72 Thame.

Biscane Iron
Abourn Rabbits
Muscovie duckes
Westphalia Hams
Inglish Saffron and Twixbury [Tewkesbury] mustard balls
Inglish oake for shiping <is good>
And Irish oake for wainscoting <wood>
Norway for deal
Nants for Brandy
and the Caribbee Iles for Rum
And so I thinke we have done
          to begin again
Scotch Collops
Second side
Studly Carrots, by Caln
Becolsly [Besselsleigh] Turnips by Abingdon
Saffron at Saffron Waldron
Nottinghame and Pumfret [Pontefract] Licquorish
Arrundel mullet as they here
is the best in England for good cheer
but at 6d the pounde tis pretty deer

The Land of carrots Studly by Caln.
          The Land of gates is between Bablock Hieth and Stimlake brode
          Norfolk Lostaffe [Lowestoft] and Yarmouth Herrings
          Cornwall and Devonshier Pilchardes
          Temes [Thames] sprates
          Turky Coffe and horses
          Persian silk and Sherbet
          East Indian Rice
          West Indian maize
          Newfoundland Poor Jack and Dorsetshire baise
          Beamdown sampier [samphire]
          Shropshire Cole
          Avon Salisbury umbers or graylings
          Severn Y and Salmons
          Glowcester Lamprey
          Pembrook new found out Anchove made of young Shad,
          Minnihed muskels

Hol barly Broth
Bartholomew faire rost pig and
Southwork faire rost pork
Brazile Sugar
French Claret and White
Biscane Cuthaleen
Libannus Cedars
Burmoodos Oringes
Russion Stergion
Holand Ling and Stockfish
Norway deal
Patney Barley
Newberry Crawfish
Glastonbury Peat and the Forest of Windzor Turf
Greenland whales and Bottell Cone noddys
Virginian Bevers
Cordovet Hatts
Cornish Tin and Sweedish Copper
Barbary gold and Potozi Silver
St. Margarets Pearls
Bristow diamonds
Jamaica spice
Norwich Stuffes   Colchester Bayes

At the bottom of the page, very blotched, a few lines set out earlier are
repeated

Arrundel mullets as they say here
are the best in England for good cheer
But at 6d the pound tis pretty dear
A Caln salamander lights Tobacco and fir coal-fyre.

JOURNEY 2
TO DOVER VIA GRAVESEND, ROCHESTER, FAVERSHAM AND CANTERBURY

This account starts on a new right-hand page. The journey was undertaken after 1670 when the ship 'Prince', observed by Baskerville, was built at Chatham. His route from Gravesend to Canterbury was the Roman road, later the A2. The handwriting is clear, cursive, and between each sentence is a larger gap than in Section 1. Baskerville started to describe in verse the land near Deal once covered by sea, see an odd page inserted at the beginning of MS Harl. 4716 (Chapter 5 'An Exploration in Verse').

An account of some remarkable things in a jorney between London and Dover

Between London and Graves End,[73] by water is accounted sixty miles, and by land 20:

The usuall passage by water for people not to mention shipps is either in tilt boats or wherrys.

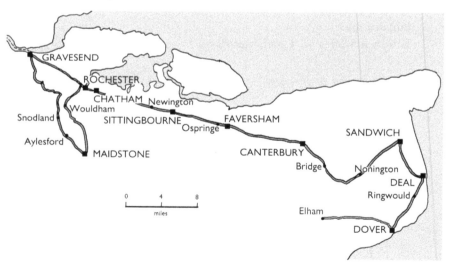

The tilt boat passengers in 1661 gave 8d a piece for theyr pass but such as go in wherreys, as they can agree but the number of people which they carrie in either of these boats ar stinted by law, tho: comonly they do transgress it for

73 Gravesend.

love of gain, when they gett from the stairs.

In 4 hours time haveing the tide with them they usually go between town and town.

Gravesend is as it were the door to London by water.

For here all shipps must give an account of theyr lading before they have leave to go forward on theyr jorney to sea.

The town and river of Gravesend is gaurded with 2 Castles tho att present but one, that on Essex side, is made use off, and unto this all wherreys or other boats going by this castle must give an account of thier buisness where they are going.

As to the towne of Gravesend, it has its subsistence by travellers both by sea and land that go too and from the Metropolitan Citty.

Tis governed by a Mayor and Common councill and hath but on church, in the church yard because stone is scarce they inscribe the names of theyr deceased Friends on loggs of wood fastned to posts att each end of the grave.

Here do happ'n because of the continuall concourse of Strangers many quarrells.

A French man while I was here behaved himself very imperiously wounding severall of the townsmen.

And when Sir Walter Rawleigh went his voyge to Guiana betwixt his and the townsmen there was a sharp contest for masterdom, but in the end the townsmen prevailed and drove many of Sir Walter men into the mudd of the river.

From hence to Rochester is seven miles in the waie you shall meet 2 Inns before you come to Gadds hill a dangerous place for robbing.[74] Being past that a mile or more as you descend the hill, the plesant scituation of Rochester is discoverd in the bottom.

This Citty is made up of 3 towns viz: Stroud on the west, Rochester and Chattam on the eastern side of the river.[75]

It hath as a man may say, 4 props to support it viz: the road from France to London a navigable river the Cathedrall and its dependants, and the residence of great part of the Royall navy when they ar unrigg'd.

It hath to unite Stroud and Rochester a stately bridge of stone - through

74 Later the home of Charles Dickens.
75 Strood, Rochester, Chattam.

eleven high and large arches proud Neptune charges the sweet purling stream of medwaie,[76] making it recoile 10 miles towards its Fountain 2 miles beyond Maidstone, a great town in Kent for so farr the industrious seamen can navigate theyr inriching vessels by the help of tides.

There was on this bridge before the barrs of iron wer sett up many robberies committed in dark nights.

Those desperate villains sometimes adding murder to their Theift throwing such persons whom they had despoyled of their goods over bridge into the water.

This Cathedral church is the worst built and most ruinated of any I have seen in England.[77]

It [hath] athwart on the eastern length of the church 2 crosses or 4 iles stretching north and south and a stone Tower and leaden spire in the midst of the church.

The Quire is handsomly repaired since our late happie change and the rest will bee with what expedition is possible, the Organ by good Fortune was preserved in a Tavern in Greenwich and now erected in its proper place.

From the body to the Quire is a circular ascent of stairs of stone and over them in the backside of the Organ they are setting up the kings armes very exquisitly carved in wood.

Nere adjoyning to the Church stands an antient Castle much ruinated that and great part of the town being environned with deep Dikes and an ancient wall.

In the river along by Chattam I told 30 stout shipps. Then riding within the command of the castle of the western side of the river except the Royall Sovereign which lay att Gillingham two miles lower.

In the late engagement before the restauration of our king between the Dutch and us she was att sea. And they told mee 700 men ar but enough to man her.

She carries between 80 and an 100 guns.

The Gun roomes for she hath 3 decks and 2 Gun rooms one under another which ar about 60 paces long.

Her stern and quarters ar curiously carved and painted with imagery work in poeticall fancies and richly overlaid with Gold.

In the lanthorn erected in the midest of the stern I stood upright it

76 The river Medway.
77 He also noted the disrepair of St Alban's abbey.

being capacious enough to recieve the properest man in England standing upright.

The Kings Cabben is richly painted and gilded and so is the great Cabbn which hath out leets into 2 Gallereys on the quarters.

Sixty men ar constantly kept in pay to keep her clean and waite on strangers, here being built for the more commodious going aboard her a bridge or waie from the banck side to the lowest ebb of water.

For her defence and to examine those that pass up and down the river a little lower do constantly ride 2 ships, whose names were the Bramble and True Love and these shipps are the utmost constant gaurds on this river.

But since the restauration of the king, some 2 or 3 years after the Dutch came up the river and took awaie the Royall Charles and had burnt the rest of the fleet had they not bin speedily sunck.[78]

The King hath now built in the ile a little below the Town of Qeenburrough[79] a strong and noble fort, for the security of these parts.

The passage from the main into this Island is less than a bow shot over, there being a large ferry boat constantly attending to carrie men and horse over.

But to return for the repairation and rigging of the Navy here the King hath his Carpenters yard, the fairest of any I have yet seen.

In one of the Docks lay the Prince little inferiour to the Soveraign for bigness.[80]

The Kings pay to the Carpenters is 2s. a day and leave to carrie awaie chipps in their armes att breakfast, dinner time, and att the ending of their days work which is att 6 of the clock att which time they likewise begin in the morning all the summer time.

Close by this yard is erected a hous for spinning and making of Cables 440 of my paces long and as long again without doors, they draw the threads because the safety of a ship depends much on the length of Cables which breaks the violence and stress of the sea when they ride it out in open roads and stormy weather.

78 In June 1667 the Dutch attacked the English fleet in the Medway, known as the Second Dutch war.
79 Queenborough, in the Isle of Sheppey.
80 'Prince' was built in 1670, 1395 tons. Crawshaw, *The history of Chatham Dockyard* (1999).

Under this house along the shoar lie plenty of great Guns belonging to the navy.

Six churches in the town and suburbs adorn this Citty.

From Rochester to Roynon 4 miles then to Newington 3 Sittingbourn the next stage for post horses 3 miles more,[81] in the waie thither and beyond grow plenty of chestnutt trees.

You cannot march the streets of this town on foot in your way but they will be earnestly calling after you to ride their horses but could I gett off as freely as come on I should say the invitation were more acceptable.

Four miles further on the road lies Green Street.

3 miles further than that Osbridge[82] where in former times strangers pilgrims had a Mazen due or hous of entertainment as the ruins now standing doth wittness to posterity.

This street standing on the road belongeth to the town of Feversham[83] distant a quarter of a mile lower on the left hand, being spacious and full of inhabitants, enriched by a creek of the sea on which hyes[84] come to the town.

It being now about the 25th of August they have a fair which dos last for 2 daies to which the Londoners and Clothiers of the adjacent countreys bring much cheese and cloath to supply the necessitys of these parts.

Hence you may go while the fair lasteth every day by water to London and att other times twice a week in Hoyes.

Two miles from this town lies Boughton.

On the topp of Boughton Hill is displayed to you one of the fairest prospects in Englang (*sic*).

West ward you shall discover a spacious plain and the meanders of the famous rivers Thames and Medwaie fertilizing it.

Noreast the rivers mouth and Azure Ocean.

Southeast 4 miles forward in a bottom the Tower of Canterburys Cathedrall and the hills beyond it.

Southward an enclosed countrey fruitfull in cornfields and Orchards.

From the topp of this hill is a fine gravelly waie leasurely descending through the midst of pleasant woods made sociable by severall booths where the good

81 Rainham, Newington, Sittingbourne.
82 Ospringe still has the remains of the Maison Dieu, now a museum.
83 Faversham.
84 Hoys.

wives stand ready to invite you tast a cup of their good liquour.

At the bottom stands a village call'd Harbledown leading allmost to canterbury which on this side is wattered with a sweet river that admitts boats some 2 miles below the town to bring commoditys from thence carted to the Citty.[85]

Canterbury

BEFORE THE INVENTION of Guns this was a strong place being circled with a formidable wall and deep dike and att the Southern end a Castle much consumed by mouldring time.

Within the walls there is a court hous erected where keep sessions for the county, 16 churches the town and its suburbs may boast off the chief being christ church the seat of the Mettropolitan of that province

The western front hath 2 towrs formed alike on each side the great Gate but they differ above that on the right hand hath pinnacles that on the left a leaden spire.

Two Crosses do thwart the length of this church and on the hithermost thrusts upp a stately tower overtopping the other 2 but without bells, in the inside hollow almost to the top before 'tis vaulted over.

Att the east end there is a peice of building carried up like a tower, equivalent in height to the body of the church but never finished.

In the body of this church I told from the west door to the iron partition where they go up into the Quire sixty eight paces.

Within these grates there is an asscent of stairs to the Quire walled on both sides breast high, and under them a vaulted passage.

From the topp of these stairs Thomas A Becket Archbishop of Canterbury after he was stabb'd was thrown over into the north Ile and buried in a little Chappell by it.

But from thence his bones were removed and diggd up and buried in the east end of the Church behind the high Altar.

The pavement over them being richly inlaid with precious stones of various collours on which stood his Shrine so much resorted too in popish times where were offerd gifts of great vallue.

In this church do likewise rest the bodys of Edward the black prince Edward the Fourth and Cardinall Poole a contemporary with Queen Mary a great favourite of hers who concluded his life when the Queen took her exit of

85 Great Stour.

this world. And Cardinal Moorton is here interr'd.[86]

The Archbishops hous is for the most part ruinated. The church and Cloysters do yet show the madness of the late sacrilegious times.

Twelve beades men ar allowed by the King to give constant [attendance] on this church, clad in blackish gowns having the letters of the Kings name embroyderd on their sleeves.

Here was also a pallace and park belonging to the Kings of England till King Charles the first did exchange it for Theobalds or Tibbaleds with the Lord Wooton.

In the great Street of Canterbury is a fair Conduit built in the reigne of Charles the first to which the King with many other Gentleman were contributors as their arms did testifie till of late defaced.

This Citty having 2 liberties that of the Bishops and that of towns in the dayes of Arch Bishop Laud[87] a man of the church libertie was araigned and condemnd to be hangd for coyning of money - accordingly executed by the mayors means tho he was disswaded from it by the recorder and common councill who told him his power did extend no further than the libertie of town.

This act as some told was a means to divert the charity of the Bishop to other places, who before this peremptory action of the Mayors towards him had a design to have built a hospitall in this citty.

2 miles from Canterbury in the road lies Bridge a small through fare town 13 miles from Dover; being gott up the hill you shall march on pleasant downs in sight of Sir Anthony Agers house in parish of Bishopford.[88]

9 miles distant from Dover, Deale, and Sandwich, the waies here parting that leads to each town.

In the road toward Sandwich that from this hill may bee seen I went by Bunington through Rowling and Winsborrough ere I gott to Sandwich[89]

86 Cardinal Reginald Pole (1500–1558), cardinal 1536 but broke from Henry VIII over the reforms of the Church; returned to England under Mary I and made archibishop of Canterbury 1556 and died two days later. Cardinal John Morton (c. 1420–1500), archbishop of Canterbury 1486, cardinal 1493.

87 Archbishop William Laud (1573-1645). He was executed for his royalism and high church principles which had contributed to the outbreak of the Civil War.

88 Bishopsbourne. Sir Anthony Aucher/Auger, knighted 1641, baronet 1666. Royalist. Buried Bishopsbourne 1692. BHO (Hasted) 9.

89 Nonington? Rowling, Woodnesborough.

formerly more frequented by seamen whe(n) the haven and river were not so chocked by sand, nevertheless hoyes and some small shipps do come up to the town in the river that comes from Canterbury which with the trade of malting constantly employing some vessels towards London keeps this place from decay.

It is fortified with a deep trench and bulwarks of earth but toward the sea some parts ar walled.

Tis beautified with 3 churches whose leaden spires att some distance comming toward the town seem to stand exactly in ranck.

On the north side almost a mile without the town is yet to be see(n) the ruins of a castle on a poynt of land formerly surrounded with the sea and serviceable in the daies of Earle Goodwin but now tis disserted by the sea which comes not within a mile or more of it.[90]

4 miles southerly on the beach of the sea stands New Deall latly built on gained ground from the sea whose dominion formerly did extend to Ould Deale 2 miles further into the land to which this new town is parish.[91]

That part of the sea which washeth this shoar is called the Downes here being so many little downs of sand blown up by the wind.

On this place is the usuall rendezvouze of such of the Kings navy that com out of the rivers when they go forth on some expedition and also for shipps of ma(n)y other as they trade too and fro.

This intercourse of shipping being the only reason that induces men to build in this place but when forreigners cast anchor here they must pay somthing toward the maintaining of lights, <constantly kept burning in the night> in this place to give warning to shipps of the dangerous places.

For land defence and security of the road here ar 3 castles, Sandown on the north side of the town Walmore[92] on the south side and Deale Castle close by the town.

Att sea here about or riding in the road ar for the most part som men of warr because England hath not any road lying more commodious to command the soveraignty of the narrow seas than this, no fleet can pass by them in clear weather without being seen of them, the land of France being between Deale and Dover in sight of such as walk on the shoar.

90 Richborough Castle.
91 BHO (Hasted) 10 indicates that New Deal had been recently built since the
    beginning of the seventeenth century.
92 Walmer.

7 miles distant from Deale lies Dover the chiefest of the Cinque Ports being nerest to France. In the waie you shall meet with 2 parishes viz: Wallborough and Ringoule both furnished with Inns.[93]

Besides this to satiate the stranger preying eys a sweet prospect over the curled Ocean and her floating inhabitants into the fertile kingdome of France.

Till in a spacious plaine half a mile on this side you ar invited to behold the Imperous towers of Dover Castle triple walled standing on a mount, cut off from the other part of the hill by deep bottoms or coomes.

On this side of the hill in the bottom under the command of this stately fort lies the town of Dover. The descent to it very steep. It lies in streets streatching this waie and that waie as the levell betweext the white cliffy rocks and sea will permitt and a good part on the sands, here being a pear made by art in the town for the safe gaurd of shipping, where they discharge their lading, close by standing a handsome wearhouse for the reception of such goods as ar brought here.

It is wattered with a sweet rivolett, streaming out of the hills[94] and adorned with 3 churches and a decayed monastry

Six miles from hence into the land is a countrey parish called Swinford[95] and in that a religious [house] called St Jones's

3 miles further in a bottom lies Eleham[96] a poor markett town 10 miles from Canterbury.

And now to speak a little in generall of Kent it is one of the best cultivated countys of any in England and great part of my way that I went being through delicious orchards of Cherrys, pears, apples, and great hop yards

In husbandly affairs they ar very neat binding up all sorts of grain in sheaves. They give the best wages to labourers of any in England in harvest giving 4 and 5 shillings for an acre of wheat and 2s[97] a day meat and drinck which doth invite many stout workmen hither from the neighbouring countreys to gett in theyr harvest.

93 Walmer, Ringwould.
94 River Dour.
95 Swingfield. BHO (Hasted) 8 noted that 'St John's, as it is now usually called, was formerly a *preceptory*, appertaining to the order of the knights of St. John of Jerusalem, to whom it belonged in king Henry II.'s reign.'
96 Elham.
97 Just possibly the symbol after the '2' is a 'd' for pence.

So that you shall find especially on Sundays the roads full of troops of workmen with their sythes and scickles going to the adjacent town to refresh themselves with good liquour and victualls, but many of them poor men paying dearly for coming hither marching of with Kentish agues which many times consumes all they have gott before they go home againe. The most dangerous places for taking this disease are the Iles of Shippy, Thanet and the adjacent levells nere the river and sea.[98]

For in these iles the waters are not so wholesome as in other parts or more especially to those not bredd with it.

Some peradventure may ask why the inhabitants of this countrey cannot do their owne work as well as in other places; in answer to this question I sall give them 2 reasons the first and main one is theyr nere neighbourhood to the sea which invites many of their ablest men to that employment, the 2nd is the neatness they use which requires the more hands to accomplish it.

For carriage all the countrey in generall do use waggons, not so high in the beds as our carts, on which doubtless they can draw a greater burden with more facility than wee can with our carts on 2 wheels with a like company of horses.

The most part of Kent is employed either to tillage orchards or woods except Rumney Marsh[99] which is great place of Grazing to which the drovers and butchers go twice a week where they ar meet by the owners of the grounds and have marketts to buy and sell as their occasion requires.

To Maidstone from Rochester and return to Gravesend

FROM ROCHESTER TO Maidstone is 8 miles.

The waie being under the hill not farr from the river side made more sociable by these countrey towns viz: Woston, Burrum, Paddington, Cutsington, in which one Mr Duke hath a handsome hous, Sandley and then Maidstone the usuall place where the Kentish assizes is kept.[100]

98 Isle of Sheppey, Isle of Thanet. It is interesting that Baskerville identified the tendency of the marshes to lead to 'ague' or malaria, particularly in Sheppey and the Wantsum marshes between Thanet and the mainland. His economic arguments about the troupes of harvest workers sound much like the agitators for poor law reform a century later, but do not mention the shortage of work at other times of year in arable country.

99 Romney Marsh.

100 Wouldham, Burham, Tottington, Costington, Sandling.

Tis watered with Medway on the west extending some houses by the help of a bridge to the other side the river.

Tis populous round formed and built on declining ground refreshed in the maine street with 2 sweet conduits of water and for the shelter of markett people are 3 common houses att the lower end of the town, hard by the river stands a fair large church capacious enough to entertain the inhabitants.

Her cheif manufacture is the making of thredd and buttons, the grounds hereabouts yielding flax for the purpose, but not so much as they use which husbandrey was brought from Flanders hither.

From hence to Gravesend is 15 miles to which they have 2 waies, that by Rochester the fairest and best for horsemen, that on the west side the river the nearest and most pleasant for footmen leading a long the bancks of Medway for 3 miles lower through Alsford a swee(t) countrey town beautified with a bridge a church and 2 fair houses my ladie Culpepers son on the west side the river and Sir John Bensteed or Barksteed on east which is stron(g)ly built with thick walls in the nature of a Castle.[101]

Along the shoar[102] here lay many Iron guns but I could not learn whose they were.

The next town New Hide Snadling Helly Cookton where Sir John Major hath a fine hous jutting on the river.[103]

From hence your waie leads on foot through Cobham Park a place which will feast the spectatours eyes with delightfull objects: fair lawns bedeckt with flourishing groves of yew oake Teile and hathorn trees under which the nimble deer and coneys do sport the time awaie.

This park or rather paradise I may call it belongs to the Duke of Richmond and Lenox[104] in which he hath att the upper end a fair pallace sourrounded with stately groves of Elme and Walnutts and such tall syckamore trees that had I not seen these I could not have imagined a Sykamore could

---

101 Aylesford. BHO (Hasted) 4 agreed 'there is a handsome stone bridge of six arches, built many years ago, and now supported by the public charge of the county'. Sir Thomas Colepepyr, of Preston-hall, in this parish, was lord of the manor, William Colepepyr, alias Culpeper, esq. was created a baronet in 1627, and in his descendants it continued down to Sir Thomas Colepepyr, bart. of Preston hall, who died possessed of it in 1723, without descendants.

102 Of the Medway.

103 New Hythe, Snodland, Halling, Cuxton (Sir John Marsham, Whorne's Place).

104 The central bloc of Cobham Hall was rebuilt 1672–82 by Charles Stewart, 3rd Duke of Richmond, 6th Duke of Lennox (1639–1672). BHO (Hasted) 3.

have attained to such height and bigness.

The hous seems to groan under some abuses offered to it in our late sad times, but the Duke is compleating that which was wanting.

From hence it is 4 miles to Gravesend.

JOURNEY 3
TO COLCHESTER FROM LONDON VIA BRENTWOOD, ROMFORD, CHELMSFORD AND WITHAM, THEN TO GREAT HENNY AND CAMBRIDGE

This journey starts on a new right-hand page. Baskerville's account of how to handle hops reflected his own experience; he wrote to his father concerning the length of hop poles some years later (see Letter 47). This journey seems to have take place in 1662, soon after the restoration of Charles II. Memories of the Civil War were obviously fresh, as the account of the siege of Colchester in the second civil war in the summer of 1648 illustrates.

He goes cross-country from Colchester to stay at Great Henny with Charles Forebench.

REMARQUES ON A jorney in Essex
The road from London to Colchester leads through Stepney the greatest parish in England for multitude of people.

Ratcliff high way, Waping, and most of the houses below the tower did in 1661 belong unto it.[105] Tis something more than a mile from London unto it.

Next to this a mile and half further on the road is Bow and Stratford both bigg enough to keep marketts were it not within 7 miles of London.

A navigable river from Ware in Hartfordshire,[106] here streaming in severall branches seperates these towns as I suppose, and is the western bounds of Essex but att Blackwall uniting again there commixing with the Thames.

Having cleared your self of these towns in your march on the left hand you shall discover Sir William Hicks his hous seated in a flourishing grove of trees

105 Ratcliffe Highway or The Highway (a Roman road) now in Tower Hamlets, Wapping.
106 River Lea.

and then Elford 3 miles distant from Stratford which at spring tides is visited by the water from Thames.[107]

4 miles more, but10 from London is Rumford a great markett town for corn and cattle 2 daies in a weeke and that for cattle one day and corn another to which the butchers and meale men of London do resort.

It hath one church handsomely beautified within.

A miles gayt from Rumford lies East Street where Mr Helmes hath a fair hous and park.

Next Brook Street then Burntwood a through fare town a mile in length, and 5 from Rumford.[108]

In the next 5 miles march you shall go through Shanvill, moneys end, by my

107 Sir William Hicks owned the manor of Ruckholt in Leyton from 1635. VCH (Essex) 6.
108 Ilford, Romford, Brentwood.

Ladie Petres house before you come to Ingarstone, a sweet town on rising ground.[109]

There I shall acquaint you that the county of Essex is so levell that thwarting it from one side to the other between London and Colchester I could not gain any considerable prospect.

Severall rivers I passed over likewise but all so slow of motion I could hardly discern which waie the current went by the hanging flaggs and rushes.

But to return to Ingerstone it hath a handsome church where the family of the Peters have an ile for the buriall of their dead and in it some fair monuments.

The Ladie now living is a widdow having a good report among her neighbours for charitable works.

Adjoining to the church yard they have a fair bowling green frequented by the gentrey hereabout.

In the next 5 miles march you shall pass through Margetts End to Wilford where upon the road I found growing Cammomell Organy and Orpins.[110]

At Wilford you shall see on the left hand Rutle a fair country parish and a little beyond it Chansford, the shire town of Essex where the five miles is compleated.[111]

Tis about the biggness of Reading, watered with a fine River and adorned with a large Church in which do lie entombed the Lord Thomas Mildmay and his Ladie who had issue 7 sons and 8 daughters as is to be seen by their effigies on a fair monument.[112]

About this town as in many parts of Essex they have large hop yards in which att the time of gathering they employ many women for 6 pence a day to pick and seperate them.

Those that are gott in Green when they ar ripe they say are the best the brown they sort by themselves, being lower p(r)ized but I have found

109 Shenfield, Ingatestone. Ingatestone Hall was built by William Petre and the Petre family remain there. The house is listed Grade 1. Historic England.

110 Margaretting, Widford. Three herbs in frequent use in the 17th century: Camomile, Origanum, Orpin; orpin is a sedum. Willes *The Domestic Herbal* (2020) 122.

111 Writtle, Chelmsford.

112 The river Chelmer flows through Chelmsford. The church became the seat of a bishopric in 1914. There is a colourful wall monument in the north transept to Thomas Mildmay (died 1566), his wife Avice and their family of 15 children. Historic England.

by experience to gather them in too green is not so good for unless they be glutinous and stick to the gatherers fingers they are not come to theyr full virtue and ripeness.

As soon as they have cleansed them from leaves and stemms they sett them to dry on killns for if they neglect them 3 or 4 days 'twill discolour them, in 12 hours time may be dried two killns but great care must be taken least they burn.

When they ar dried it is good to lett them lie a weeke or more in the heap to air for if they are putt in baggs too soon they ar apt to grow mouldy.

But let us pass forward to Springfield by which in the Road you shall have a view of that stately mansion New Hall which owned the Duke of Buckingham for lord in (62).[113]

From the high waie it hath a stately walke or riding to the house sett on both sides in exact order double rowes of Lime and hornbin trees at such distance that att the end of this flourishing walk you may discover the front of the Dukes magnificent pallace which with desires to have further satiated my greedy gazing eyes I left behind and came to Boorham[114] where one Mr Cammock[115] hath a neat house and garden finly planted with out landish trees whose ever verdant topps overlook the vale adding delight to travellers that pass that waie.

To the next village called Alford is 6 miles from Chansford to Wittim another markett town. Here St George on his horse encountering the draggon is carved in wood on a sign post in full proportion.

Hence through Riblam to Kilding is 3 miles where there is a river.

To Fearing and Stanaway 5 miles more and from thence to Colchester 3 which compleates 11 miles from Wittim but before you come thither you shall pass through Lextone a pretty little town within the liberties of Colchester.[116]

---

113 New Hall, Boreham, Henry VIII's former palace of Beaulieu, of which only a wing survives. The gardens were possibly designed by John Tradescant the elder. In 1656 John Evelyn noted in his Diary the New Hall, the wilderness and the fine south approach, then planted with four rows of limes. In 1660 George Monck, Duke of Albemarle, lived here splendidly but a legal problem meant he did not own it until 1662. House and grounds are separately listed by Historic England.

114 Boreham.

115 Cammock is a surname found in Essex and there are a number of large houses in Boreham.

116 ?Appleford, Witham, Rivenhall, Kelvedon, Feering, Stanway, Lexden. (So here, as in Kent, he followed the Roman road). Stanway House is now in the middle of

Colchester

THE FOUNDER OF this town was Coellus or Coile Earle of Colchester and King of Brittain who began his reign in the year of our Lord 262 ruling it for a certain time to the content of his subjects till Constantius appointed by the Rommans passed over into this Ile with an armie which putt Coyle in such dread that he imediately sent an Embassage and concluded a peace covennanting to pay the accostomed tribute and give to Constantius his daughter in marrage called Helena a noble Ladie and learned who was the mother of Constantine the great.

Shortly after Coyle dyed, after he had reigned as some write 27 years or as others have but 13 years.

But to this day the townsmen of Colchester in remembrance of King Coyle their founder do keep in repairation a well rayled about in the chiefest street of the town and on the topp of the pump the Effegies of K Coyle and on each corner of this Inclosure the town armes.

Conduits they can have none because the scituation is on ground as high or higher than any here abouts, I mean that which is walled.

Sixteen churches and a ruinous castle for publick buildings ar reckoned within this town and her preimeter

The castle now a prison for the county was the pallace of King Coyle, of late years made famous for the sufferings of those 2 worthy knights Sir George Lile and Sir Charles Lucas who were here shott to death.

In that place where they fell the grass att this day doth not grow or hide the earth although it grows thick and plentiful round about.

7000 came into the town with my Lord Goring and those 2 knights being hottly persued by the armie under Sir Thomas Fairfax so that they had no time to make provision, and yett for all that they held out eleven weeks with a great deale of Gallantrey against the enemie being driven by extreamity of hunger before they did yeeld it up to eat their horses.[117]

In this siege the suburbs of the town were much endamnified but since for the most part repaird but St Buttalls[118] one of the fairest churches of the

Colchester Zoo. It contains some timber in the roof of the original grand house built by presumably built by John Doreward (d. 1420), a Speaker of the House of Commons in 1399 and 1413. VCH (Essex) 10; HoP.

117 In the summer of 1648 a Royalist army was attempting to raise support for Charles I; it was pursued by Sir Thomas Fairfax and the Royalists retreated to Colchester, where, as TB says, it withstood a siege for 11 weeks.

118 Botolph's.

town is yet a ruinous spectacle by means of the seige. They after surrenderd and paid £1000 for composition to the parleament.

The chief manufacture of this town does consist in making of Ruggs and bays which doth employ so many hands that they ar able to make 10000 able men.

They have likewise enrichments from the sea by a river navigable for hoyes to St Leonards a part of the town.

Att the mouth of the river lies Cole[119] their port town.

Five miles from Colchester in the road to Ipswich lies Naylam a little markett town in Suffolke sourrounded with Rich meaddows mellowed by a river runing through the town and halfe a mile from it lies Stock on the top of the hill, a town as bigg as Naylam.

And between this and Sudbury on the river Stour which runs to Colchester lies Buash Lamash and Hene Magna, where my worthy Friend Mr Charles Forebench formerly parson of Sandford in Oxfordshire by Oxon doth live and is now Rectour of this place 1662 att whose house I had a hearty welcome for some weekes.[120]

About five miles from this Gentlemans hous on the Edge of Suffolk lies Sudbury a fair markett town scituate upon the river Stower a part of it called Ballington[121] being in Essex. Tis beautified with 3 fair churches whose towers and steeples att some distance as you come out of Essex through Ballington, seems to stand in the forme of an aequilatour [equilateral] triangle; the churches names are St Gregorys, St Peters, and Alhallowes, in the last the Family of the Edens who live now at Ballington hath a fair monument.

By this church there was a priory now the hous of Mr Hows.

Here was likewise an Abbey sometime the residence (or else the town was his birth place) of the learned man Simon of Sudbury afterwards archbishop of Canterbury[122]

Thomas Baskervill

---

119 Has TB confused the river Colne with the name of the port? The quay area was called Hythe.
120 Nayland, Stoke, Bures, Lamarsh, Great Henny; Charles Forebench, rector of Great Henny 08/08/1634 - 00/09/1664 (deceased). CCEd.
121 River Stour, Ballingdon, Sudbury.
122 Simon Tybald, or Thebaud, or Theobald was born in Sudbury, archbishop of Canterbury from 1375 and chancellor of England from 1380, beheaded during the Peasants Revolt in 1381. https://www.britannica.com/event/Peasants-Revolt

The signature at the bottom of this page suggests Baskerville thought he had finished that particular journey. It also suggests he wrote the previous pages. On the facing page there are notes in a slightly different hand relevant to Essex, the subject of the journey just described, but implying he had travelled the road from Chelmsford to Braintree on a different occasion.

Essex for the generallity is a level and enclosed country, not soe well planted with fruit trees as Kent, but in other respects as neatly husbanded. Out of this country and Suffolk they drive like flocks of sheep to London great legues of turkys.

A large space beneath this last sentence

In Essex is a market Town called Hasted built on the declivity of a hill, and in the bottome a river, here Sir Samuel Trayn hath a fair house. Anno 1662.

Five miles farther in the road to London is another large market town called Braintree, on the top of a lowe hill, having adjoyning to it another handsome Towne called Bockhen and by that a river; between this town and Chansford in the road formerly described is accompted 10 miles[123]

To Cambridge from Sudbury

A half page here, apparently a draft for further remarks on Kings College Chapel, Cambridge, is placed with the description of the Cambridge colleges below.

The account of saffron growing (in 1681) adds to the account in Journey 1 above, to which he refers.

FROM SUDBURY TO Cambridg is accompted 20 miles, but I found them long ones, the nearest way leads through Bulmar; next water Belching which is about 4 miles from Sudbury, there is one Parish more calld Assington I went through before I gott out of this by-way to Stoke, which hath 2 Inns in the road from Sudbury to Cambridg. Here one Sir Jarvis Alloway hath an ancient house formerly some monastery.[124] Here is to be noted, that this

123 Halstead, Bocking.
124 Bulmer, Belchamp Water, Ashen, Stoke-by-Clare. The road through Bulmer suggests TB actually went from Great Henny to Cambridge. At Stoke-by-Clare there had been a cell of the monastery of Bec, but as an alien priory it was dissolved and in 1415 became a collegiate church. VCH (Suffolk) 2. The College and manor were bought by Sir Gervase Elwes (died 1705). The name Sir Jarvis Alloway is close to the actual name, as often with TB's spelling of names.

place is in the county of Suffolk which is devided from Essex by the river
Stower, that about Haverel hath its fountain which is a throughfare Town on
the road 4 miles nerer Cambridg, and about 10 from Sudbury.[125] The making
of fustian and dimmety is here a great trade, alsoe about these parts safron is
much planted. But as to the discourse of the husbandry and planting of it, they
gave mee this acompt, viz: about midsummer when they design to new plant a
ground for they usually lett the roots stand 3 or 4 years they digg them up and
dung the ground and then set them again, as thick as they can plant them and
5 inches deep, that soe they may howe of the weeds for 3 or 4 years without
spoyling the roots, for they lett the weeds growe all the summer for cattle to
feed on, and howe them of about the middle of September a little before the
saffron flowers begin to rise.

In the first years planting the roots doe yield but few flowers, the second and
third years they bear flowers plentifully, and in the fourth year are dugg up
again to be dungd and planted as above said. When the flowers come up the
people are dilligent to gather them in baskets, and to take out the Chives in
the middle of them of a reddish colour and that is that which they call safron.
Then these Chives are dried in a iron pan over the fire, till they are soe well
dried that they are not apt to be mouldy, thus cured a pound is vallued at 25
shillings in these dayes, but formerly it was doble the price of the weight of
silver for safron.

These safron heads or roots are grown so cheap that you may now in these parts
buy a bushel of them for one shilling and sixpence and sometimes a shilling, as
this year 1681 the man at the *Dog* at Melsome[126] in the road between Royston
and Cambridg told mee.

A little beyond Havrel is Cambridgshire.
       From Havrell to the University of Cambridg they have 2 wayes the one
leads through a market Town if I am not mistaken cald Linton which is the
farthest, and the nerer through Ratton[127] a rotton place in which is a poore Inn
where I was glad of a bed as hard as a board, and the country hereabouts is a
verry rotten soyle for the men as well as the women are forced to goe in high
iron pattens.

125 Haverhill.
126 Meldreth or Melbourn?
127 Linton, ?West Wratting.

Four miles forward and not far from my Lord Allington's house I went by Bassim <Balsom> over new market heath where there is a deep ditch thwarting the plains or heath commonly cald Divel's ditch, cast up as I suppose for a boundary, between the East Angles and Mersians.[128]

The way leads along the side of this ditch or trench from whence you have at 5 or 6 miles distance a goodly prospect of the famous University of Cambridg, seated in a spatious Level; by an easy descent from these hills you shall come to Fulbourn,[129] a country Town but remarkable because it hath 2 churches in one church yard, built by 2 maids, and covered with more reed, and are 2 distinct parish churches as people then told in 62, from whence I went to Chesterton, for the description of which Town and Cambridg I shall refer you to another journey, and speak but a little of it here.

Cambridge

CAMBRIDG SITUATE ON the east side of the river Came might have its name from thence, although some historians derive it from Cantaber, who 375 years before the incarnation had there setled the muses seat, and albeit in many ages this city like many others hath tasted many wofull fortunes, yet now it is beautified and fairly adorned with 16 colledges and Halls full stored with painfull students. The most magnificent for building are Trinity, and Kings Coll: joyning to which is that famous structure built by Henry the Sixth but finished by Henry the Seventh cald Kings Colledg Chappel, for elegant workmanship equal if not superior to any church work elsewhere in England having in it on the right side a fair Library; this chappell runs in length with out any pillars in the body to support the rough, or isles thwarting from north to south as in most Cathedralls, having curiously carved in stonework upon the inside of the walls the arms of the then present Kings, being divided in the midst to distinguish the Quire from the body by a rare partition of joynery work, on which is erected a beautifull Organ. At the west end of the chappel on the right side is a stair-case by which I ascended the ledds, where besides the vew of Came's meanders courting fair Cambridg with embraces I discovered a spacious plain, of the largest extent that I have seen any in England, soe that in this she doth outstrip her sister Oxford, but for sweet air situation and magnificent building much beneath her, excepting this fabrick on which I stand, which yields to none in England. Upon the chappel at each corner

128 Balsham. Devil's Dyke.
129 There were two churches in Fulbourn within the same graveyard, St. Vigor's and All Saints. All Saints was ruined in 1766 when its tower and bells collapsed and it was later demolished. https://www.fulbournpc.org/about-fulbourn

mounting above the ledds are fower spires or tall pinnacles and between these on the sides and ends lesser pinnacles.

The schools of Cambridg are not to be compared to the durable monument of Bodely's in Oxford, yet they have a fair market place which Oxford wants, and at the upper end a conduit.* St. Mary's church here is well nigh as fair a building as ours at Oxford but the black durty streets doe eclips the splendour of their buildings Ann: 1662

*The faire conduit above mentioned was built at the Charge of Hobson a Carrier in the year 1624[130]

A paragraph on an earlier page concerning King's college chapel, perhaps written hastily, is added here.

Besides the magnificency of the structure of that Famous Chappell of the Kings Colledge founded by Henry the sixth within are two things very remarkable: a stone that hangs by Geometery in the top of the Chappell, you may see round it into the Quire and may stand upon it as securely as upon any other part, yet seeming to do your onswing; the other remarkable is an emblem of the resurrection carved so to the life upon part of the wainscott going into the Quire, which supports organs, that it hath been and is the admiration of all Arttist and travellers, tis contained on a small peece of the said wainscott going into the Quire as aforesaid. Yet £500 has been offered to the Colledge for it and refused.

JOURNEY 4
TO SOUTHAMPTON FROM ABINGDON VIA NEWBURY AND WINCHESTER

This section contains the only reference Baskerville made to going to Newfoundland. In his Memoir of Tom Hyde (see Chapter 6 'Miscellaneous Writings') he mentions that two of his brothers went to Greenland to make whale oil, but his purpose in going to Newfoundland is not stated. This account makes clear that the manuscript is a composite of information, including on another occasion sailing from Plymouth through the Portland race; some is in note form, and some incorporates later observations. The journey may have been in 1649 and also 1679

130 Asterisk and note added in a ?different hand.

REMARKS UPON THE way from Abingdon to Southampton And other Places

From Abingdon to Newberry is accompted 15 miles the way lyes through Ilsley a Town of small note seven miles from Abingdon and eight from Newberry.[131]

Newberry is seated on the banks of Kennet that parts it from Spinnum Lands,[132] being a place known to many by the rich manufactures hatts and cloth, but more notorious to the nation by fighting 3 unhappy battles near it.

About a mile from Newberry in the road back again towards Abingdon upon a hill on the left hand stand the ruins of Dennington Castle, and a mile of on the right hand at Shaw Mr Doleman hath a fine house.[133] And upon the hill by Dennington Castle, you have sight about 4 miles of, of a stately house built by the Lord Craven since the restauration of the King, but the time when I went this journey was but a few months after the beheading of King Charles the 1st.[134] Att the sign of the *Bear* at LYMINGTON

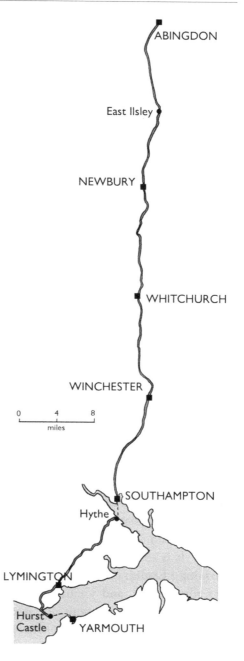

131 East Ilsley is on the modern road from Abingdon to Newbury.
132 Speenhamland.
133 Donnington Castle. Thomas Dolman, clothier of Newbury, started to build Shaw House in 1554 and it was finished in 1581. Sir Thomas Dolman was the owner when TB saw the house. VCH (Berks) 4.
134 Hamstead Marshall was built for William Craven as a residence for Charles I's

Spinnum lands now lives Mr Phillips who keeps good wine, a bowling green and a cockpit.

Newberry hath one fair Church, and a handsome market house in a pretty large market place.

It is well served on Thursdays and Frydays with sea fish because it Lyes in the road to Oxford, and for River fish it hath delicate trowts, jack, and excellent Crawfish with such other sorts of fish as the river Kennet affords.

It is a corporation Town, but they send noe Burgesses to Parliament.

They are a sociable people, and to encrease trade do keep great feasts, each severall company they and their wives feasting together, especially the Clothiers and hatters.

For coming one day through the Town and staying at the *Globe* Inn to dine, one of the company's they and their wives after they had heard a sermon at church were met at the *Globe* with the Town musick, who playing merrily before them, the men in their best clothes followed them, and after them the women in verry good order 2 and 2 neatly trim'd and finely drest all in steeple crowned hatts, which was a pleasant sight to behold.

From Newberry wee went to Whittchurch[135] in Hampshire a poor through fare Town on London road from the western parts, the country about it hilly and well stored with flocks of sheep, the hedg rows and enclosures sett and adorned with yew trees here plentifully growing in these parts thow rarely fownd in other places.

About 2 miles from Whitchurch the Lord Dellaware hath a good house seated by a fine river.[136]

Winchester

WINCHESTER ABOUT 30 miles from Abingdon the chiefe and onely City in Hampshire is the next eminent place in the roade to Southampton whose situation is in a pleasant botome by a sweete river running among the hills. It is strongly immured with deep trenches, the wall that ingirts it containing 2 English miles or more. It has a Castle but now allmost demolish'd. It has allso 7 gates, and 7 Churches besides that stately ancient fabrick the Cathedrall, under whose vault doe rest the bones of divers Kings, some of whose bodies lye in chests of stone upon the walls of the quire neare the high

    sister, Elizabeth of Bohemia, although she died before construction began. It burnt
    down in 1718. It is 4 miles from Newbury as TB said.
135 Whitchurch.
136 The river Test. Lord de la Warr owned Wherwell until 1695. VCH (Hants) 4.

altar. These sepulchers since the King's resauration have bin beautified - and adorn'd with colour, the oversight of these and other reparations in the Church being left to the care of my worthy friend Dr. Dayrell[137] one of the Prebends, who has here built for himselfe and his succeeding prebends a very faire house. He has allso belonging to it a very fine garden, on one side of which there is such a wall of flint as for height the like is not to be seen. At the West end of the Quire (to which there is a faire ascent) did stand in brasse the Effigies of King James and Charles the 1st; but before our return (we then goeing a voyage to Newfoundland a few weeks after the beheading of the King) they were pulled down, but since the restauration they have bin set up again.

Here is erected by this present Bishop Morley neere the Church, a good almes house for such Clergymen's widows as stood in need of his charity.[138]

This city has bin formerly adorned with many more Churches, whose ruines are now scarce discernable. But at the West end of the Cathedrall there still remaines some part of a heathen temple. 'tis a greate thick piece of wall built of lime and flint, now more like a naturall rock than any artificiall workmanship,' tis so strong cemented.

And as touching the walls of the city, being built with the same materialls, where any part has fallen, it lies like rocks severall yards in length without separating; so skillfull were they in former times in this sort of building

Touching the antiquity of this City historians tell us t'was built by Rhudhadbrasse 900 yeares before the nativity of our saviour, and under the vicissitude of her owners has had these severall names imposed: by the Britaines t'was called Caer-Gwent, by the Romans Venta Belgarum, by the Saxons Windanearder, and now Winchester; in which revolution of times it was twice consumed with fire, but by the Saxons it was re-edified the walls built, and made the chiefe seate of the West Saxon Kings, and the Metropolitan see of their Bishops, wherein were crown'd Egbert, and Elfred, and Henry the 3rd born.

When the Danes did incroache upon these Kingdoms, here was a combat fought between Colebrand the Danish, and Guy Earl of War. the English Champion, in a place called Hide meade, where that - swaggering Lordane was slaine to the greate joy of King Athelstan[139] and his good people.

Here is now kept one of the most famous schooles in England, from

---

137 Walter Dayrell, student of Christ Church, a canon of Winchester from 1662 until his death in 1684, aged 74; archdeacon of Winchester 1666. Son of Walter Dayrell of Abingdon. CCEd.

138 George Morley, bishop of Winchester 1662-1684. CCEd.

139 Heavily overwritten and finally rewritten neatly on the next line.

whence doe yearely goe some hopefull scholars to New College in Oxon.

Half a mile without Winchester, in the way towards Hampton[140] whither wee are now going doth stand St. Crosses Church and Hospitall being endowed with good revennews.

2 miles on this side Hampton accompted 10 miles from Winchester wee had a pleasant prospect of the Town and shipping in that haven, as we came to the north gate for entrance we saw the effigies of 2 gigantick men in paint on the walls on each side of the gate, perhaps the famous Sir Bevis and some other gallant.[141]

This being a seaport-Town and now strongly garrison'd, wee were strictly examined by the guard from whence wee came, and what we did there, and at night a gentleman from the governor came to the *Rose and Crown*, where wee lay and took our names in writeing and thus they doe to all strangers.

To give some accompt o(f) the buildings of this Town it is strongly wall'd on which doe stand 29 fair towers, and it hath seven gates, 5 Churches, an hospitall, and on the top of a hill cast up by men a strong double wall'd castle, from whence may bee seen 2 fair havens for ships to ride in.

It has one fair and broad street <besides other of lesser note> running in length from the North gate to the South gate, where is a fair Key to land or send aboard goods as also to take boat to goe to the Isle of Wyte,[142] for which purpose they have good boats constantly attending.

Here is also another fair Key at the West gate.

The trade of this Town is much decayd of what it was in former dayes, for then much French wines and goods were landed here, and carried into the countries, but now that trade is diverted to other places.

To Hythe, the New Forest and the Isle of Wight

THE SEA OR river is navigable from Hampton, as far as a Town called Rummsy, and 10 miles to seaward of Hampton stands Callshott castle which commands the entrance of the haven.[143]

Takeing boat at the south Key wee crost the haven to a small village

---

140 Southampton.
141 The legend of Sir Bevis of Hampton is, according to expert Jennifer Fellows, 'arguably one of the most important non-Arthurian romances in Middle English'. A story of many adventures and the successful reclaiming of his patrimony of Hampton. https://historicsouthampton.co.uk/bevis/
142 The Isle of Wight, variously spelled, is mentioned a number of times.
143 Romsey, Calshot.

called Hiethe,[144] within the virges of new forrest.

From whence it is about 3 or 4 miles to Limminton[145] a small seaport Town, here is also another passage where boats attend to carry men and horses to the Isle of Wyte much nerer than that at Hampton, for it is not much above a league over here between the main land of England, and the Isle of Wyte, and it is the safest passage, for in the other passage between Hust Castle[146] and the Town of Yarmouth the tides runn verry rapid, being streightned in their current by the nearness of the land between Hust Castle and the west end of the Isle of Wyte, which is scarce a mile assunder, and in part of the way there stand up some high whiteish rocks above the sea which they call the needles.

This Town since the act of forbidding French wines to be brought over lies verry commodious for stealing wines ashore,[147] and that perhaps of late has contributed to their wealth, for here are now built some handsome houses. Here in the year 1679 being in company with Mr Weeks Huntley a gentleman related to mee,[148] wee fell aquainted with one Mr Dore a lawyer, who conducted us through the forrest to find out Mr Gorge Rodney one of the Rangers, and it was but need enough for wee rodd some 6 or 7 miles through woods, trees, and winding paths, soe that sometimes that Gentleman himself was at stand which way to goe, but at length hee brought us to Lindus[149] the Kings house well built, with good stables belonging to itt. Here at this time happning to be a court kept for the Forresters were much good company meett together, and they had a great feast at a small Inn nere the Kings house where this worthy gentleman Mr Rodney treated us verry liberally with good Cheer and wine, and sent a guide with us to conduct us through the forrest to Rummsy.

This Forrest was made by Will: the Conqueror depopulating many parrishes after his conquest of England, that so in case of rebellion his people might have more freedome to land, and it is at present I suppose one of the greatest forrests in England.[150]

It is I suppose about 4 miles between Limmington and Hust Castle, in the way thither the hedge rows especially those nere Hust Castle look as if they

144 Hythe.
145 Lymington
146 Hurst Castle.
147 The Prohibition by act of parliament 1678 (29 & 30 Cha. 2 c. 1).
148 See Chaper 2 'Life and Kin'.
149 Lyndhurst. The King's House was the former manor house.
150 This paragraph was omitted by HMC.

were shorn with a pair of sheers, soe sharp and cutting is the cold weather and winds that blow here from the sea, and the oaks for 2 or 3 miles riding being not able to weather it or grow upright, doe extend themselves to landward in an arbburing way, some of them 9 or 10 yards in length.

Here along are many salt pans, or places into which they lett the sea water to stand and be heightened by the suns heat, and then in their coppers for which here are many houses for that purpose it is boyld up to the consistance of salt.

Hust Castle stands upon an Isthmus of land, which in former times att high tides was wont to be covered with the sea, but now since the waters have grated a channel neerer the Island it remains dry land.

The castle is round and low built commanding the entrance of the channel between this point of land and the Needles.

When the King was kept prisoner at Casbrook[151] Castle in the Isle of Wyte, he stayd some dayes at Hust Castle in his passage thither.

The tides doe here run soe strong at the Needles the waters being streightened by the neerness of the land especially the ebbing water when at strength, that ships with a strong winde can hardly stemm it, or sayl against it. Here are in these seas 2 dangerous Races, the one called St. Albons[152] the other Portland Race. For comeing by sea from Plimouth[153] to Portland, the wind was then soe calm we were feyn to tide it most part of the way. Here was in this race such a strange chopping leaping sea which made mee much admire it, and yet not a way (*sic*) of wind stirring to disturb the water; and some of our marriners told mee that if ships venture to sail through it in tempestuous weather they are in danger to be swallowed up of the sea, soe perrilous is this place.

Tis about a league between Hust Castle and the Tow(n) of Yarmouth in the Isle of Wyte. Here wee met with a boat to carry us thither, and left our horses at a poor Inn by the Castle, the boatmen told us they did usually carry over horses, but the boat did seem to bee to small to carry over such bulky creatures, and doubtless tis dangerous for in the midway the sea was verry rough and troublesome <although we had but little wind.>

Yarmouth is a little Town built on the brow of a hill in an Island within the

---

151 Carisbrooke castle. Charles I was imprisoned there for just over a year from 13 November 1647.
152 St Albans Race or inshore passage.
153 Plymouth.

main island, the present Governor haveing lately cutt a passage through some
land to lett the sea round it and make it more fortifieable, since wee had some
fears of a French invasion,[154] whose man went verry civilly along with us to
show us the Town and fortifications. It has also in it a verry strong castle to
command such shipps as sayl by it on the sea, and all shipps are oblig'd to
Lower their top sayles as they sayl by the castle, if not they must endure the
summons of a great gunn.

For it happen'd while wee were eating our dinner of fish at one Mr Dods
house an Inn keeper of the Town that a shipp bound for France endeavoured
to pass by without the performance of this duty, which the Governour seeing
commanded a gunn to bee fired att him, but those in the shipp still refusing
to strike he fired 2 or 3 more with bullets which kept a plaguey singing in the
air, and then he commanded the boatmen that brought us hither to bring the
master of the shipp prisoner to the castle. who was forced to pay 40 shillings
or more money for his presumption before he had liberty to proceed on his
voyage. The masters name of this shipp was Phillips, and he told mee Mr
Bishop the milliner of Oxford was his uncle, he pretended when he was
brought before the Governor, that the sunn shone soe in his eyes that he could
not see the castle but as wee went back again with him towards his shipp for we
could get noe horses to make a farther progress in the Island, he told us he did
it purposely, and for hast made so much sayl that hee was like to have drawn
his long boat astern under water.

There follow a number of notes in different hands (not transcribed by HMC)

Trinity Church in Winchester is 178 yards in Length, this was measured by my
Cosen John Holloway brother to Mr Charles Hollow of Oxford. This church
Containes this measure within it.

The Fishermen about Pool for the most part serve the Ile of Wight and the
shores on tother side to Linnington and other parts with fish especially
operhors? as people told me - but at Hurst Castle wee bought some whitting
Cole or larger whitting newley taken here about which were drest at Yarmouth
for our dinner.

---

154 In 1662, a moat was cut round the eastern end of the town through the narrow
     neck of land that connected the Yarmouth peninsula with the Island mainland.
     Hist. MSS. Com. Report XIII, App. ii, 288; https://www.iwhistory.org.uk

Two fairs in the city of Winchester the first on the first Munday in Lent and the second a fortnight after Michaelmas.

Two fairs are kept without the Town one upon Maudlen hill on the 22th of July the other on St Giles hill on the first day of September.

The King's house at Winchester is 107 yards in length on a square as you enter.

Mr Holloway and his wife gave me this account Innkeepers in Winchester.
Mr Holloway is brother to Richard Wests wife of Sunningwell.

JOURNEY 5
TO NORTHAMPTON FROM OXFORD VIA BICESTER, BUCKINGHAM AND TOWCESTER, THENCE TO THE WEST VIA WARWICK

The account starts on a new right-hand page. The handwriting is more cursive than the last section, is better-written and more generally literate in spelling. The date of the journey appears to be February 1673, not long after the Northampton parliamentary election of 1670 but before the fire of 1675. A typical example of Baskerville's incorrigible enthusiasm is his return visit to Northampton after the great fire, information on which he added to his account of the 1673 journey.

R EMARKABLE NOTES ON the rode to severall inland Towns in this nation.

Louse hall 4 miles from Oxford nere Gossard[155] bridg famous for ale and an old woman that always wore a ruff whose picture is yet to be seen in many alehouses.

Islip a throughfare Town on London rode and 6 miles from Oxford ann: 1673 at the sign of the *Georg* where wee dined, with good usage, lives one Titmash a merry man formerly a souldier under Char: the first.

Towns on the rode towards Bister[156] Weston on the Green - there lives an honest gentleman called Sir Edward Norris.[157]

---

155 Louse Hall in Gosford, part of Kidlington parish, now the *King's Arms* public house. Historic England. It was repaired by the overseers of the poor and a pauper sent there. VCH (Oxon) 12.
156 Bicester.
157 Sir Edward Norreys was an MP for Oxford or Oxfordshire from 1675 until 1705.

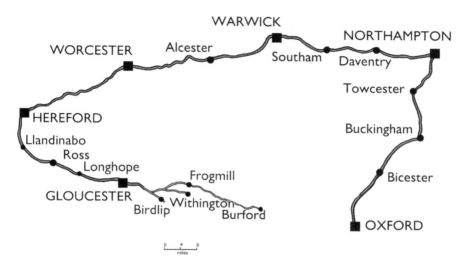

In the rode as you goe towards Bister, you shall see about a mile or 2 on the right hand a Parrish called Marten[158] and on the left Chesterton to which a large meddow belongs, and 5 miles distant from Islip stands Bicester a market Town on frydays haveing on[e] fair Church and a pretty brook of water running by it. here now lives an honest gentleman of my acquaintance on(e) Mr Francis Blower.

From hence to Buckingham is some 7 or 8 miles. Wee went by a village calld Catswell and another named Tingish and soe to Buckingham, which is seated in a valley by a small river that runs into Ows that passes by the Town of Bedford.[159]

It being St. Mathias day here was a great fair for cattle and other commodities. The Town is pretty large surrounding a green mount on which remains some ruins of a Castle.

It being the county town of the shire, the assizes are usually kept here, but haveing no Town Hall for the judges to sitt in, they doe erect sheds for the purpose against the ruinous castle walls. It hath but one church with a ledden spire, and some good Inns for entertainment.

From hence wee went to a Town called Tortester by a place called Lilingstone Dorrel, of which one Captain Dorrell was Lord his estate being said by a

HoP.
158 Merton.
159 Crockwell, Tingewick, Ouse.

knowing man to bee worth £600 per ann: being lately dead hee was buried this day as I heard at the Inn where I lay that night in Torster.[160]

Passing by Lillingston Dorrell wee rodd through Whitleberry forrest, haveing on the other side the wood next Toster, a small village called Whitleberry, where is an ale house.[161] Tortester is about 2 little miles beyond this village in the rode towards Northampton, where wee lay at the sign of the *Talbot* one Mr Jones a gentile man who hath a neat dame to his wife being the present master of the Inn who are curious in their house and gardens.

Tortester is a fine Town seated by a small river which runs through Northampton, and hath one Church with a great Charnell house[162] under the Chancell and some verry good Inns for entertainment. Here you may buy boots and shoes verry cheap.

Some half a mile without this Town on the other side of the river there is a village called Eson,[163] where Sir William Farmer hath a good house and park. Not long a gone he and the Lord Bryan were compettitors for a Burgess's place in Northampton, one Sir Yelverton another burgess of it dying at that same time they were both elected.[164] Sir William Farmer, I was told, hath the Toll of Northampton market.

Northampton

HAMPTON[165] IS ABOUT 6 or 7 miles from Tortester, wee went through a village call'd Milton, and being come within 2 miles of Northampton, wee had a fair prospect of that Town seated by a river, on ground gently rising on the other side the stream, to which the way leads over a stone bridge and about a mile on the right hand in another rode stands a fair Cross with the Effigies of some Kings and Queens cutt in stone work.

---

160 Towcester, Lilingstone Dayrel. Peter Dayrell was an active royalist; he died in
   1667. VCH (Bucks) 4.
161 Whittlebury.
162 The Crypt.
163 Easton Neston.
164 Sir William Fermor [Farmer] of Easton Neston, 2nd Bt. MP for Northampton
   1670 and 1679. 'Fermor stood for Northampton in 1670, where he had a 'fair
   house', at the first vacancy after he came of age; he was opposed by Lord Ibrackan
   (Henry O'Brien), but the other seat also became vacant and they were returned
   without a contest.' [Married 1671 Jane, daughter of Andrew Barker of Fairford
   (died 1673)]. Henry O'Brien died before the next election. Sir Henry Yelverton,
   2nd Bt. (1633-70), of Easton Maudit, Northants was the other member who died
   suddenly on 3 October 1670. HoP.
165 Northampton.

The Town seems to bee not much less than Oxford, having fair streets and strong built houses of freestone of an Oker colour in many places, with fair Inns and a verry spacious market place, it hath likewise to adorn it 4 Churches, viz: St. Peters, St. Sepulchers, Alhallows, and St. Giles; and at the end of the Town which leads towards Daintree[166] an old Castle.

This town some years since this journey hath suffered under a dreadfull conflagration 3 parts or more of it being totally ruind by that furious element, but tis since Phoenix like risen out of her ashes, in a far more noble and beauteous form, the houses of the streets being now built in verry good order with excellent freestone and bellconies, and some of the Inns are such gallant and stately structures that the like is scarcely elsewhere to bee seen.

Some weeks after the fire I went thither to see this ruinous heap, when I found about the midle of the Town an indifferent house standing and all the other houses for a good distance round about it burnt down, and yet the upper storys of it were only studded with lath and plaister work, twas a small Inn and had for the sign a shoomakers last with this motto 'I have sought for good ale over the Town and here I have found it at last'; the straingeness of this preservation made mee alight to discours the Innkeeper how it could possibly bee effected, who told mee by the help of some friends hoisting some hogsheads of beer out of his sellar, and being verry dilligent to coole those parts of the house which were verry hott they did preserve it.

Sir William Farmer before spoken of having a fair house at the Lower end of the Town was turned into an Inn immediatly after the fire, and soe were some other gentlemens houses in the outward borders of the Town.

Here is kept on St. James's day a great fair where many good horses are bought and sold as also at other fairs held in this Town when the dayes come.

Kingsthrup[167] a mile from Northampton was the ancient Town and market as country people here told mee. Here is also a village nere it called Abingdon.

As wee went towards Daintry wee saw Holmby[168] one of the Kings houses some 2 miles distant on the right hand, this house I have since been att but there is little now left save ruinous walls, but those shew the structure to have been verry noble. It stands in a delicate place for prospect, here commanding the view of the country round about, especially the Earl of Sunderland's house,

166 Daventry.
167 Kingsthorpe.
168 Holdenby.

nobly built and seated in a fine park.[169]

Holmby is about 4 miles from Northampton, and 'tis about 7 or 8 miles betwixt Northampton and Daventree.

At Daventree wee lay at the sign of the *Swan* near the church, Mrs. Bostock, a widdow a propper gentilewoman, the landlady of it Ann:1673 and formerly the wife of a handsome tall gentleman of that name, who did usually come to the Lent fair at Abingdon with good horses to sell, where I first gott acquaintance with him. This Town hath one fair church in it and divers deep wells along the great street, and verry good Inns for entertainment.

From hence we went by higher and nether Shugburrough, where one Mr Harvey hath a house, and soe through a small market Town called Southam, where much cattle are bought and sold on Mundays, it is accompted 9 miles betweene Daventree and Southam, and 9 miles more from hence to Warwick, in the way thither lys these villages viz: Upton, Radwill, and Limmington.[170]

Warwick

WARWICK IS A famous Town on the river Aven over which a bridg of 12 arches or more leads to the Castle which for beauty situation and stately structure, yields to none but Windsor within this Isle. The Lord Brooke a courteous gentleman in whose company I have been at Bathe is the present owner of it who keeps many men now at work to repair it, it is built upon a rock of excellent freestone, and out of the dike surrounding the wall they drew the stone which built this brave edifice.

In the court without the castle are lately built verry fair stables after the new mode, being come within the gate (haveing at the corners of it square high turrets) is a fair court, and within that encompassed with a palle a dainty bowleingreen, sett about with lawrell, Firs, and other curious trees. Upon the south side this court respecting the river is the dwelling house, in which are noble rooms, and on the western square of the castle is a mount well nigh as bigg as that at Oxford, but devided in the midst with a strong wall, one half lying within the compass of the castle court, and t'other without open to the garden, into which being come, wee went up fine winding walk sett with hearbs and various trees till wee came to the top of the mount where grew within a circle of laurell a Scottish Firr-tree here (as the gardener told us] before wee had a full prospect of all the garden at once, and I must confess it was

169 Althorp Park. Robert Spencer, 2nd Earl of Sunderland (died 1702).
170 Lower Shuckburgh, Southam, Ufton, Radford Semele, Leamington.

verry delightfull to behold the curiositys below, viz: the winter greens,[171] with other trees shedding their leaves, (it being now the month of February) the pleasant walks, and curious knots, pretty flowers, arbours, and summerhouses, and under all close by the walls of the garden which are a good height above it glides the sweet river, haveing on t'other side verdant meadows and goodly walks of Elms and other trees, extending some 2 miles of to a Lodg in a Park. From hence you may likewise view the Town and Castle, you have here also a large horizon with the site of a goodly vale and hills a dozen and 20 miles off, soe that taken all together t'is one of the best inland prospects our country doth afford.

As touching the Town it is fairly built, with wide streets haveing for publick buildings to adorn it 2 churches and 2 gate houses, and over one a chappell, and close by an hospitall for 12 men the Earl of Lecesters gift. Here is also now a building a fair market house supported on rows of pillars, and they have since built a noble Town-hall.

Here are in this Town capacious Inns and good entertainment as to wine and other necessaries for mans delight.

The north eastern side of this Town Sir Henry Puckerton hath a fine house.[172]

Wee lay at the sign of the *Swan*. Mr Holloway being present Landlord.

To 'the three choirs' cathedrals: Worcester, Hereford and Gloucester and return to Burford

FROM WARWICK TO Worcester is accounted 22 miles. In the way thither wee went by Esquire Heales house and park, and soe in sight of another great house now owned by Sir Charles Lee and soe to Oster[173] a small market Town 10 miles from Warwick.

From Oster it is 12 miles to Worcester. Wee had a fair prospect of it from a hill in the way a mile or more before wee came to it. The way to this city is a reddish earth and verry bad for travellers in winter, soe that for the benefit of horsemen in durty weather they have made a caussway extending some miles from the Town.

171 Evergreens.
172 Sir William Newton, 2nd baronet, in 1654 inherited the estates of his uncle, Sir Thomas Puckering and moved to Sir Thomas's residence, the Priory, Warwick; he adopted the name Puckering (1618-1701). HoP.
173 Alcester. Charles Lee owned Billesley manor between 1600 and 1689. VCH (Warks) 3.

Worcester

As touching the city of Worcester I think 'tis bigger than Oxford and very full of people, but the streets excepting that running through the city to the bridg and another thwarting the upper end of this street, are narrow, and old decay'd buildings.

Here are in this Town 12 or 13 churches, with that on t'other side Severn, to which a fair bridg with 6 large arches big enough for hoys to pass under gives the passage.

This river is navigable for these kind of vessels to Shrewsbury and further, and from those parts they bring down abundance of Cole to serve this citty and other places beneath it, and from Bristoll they bring marchantable goods up streame again to serve these parts.

Along the banks of Severn here which is well nigh a bow shott over, running with a nimble clear current are large fertile meadows, but that which is most remarkable, as touching ingenuity on the shore of the Town side is a waterworke which the stream of the river without the help of horses haveing a wheel which gives motion to suckers and forcers it pumps the water soe high into a ledden cistern, that it servs any part of the city never the less that water may be more plentifull they have horses also at work to force up water; and here also which I have noewhere els seen, save in the City of Ely, they fetch water from the river upon horses in lethern bags to sell.

The Cathedrall of this city is a grave ancient structure with 2 crosses thwarting the body haveing upon the first as you enter a verry big and high tower, with pinnacles on the corners to small and short for the bulk and height of such a tower; the stones of this fabrick are of a reddish grey, as be also that of a large cloyster leading toward the river side which is hard by. Here was now noe Bishop resident but since Dr Blandford bishop of Oxford a worthy gentleman of my acquaintance[174] is removed thither who since his decease has left an estate to maintain some almsmen in their gowns.

This city is enclosed with an ancient wall haveing over one of the gates the greatest diall that I have seen, whose style is a long ferrpole, here is also erected att the upper end of the high street at the charge of the Townsmen upon a pedestall of stone the effigies of Charles the 2nd and upon a stage hard by a woman representing Justice.

The butchers of this Town as man may say keep Christmas all the year round

174 Walter Blandford, bishop of Worcester 1671-1675. CCEd.

for they dress their meat on market dayes with rosemary and bays.

Wee lay at the sign of the *Reigndeer* where one Mr Wells a comely grave man of seventy years was our Landlord who had a handsome maid to his daughter, who was betrothed to a yong baker of this Town, who intended to marry her as soon as his prenticeshipp was over, but falling sick of the small pox he died before the time was expired. He gave his sweetheart who tenderly lookt to him in his sickness £20 which was all he was then master of, and she in kindness to his memmory spent £6 of it treating his friends with a good supper that night wee lay there.

From Worcester we went to Hereford 20 miles nerer the confines of Wales, the way in this month of February verry foul and dirty and through many narrow lanes, but as to the prospect of the country 'tis delightfull consisting of hills and valleys of a reddish earth bedect with fruit trees large woods and groves of oak, hasle, and Elm, Burch, Ewe, Holly, and Juniper, and many large hopyards; it being the husbandry of the country to plant their hopyards and orchards together of red streak aples or els to sow corn between them, and turneps in their season. But when the trees doe come to some perfection they lett their hops decay, the hoppoles are sett up in the same ground in round heaps all the winter with the great ends upward. Many of their poles are forked.

Here and also in Worcestershire when fruit trees grow old they saw them of in the main body and graft them, and they thrive and grow yong again, and they also stick sharp pointed sticks in the Lome or clay to keep the crows from spoyling the grafts.

The villages as well as I remember in the way are call'd first Stiffern, then Seed where Mr Barkley dwells whose brother an acquaintance of Mr Blowers came to Bayworth to see mee he is a lawyer, and lives at Pharnum in Hampshire an ingennous man and writ that sang of the Isle of Pines.[175]

The next is Castlethrow, westHide, Withington, and so over a bridg on the river Lugg a mile from Hereford where is a good Quarr of grinstones.[176]

Hereford

HEREFORD IS A Strong wall'd Town - with a moat surrounding it, it being a frontire garrison in former days of great concern before Wales was reduced to the government of England. It hath the river Wye famous for

175 Stifford's Bridge & Seed Farm or Steen's Bridge indicate the approximate course of TB's route, close to the A4103 today; Farnham in Hampshire.
176 Castle Frome, Westhide, Withington.

salmon and other good fish running by it, under a stone bridg of 6 arches, which joyns with Lugg some 2 or 3 miles below the Town not far from Hom-lacy[177], where my honoured uncle the Lord Scudamore now defunct did live, a person to which the whole county is obliged for his worth, he being the man that brought the now soe much fam'd Redstreak sider to perfection call'd by the Prince of Florence or Tuscany when he came to see Oxford and had drunk of it vin de Scudamore. He hath rare contrived sellers in his park for the keeping of sider, with springs of water running into them, but as to the contrivance within I was not so fortunate to see it, his bailif who had the keys in his keeping being then gone to the town of Lemster[178] a place famous for fyne wool, and my uncle then alive was at London at his house call'd Petty France in Tuttle Street. Here is a good old house built with brick and a fair park belonging to it, but people tell mee his sone has now pulled it down, and hath built a fair house of freestone in the place of it.

But to return to the description of Hereford it hath 6 churches, but that on t'other side the bridg was destroyed in time of war.

St John Bap: the Cathedrall is a well built church, but less than that at Worcester the spire upon the Tower is covered with ledd, and at the west end it hath another Tower of stone.

The vicars and singing men are here well provided for living after a Collegiate way, haveing nere the church a handsom house where they dine together, haveing Cooks, Bakers, Brewers, and other servants belonging to it, goeing to see it they gave us the curtesy of the place, viz: some bread and beer.

Here is now at the cost of Dr Gardner lately cannon of Xte Ch: a fair hall a building for these people to dine in, but at present they make use of a room above stairs, they told me such gentlemen as are minded to stay in Town may take their commons with paying the usuall rate.

Sir James of Craft[179] the now bishop of Hereford lives at his own house by Lemster, who being offended with the Townsmen of Hereford hath removed the court formerly kept in this Town to Lemster, to the prejudice of the Herefordians who grumble at it.

Wee lay at the *Black Swan*, Mr Jones an honest ingenuous man our Landlord, whose wife is a distiller of incomparable strong waters; here wee drank brave

---

177 Holme Lacy. His father's half-brother, Sir John Scudamore, created baronet 1620, Viscount Scudamore of Sligo 1628, died 1671.

178 Leominster.

179 Herbert Croft, Bishop of Hereford 1662-1691. CCEd.

redstreak sider, and had beer for our mornings draught of 2, 3, 4 and 5 years age, for which purpose he has lusty great vessels to keep it. Here my landlord I haveing not eaten any of that kind of flesh before for half a crown bought a young kid for mee, it being small wee rosted the 4 quarters at once and found it verry delicate meat. Here the people of the country bring their butter to sell in piggin pails and here they make verry good gloves to sell.

Here is a litle without the Town a good almshouse, goeing to see it wee went into one Mr Cunnisbys chamber, a stout man, and formerly a souldier for the king in the dayes of Charles the first. Being falln into poverty he had a place in this alms house given him, where to divert himself he has a forge and tools to make such things as he has a mind to and when he is wary of that employment he goes abroad to wait upon gentlemen, to whome he is verry acceptable because of his former loyalty.

About this Town is much safron planted and all over the country fruit trees and hopgardens abound, but the most famous and best reputed redstreak sider is made at and about Kingscaple,[180] for they are an industrous people and verry civill to strangers.

Staying at Hereford some dayes I went 2 miles from thence to a place called Monk -horne with my landlord Mr Jones to gett some redstreak grafts, and was thence invited to Dewswell[181] by Sir James Bridges, a worthy gentleman and as I after found by discourse my kinsman who is since created Lord Shandos and lately sent by his Majesty embassadour to the great Turk, who kindly treated mee with a good dinner and excellent sider.

    Mr Barnerd his father in law an east India merchant, whose daughter Sir James had married an ingenuous, grave, courteous man was then with him and his wife.

    In the time of the wars Sir Barnaby Scudamore long since dead brother to the Lord Scudamore and uncle to my self was governor of the City [of] Hereford for the king.

From Hereford to Glocester is accounted 20 miles, in the way from Hereford

---

180 King's Caple (south of Hereford).
181 *5 lines crossed out and a line drawn across them linking to the name Dewswell; the lines are then repeated as far as the great Turk, except that the name of Sir James Bridges is missing from the first version.* Monkhall farm is close to Dewsall, south-west of Hereford (4 miles rather than 2).

thither wee went through Bier, and Landinabo where I gave a woman 12 pence
for a dozen right redstreak grafts which when I came home I grafted and they
grow and are the fairest fruit of that kind I have seen.[182]

Ross a market town 8 miles from Hereford upon the river Wye, lyes in the road
way to Glocester. On this side the river stands the ruins of Sir James Bridges his
house demolished in the wars because a garrison, and here is a long bridg over
the river into the Town of Ros.[183]

     From Ros wee went to a place called Longhope and turning a little out
of the road saw the furnace or kill [kiln] where they melt iron, the bellows
being verry great which give furious blasts to fire, are driven like an overshott
mill with water, haveing a great wheel divers yards in Diameter. The fire to
melt the oare in the furnace made of stone which may be 7 or 8 yards from
bottom to top or in height, is made of charcole burning day and night for some
months, viz: soe long as the water which is but a small stream and commonly
dry in summer doth last. The flame mounts fiercely a good height above the
furnace, here is also at the bottom of the furnace a hole as bigg as that of an
oven, which lets the dross runn away in fiery streaming flames from the melted
mettle or oare, which metal once in 4 howers is lett runn into barrs or other
forms of iron, but the dross when cold becomes a green glassy stone, of which
they have vast mounts or heaps about the house and good for nothing but to
mend the high ways. The heap of charcole was also great, and the men worke
day and night in their turns.

Turning again into our way from Ross to Glocester which is accompted 12
miles after wee had passed by Long hope the way lay in the bottom between
steep hills, when at length wee came by a fair park of Deere, belonging to Mr
Cook[184] who hath by it a fair house built Quadrangular after the new fashion,

182 Much Birch? Llandinabo. The Redstreak apple may have been introduced from
    France by Sir John Scudamore in the 1630s ('Scudamore's crab'), or by Thomas
    Beale who wrote on orchards. Generations of the Scudamore family were closely
    associated with the Beales. Redstreak was the pre-eminent cider apple but is now
    lost. Margie Hoffnung, 'A history of traditional orchards in Gloucestershire and
    some questions for the future', The Wider View 2 (Gloucestershire Gardens and
    Landscape Trust 2021) 48-9.
183 Wilton castle, held for Parliament, was sacked by the royalists. Eldest son of the
    Bridges family also Lord Chandos. Related to the Scudamore family of Holme
    Lacy.
184 Highnam came to the Cooke family through marriage to the heiress in 1605.
    Sir William Cooke was sheriff of the county in 1663 and Mayor of Gloucester

with large fish ponds adjoining.

Gloucester

BEING COME WITHIN a mile of Glocester wee went over a high bridg thwarting Severn with 6 or 7 large arches, which is divided above Glocester, for another stream runs under the walls of Glocester, and soe for the spring tides from the sea and some miles above it doe make the fresh waters recoile, as we saw by the ose or mudd lately moistend by the flooding water.

The river is navigable for pretty big vessels to this Town from the sea.

From the top of St. Marys tower a lofty pile and curious work, I told 6 churches, they say there were more in this city before the wars. In this cathedrall are intombed the bodyes of Robert duke of Normandy and Edward the 2d who had a spitt thrust up his fundament; in this church wee likewise heard and saw that soe famous whispering place. Here is a fair cross and conduit in the midst of the high Street of the city and it is wall'd with strong gates for entrance.

Att the lower end of the Town nere the river is a glass house, where they make great store of glass bottles, selling 15 to the dozen, for which I was fain then to pay 4s for every dozen quart bottles. Here I eat of the yelver cakes: they are made of young Eels, which in their season come so numerously up the river that the people skim them up in rangers, and soe by an art they have to cleans and strip their skins after boyling are press'd into cakes for food.

Marked change here as far as the bottom of the page to an elaborate hand for what appears to be information added later.

At this glass house now 1682 in Glocester they sell 12 quart glass bottles for 2s-6d.

The Effigies of Robert duke of Normandy is curiousley carved in Irish oake and laid upon his Tombstone, at the upp end of the quire beneath the Communion Table. Here lyes also intombed Bishop Goodman late of this diocese[185] who sometime came down from London goodman Byshop. The roof or vaulting of this Quire is very curious work but the pillers in body of the church are ordinary viz - round and short - yet these like a foyle do set of the more exquisite workmanship of the eastern end of this fabrick.

The Pinnacles of the Tower its battlements and those of the Church are

---

in 1672 and he later represented the city in Parliament for several years. VCH (Glos) 10.

185 Godfrey Goodman bishop of Gloucester 1625 to 1640 when he was deprived. CCEd.

open Airie work for you see through them. In the middel of the Whispering place is a little Chappel where he that attends confession may easily here such as confess, though they do but whisper and yet never see them, and so give Absolution. Adjoining to this church is a faire Lybrary, and a great and lesser Cloyster fairely built and Cleanly kept. <In the lesser Cloister now lives Dr. Washborne[186] whose sone Charles was my great acquaintance.>

The handwriting reverts to previous cursive style

Near this Church lives one Mr Sims a schollar of Oxford who bid us welcome to his mothers house, viz, Mr Thomas Baskerville Mr Thomas Cary, Thomas Stevenson in Jan. 1682/3 when wee brought Mr Stedman[187] soe far forwards in his way towards Wales.

Here wee fell acquainted with one Mr Baker an aturney by means of one Dr Clutterbook whome wee mett on the road at Frogmill, a fellow of All Souls, these civill gentlemen shewd us the Town and its rarities amongst which the prison or goal must not be forgotten being esteemed for a house of that use the best in England, soe that if I were forced to go to prison and make my choice I would come hither.

Mr Langborne the keeper or chief master of the prison entertaind us kindly and gave us good ale, and while wee were there one Mr Powell a minister read prayers to the prisoners, for which he and another have an yearly allowance to read prayers to them twice a week.

Here is within the walls of this goal a fair bowling green, and hither the Townsmen come to divert themselves, the jaylors wife also deserves to be commended for adding to the beauty of the place a neat garden.

Here are also in Town 2 market houses and a fair hospitall called St. Bartholomews not mentiond in the former dy(s)course, and a fair key by the Town side where they land a great deal of goods. But of the 2 streams which part at Maresmore[188] a mile above Glocester where wee found verry good ale, that which runs by Glocester though seemingly narrower is the deeper channell, and through that the boats goe up to Worcester, the other being broader and shallower. Here when oysters are in season the usual price is 6 pence a hundred,

186 Thomas Washbourne, created D.D. 1660; canon of Gloucester 1660; died 1687, buried in Gloucester cathedral. For Charles *see* Chapter 3 'Oxford'.

187 Mr Sims probably John Sims of Hempstead, matriculated 1637; Henry Stedman, matriculated 1674, described as chaplain of All Souls College, Oxford, 1680; presumably on his way to his new appointment as vicar of Llandegley, co. Radnor, 1683. BHO Foster; CCEd.

188 Maisemore.

which are taken about Milford haven and those parts of the sea nere Wales. The best wines to drink in Glocester are canary, sherry, white wine, for wee neither drank nor heard of any good clarret in Town, but Worcester surpasses this city for all sorts, where not long before wee drank excellent canary, sherry, and clarret, canary 2 shillings, sherry 1s. 8d claret 1s as good as in London, but for cyder and ale Glocester doth surpass Worcester, for here wee had excellent redstreak for 6d a quart, and good ale 2d a flaggan for here the people are wise and brew their own ale not permitting publick brewers. For curiosity of trades seldom found in other Towns, here are 2 or 3 hornmakers that make excellent ware of that kind, viz, clear horns for drinking powder horns ink horns, crooks, and heads for stalves, hunters horns, and other things. Dr. Frampton Byshop,[189] Mr Web mayor of this Town of Glocester.

As to Inns which are the chief things which a traveller is to look after that hath money in his pocket these are the best *The Swan*, the *Sun*, the *Fountain* a tavern and coffee-house Mr Vaughan master, the *Old Bear* Mr Crump and his wife Inn-keepers where wee lay, and the *New Bear* without a sign a large square brick built house.

Glocester is 20 miles from Hereford 15 from Circiter 10 <20> miles from Worcester, and about 10 or 12 <7> miles from Tewxbury,[190] and about 21 from Burford to which the rode lyes thus :- As you goe out of the Town towards BarnWood parish, you see 2 hospitalls as they say built by 2 sisters calld St. Margrets and St. Magdalens hospitalls with little chappells adjoyning to them.[191] In Barnwood I saw a great heap of crabs Jan 17 lying at a house and in the open ayre being so prepar'd to make cyder which was not to be made till towards our Lady day and then rotten and sound are pounded or ground together thus ordered they say twill be a strong liquor in summer.

Next Hosbury bridg[192] a good Inn 4 miles from Glocester through a long dirty lane leading to it. Here Thomas Stevenson did kill a strange bird which none in the country hereabout or els where had seen before, this strange bird having another by it on the tree where wee kild it is nere upon as big as a wind thresh, upon the head and bill which something resembles that of a Bulfinch,

189 Robert Frampton, Bishop of Gloucester 1681-1690, when he was deprived. CCEd.
190 Cirencester, Tewkesbury. The different miles (in brackets) were written in above the names of the places.
191 This page gives the impression of being written as it was being composed, and so suggests this is Thomas Baskerville's own hand.
192 Over the Horsbere brook.

it hath a fine tuft of feathers of a cynamon colour, the feathers of the neck brest back and part of the whings something darker, the upper part of the tayl where the feathers join to the body is ash colourd, then a ring of black, and on the extream part of the tayl feathers a ring of aurora flame or gold colour, but under the tayl a perfect cynamon. The prime flying feathers of the whing are curiously diversified, for upon each whing, whose feathers are for the most part black are white spots answerable to each other. Then the extreme points of 9 of the longest pinion feathers are tipt with white and lemmon or gold colour, the lesser pinion feathers which are 7 in number, are tipt with white; and the extreame part of those seven feathers on each side are of a pure vermillion colour, but these vermillion tips are noe feather but of the nature of the stem of the feather though dilated broader at the ends. At Hosbury bridg the road does part, the right hand road towards Circeter, and the other towards Frogmill, that to Circiter goes through Burlip[193] where are divers good inns, and the road that leads to London goes through Barnsly leaving Circiter 2 miles on the right hand. <But the road from Burlip to Cirencester where you first get in the way 2 miles on the right hand in woods Mr Sands house, goe by 4 and 5 miles houses Inns at that distance from the town.

As to the way from Hosbury bridg to Frogmill, you goe through Brockworth parish and see Sir John Guise his house on the left hand,[194] and soe ascending these hills Mr Cartwrights house on the right and soe having got the top of these downs you descend again towards Cubberly[195] where now lives the widdow Castleman a courteous gentlewoman, who not long agone gave my self and some gentlemen a verry good treat at her house. Here in the way above Cubberly doth arise the highest spring of Thames, that runns to Cyrencester, and below this a little above Cubberly do arise seven springs or wells, which presently make good fish pools, and heard by the house other great springs doe arise, soe that for trouts carps tench perch and such like fish the pools are soe large and many they may have great store. This ladys husband[196] some years agow broke his neck with a fall from his horse as he was rideing a coursing, his picture now in the house shows him to have been a handsome man. And as to madam Castleman now about 30 years of age, she is a well shapd woman,

193 Birdlip.
194 Brockworth Court was held by the Gyse family from 1541. It was built for Richard Hart, the last prior of Lanthony 1534-9. Historic England. Sir John Gyse of Brockworth paid tax on 10 hearths in 1672.
195 Coberley.
196 Paul Castleman paid tax on 26 hearths in 1672.

a good historian as wee found by her discourse, and I believe well skilld in musick, for in the parlour was a fair organ, violls, and violinns, and about the house the greens gardens and walks were neat and well kept. Her maiden name was Barefoot, being the daughter of Mr Barefoot who kept the *Devil* tavern in fleet street by temple barr. This Mr Barefoot immediately after the great fire of London was then alive in that tavern, and my friend Mr Edmund Bostock now defunct goeing thither with mee to give mee a glass of wine, Mr Barfoot came into our company and told he was lord of Little Balden in Oxford shire.

In December 1682 my self T B Mr James Stonehouse Mr John Pollard Mr Xtopher Blower senior and 3 of our men came to Cubberly to buy colts of Mrs Castleman where she gave us a good dinner and envit'd us to stay all night it being then a great fog or mist over all the downs, but being loth to give her that trouble because wee were soe many we resolved to lye at Frogmill and her man went along with us to shew us the way and brought us within half a mile of Coldcomfort an Inn a mile from Frogmill, and soe giving directions left us to goe forward on our way in the fog but we not giving soe good heed to his words as we should have done took the wrong instead of the right, and soe after half a miles riding comeing to the place where the ways part; the left and greatest road being the way to cold comfort, wee went the right hand and lesser way, and soe instead of seeing cold comfort after 4 or 5 miles rideing, without any sight of houses or people to enquire the way, wee found our selves shut up in darkness upon these comfortless downs, where I knew wee might ride 20 miles forwards and perhaps not find a house, and upon these verry downs Captain Stonehouse of Cockrup told mee he lately lost his way, being faine to ride and walk a foot all the night and when the daylight apeard he found himself falln dow(n) towards Ferford. But this evill ready to fall upon us was prevented by meeting a man on the road with horses goeing to Cheltnam who told us this way lead to Chidworth,[197] and that at Withington a mile in the bottome on the left hand we might find a good Inn to lodge at, so blundering in the dark as well as wee could to our great comfort at last thither we came, where wee found excellent ale good entertainment and a conscionable Landlord and Landlady, for being 7 men and horses we had good fires excellent ale of which wee drank verry freely a good dy(s)h of stakes or fryed beef a dysh of birds wee had kild well rosted strong water and for B(r)eakfast bred and cheese and a cold neats tongue well boyld, hay and each horse his peck of oats and all this for 17s.[198]

197 Cheltenham, Chedworth.
198 In his verse account of the stay in Withington, TB named *The George* and said

But to proceed in the road from Glocester towards Burford you goe by the afforesaid Inn or alehouse cold comfort, to Frogmill where the widdow Powell keeps house, here in the bottome you see 2 parrishes nere togather, viz, Shipton Olive, and Shipton Salice and Mrs Haydens house.[199] Above these Towns on the stream which drives Frogmill is Brockington and Sinnington where people tell mee the highest springs of this stream which goes to Ferford break forth, and at Compton in the hole in the road from hence to Norlidg[200] other springs doe rise in the high way which joyn with those above said at Withington but this Town lyes on the right hand of the great road that goes toward Burford. Norlidg is 14 miles from Glocester 7 from Burford.

JOURNEY 6
TO BRISTOL FROM BAYWORTH VIA FARRINGDON, HIGHWORTH, MALMESBURY AND PUCKLECHURCH

A different and more elaborate hand compared with the facing page, using a lot of capital letters and generally 'modern' spelling. The date of writing this account is stated several times to be early in 1681/2. Baskerville's visit to the area appears to have been in 1665.

THE DESCRIPTION OF Townes on the roads from Farringdon to Bristow and other places. vizt

From Bayworth to Farringdon as we account, is ten miles the way layes through Sunningwell and Blagrove Leaz (where now lives an honest gentleman and my neighbor Mr Richard Hyde <1681>).[201] The next Villages are Called Sandforde and Cottwell wherein the Quarrs hard by, you may have good sand to scowr Pewter, from hence passing through Tubney Wood where is a good Warren for Rabbets and by it a handsome house formerly Dr Langley's (now

there were 17 altogether in the party including horses. Using the Measuringworth website, 17 shillings might be equivalent to £130 to £143 in 2021. https://www.measuringworth.com

199 Shipton Oliffe, Shipton Sollars. Memorials to the Powell family of Frogmill exist in Shipton Sollars church, to which parish the Frogmill belonged.

200 Brockhampton, Sevenhampton, Fairford, Compton Abdale, Northleach.

201 Faringdon, Blagrove (Farm).

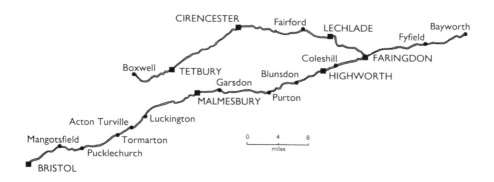

defunct) you come to Fyfield where my loving friend Doctor Parret hath Lately built a fair house and hard by that is the Mannor House belonging to Mr White. A small mile forward on the Road layes Kingstone formerly Mr Latten's lordship but now in the Mannor House beautified with finde Gardens lives Mr Fettyplace, my Loving friend.[202] The soile of this Town as also from Sandforde to Farringdon is sandy, the Road for the most part being as good for Travellers in winter as sommer especially if you go a little about by Pissy and Wadley; at Pissy now (Anno dmi 1681/2) Lives Widow Dunse whose husband not long ago was high shrieve of Barkshire, and at Wadley Sir Henry Purifoy.[203]

From Wadley it is two little miles to Farringdon over a finde green or Carpet Countrey with spacious prospects over the vale to the downes, and within half a mile of Farringdon they have lately made a delicate bowling-greene, where in the sommer time the Gentry of these parts meet to divert themselves in this pleasant air. At Farringdon Sir Robert Pye hath a fair house and good Estate belonging to it.[204] This Town was a Garison in the Late unhappy warrs and much of it was then burn'd, but now is pretty well built, with some good Inns for Entertainment of which the *Crowne* is Chiefe, Mr Stibbs the present Landlord of it being seldome or never without good wines and such other

202 Dry Sandford, Cothill, Tubney Wood (Tubneywarren House on OS 1880s), Fyfield, Kingston Bagpuize.
203 Pusey, Wadley. Edmund Dunch, 1st Baron Burnell of East Wittenham (1602–1678) was a Parliamentarian. Sir Henry Purefoy, created a baronet in 1662, in his father's lifetime and when only five years old; died 1686. VCH (Berks) 4.
204 The Pyes, lords of the manor of Faringdon from 1622-3, were Parliamentarians. They lived at Faringdon House. Sir Robert Pye died 1701. VCH (Berks) 4.

provisions as are fitt to salute his Gests, here is kept on Whitsun-tuseday a great fair for horses, Cattell, and other goods.

From this pleasant Town of Farringdon in Barkshire Travellers may go two ways to Bristow, either by Leachlad in Glocestershire or by Hyworth in Wiltshire.[205]

In the way to Hyworth from Farringdon which is accompted 4 miles you shall go by Coltswell[206] where Sir George Pratt (now defunct) hath built a noble house with curious gardens, seated on the side of a hill which commands as noble a prospect. Here I may take occasion to speake of that Ancient Land-marke or Remarkable worke of Antiquity which gives name to our Country the Vale of White Horse, for in the way betwixt Farringdon and Hyworth some 5 or 6 miles distante you have the best prospect of the white horse, cut in the side of a white Chalky hill a mile above Uffington, the Manger as they caleth it, or sides and bottome where this horse is cutt is now in the possession of my Loving friend and neighbor Mr Wiseman of Sparswells Court[207] and some that dwell hereabout have an obligacon upon their Lands to repair and cleanse this Land marke, or else in time it may turne green like the rest of the hill and be forgotten.

My loving friend Mr Ellis who wrote this relation for me, going thither to see it, and paceing the taile of this Horse, saith it is about 60 yards in Length.

But the belly where I took this prospect in the way between Faringdon and Coltswell, appears too gaunt and slender for the Length and proportions of the Horse; therefore such as are concerned in the worke might do well to make the belly bigger.

As touching the originall of this eminent Landmark which gives its name to one of the best Vales of England, I heard my Father say who was a man well read in Antiquitys that he thought it was Hengist the Saxon Conqueror who in Remembrance of his Exploits, this being his Armes or Crest to them Caused this figure to be cut here. This Hengist came into England anno domini 450 being sent for by Vortiger to assist him in his warres.

205 Lechlade, Highworth.
206 Coleshill. 'Coleshill House, on the south-east side of the village, was built in 1650 by Sir George Pratt, and is one of Inigo Jones's best-known works.' VCH (Berks) 4.
207 Sparsholt's Court, West Hendred, a large house demolished in 1721. It was owned by the Wiseman family from 1613. VCH (Berks) 4.

Hyworth is a Town in Wiltshire of which I can say little, save that it is seated on a hill hath weekely a great market for Cattle and on Lammas day a very great fair for all kinde of beasts especially sheep.

Here groweth in Hyworth Church yard nigh the Tower a tree as high as the Tower which to the Vale Country people about Lechlad seem's to be two Towers.

Here many people for want of wood do burne Cow-dung, and to drye it in the summer, do daub it up like so many Cakes against their walls and houses.

At Hanyngton on the right side of the Road Esquire Freake hath a fair house, and at Berryton a mile farther on the same side Sir John Earnly hath a house, and three miles from Hyworth at Little Blunsdon Mr Cleeve the father of our Cleeve at Wootton hath a great house, anno 1665.[208]

From hence to Benton[209] in the parish of Purton is two miles.

Purton church standeth on a small hill a mile from the road on the left hand. Remarkable to Travellers for having a Tower and a Steeple, 5 miles forward on this road which leads through Brayden Forest, layes Gazing, here Mr Washington hath a fair house and a walled Parke.[210]

Mr Milborne and Mr Esex have likewise fair houses in the same parish; at Charlton, hard by layes the Earl of Barkshires house.[211]

Masberry or Malmsbury a market Town two miles forwards in this Road was heretofore more famous for a great Abby in't and yet tis not decay'd as it is in many other places for the Town makes use of the Abby Church and keep it up, and Sir Thomas Ivie now ownes a house in the Abby and makes it now his dwelling place, who is so Curious in his gardens that it's worth a Traveller's pains to go to see it, for on the walls of the Abby which are high and broad, he shall finde curious borders set with various flowers suetable to evry season, which affords a delicate sent, and sight to the eye, as you go from his dwelling house to a finde Banquetting house a furlong from it on the wall; here likewise from the height of this wall as you walk you see under it a finde purling River which affordes good fish and many moorehens sporting and

208 Hannington, Bury Ton (Farm), Little Blunsdon.
209 Bentham.
210 Purton, Bradon Forest, Garsdon. Garsdon Manor was probably occupied by the Moody and Washington families in the 17th century.
211 Charlton Park was a 'great' house, now listed Grade I, and was imparked in the later 16th century; it was owned by the Howard family, Earls of Berkshire from 1626, later also Earls of Suffolk. VCH (Wilts) 14.

playing in it, and within the inclosure 'tis well sett with excellent fruits and garden stuff for the potte and phisicall uses. Here is a Tower built to hold bells at some distance from the Abby Church since the Monkes were forced to leave this place. Between Faringdon and Malmsbury they accompt 15 or 16 miles.

Two miles forward on the Road to Bristoll layes Boxly where Mr Oliver hath a house, there to Luckington 3 miles, Turbithanton 2 miles, Turmington 2 miles, Hinton 2 miles, and then to Puckel-Church[212] 2 miles more, and 5 miles farther layes Bristol. Here at Puckle Church, the London and our Countrey roads meeting are good Inns for Travellers to lodge at.

Here lives in this Town a worthy Gentleman by name Mr John Denis who is near related to my brother Morgan. Himself, brother, and mother, are single people and live togeither, they have a good estate in Lands and Coal mines, and do keep a plentifull house as I found for Anno 1680 goeing thither with my brother to see them they treated us nobly for 2 or 3 dayes. At a mile distance from their house they have a pretty little parke with a finde Lodge and some deere in it, but they rent it of another Gentleman.[213]

In the way from Puckel-Church to Bristol you go through Margar-field and the Forrest of Kings-wood where be many Coalpits.[214]

An alternative route via Lechlade, Fairford, Cirencester and Tetbury, but ending at Boxwell

Now to give some accompt of the other way from Faringdon to Bristol these are the names of the Townes, as followeth.

About 4 miles below Faringdon layes St Johns Bridge and Leachlad a small market town a little beyond it, in Glocestershire.[215] But to looke back a little before we go out of this Country, here is yearly kept on the 29 of August in a Meadow by St John's Bridge a very great fair for Cattle, Cheese, and other commodities, more especially sage Cheese in various shapes and colours

212 Malmesbury, Foxley, Luckington, Acton Turville, Tormarton, Hinton, Pucklechurch.

213 Court House, now Courthouse Farm, a late sixteenth and early seventeenth century house with a big barn adjoining and a massive central brick stack with six diagonal chimneys. Historic England . John Dennis died 1687. With the death in 1701 of William Dennis, two daughters were co-heiresses. The park was possibly Dyrham.

214 Mangotsfield, Kingswood.

215 Lechlade. The term 'below Faringdon' suggests Baskerville has a map with east at the top, as St John's Bridge is west-north-west of Faringdon.

which I have scarce seene any where els to be sold. And because the meadow is surrounded with the River navigable from Oxford hither 'tis thick set with boats full of provisions brought from thence to entertaine such people as come hither, and they go laden back againe with such goods as are bought at the fair to go down streame.[216]

Here is hard by the bridge a very good Inne for entertainment and they have Commonly strong march beere in bottles to sell and pretty good wine for as I remember in Leachlad there is no Taverne.

The next Town in the Road forward where are good Innes to Lodge, is called Ferfett 3 miles from Leachlad.[217]

A little without the Town on the right hand is a great square new built house where Esquire Barker Lord of the Mannor now lives, who hath the Royalty of the River running by the Town in which are very good Trouts.[218]

For the Effigies of Saints in ancient painted glasse you may see more in the Church windowes of Ferfett than in the riding of many miles elswhere.

From hence 'tis about 6 or 7 miles to Cyrencester, but in the way thither scarce a house yet if yee are benighted some 3 miles on this side Cyrencester you may turne off on the right hand to Barnesly[219] but a mile distance where Mr Fage and his wife will give you excellent entertainment. They have also for divertisement a very good Bowling-green much frequented by the Gentry hereabouts.

And from hence 'tis but a little above two miles more to Cyrencester.

Cirencester is a Town about the bigness of Abingdon having in it some fair streets, good houses and Inns of which the *Kings Head* is chief, Mr Dancy is now the master.

It hath also in it a great and beautifull Church with a tall Tower conte(n) ing 8 very tuneable bells, with which the young men are much delighted as also with the art of singing. For lying at the *Kings Head* in the Christ mass holidayes in the morning before day as I lay in my bed, I heard them sing some Christmas Carols very musically in the streets as they went towards the Church to ring.

216 TB wrote about this bridge again. See St John's Bridge below.
217 Fairford.
218 Samuel Barker's new house at Fairford was illustrated in 1712. *Johannes Kip, The Gloucestershire Engravings* ed. Anthea Jones (Hobnob Press 2021). *See also* Cirencester below.
219 Barnsley.

Here runs by this Town a small river being near the head or springs
of Tems, and at the west end of this Town my Lady Poole hath a fair house.
Little more can be said of this place save that the great Road or Fossway goeth
through it. <Mr Masters hath also here a fair house.[220]>

From hence 'tis accounted 7 miles over a dainty Cotswould Country to Tetbury
alias Tedbury and in the way thither on the downs you commonly see some
flights of sea-meaws which birds if you cary a Gun with you will aford you
Recreation, for when you have kild one, if sometimes you swing him in your
hand and sometimes lay him on the ground, the rest will sore over you so that
you may shute them at pleasure.

Sir William Kyte of Ebberton or Ebrington[221] <my worthy friend> had a gun
made for the nonce, which had a barrell contrived with two bores in one stock,
which when they were chardge(d) he could fire as he pleased one after another.
By this means he quickly got a good dish and as he told me they were pretty
good meat.

Tetbury is pleasantly seated on the plain of a hill in a very good Ayr
with finde bottomes about it in which runns some small streams. In this Town
are fair streets, han-some houses, good Inns, and one Large Church with a tall
stone steeple, here is also a pretty good Market house where on the Market
dayes a great deal of wool and yarne is to be sold, mutton and lamb is here sold
Cheap.

Three miles from this Town, but a little out of the Road to Bristo at a place
called Boxwell, now lives my Loving kinsman Mr Matthew Huntley Lord of
the Mannor of Layterton and Boxwell in which tho' but a small parish are two
Churches, the present Incumbent of them being my Loveing friend Mr Cox
now by his long stay there growne old upon them, by means of the pure Ayr
he there injoys.[222] My uncle George Lyte of Layterton when I came thither
one time to see him, told me there had not been a Corpse buried in Layterton
Church or Church-yard in above a dozen years, and as I remember for my dear

220 Johannes Kip also made an engraving of Allen Bathurst's seat in Cirencester
(which shows an exaggerated church tower), and Cirencester Abbey, the seat of
Thomas Masters.
221 The Kite family have a number of monuments in Ebrington church. Their seat
was at Norton in the parish. Sir William Kite died 1702.
222 Richard Cox, rector of Boxwell with Leighterton 1640-1688; possibly
matriculated 1633 aged 17, at death aged about 72; BHO Foster.

Uncle is now dead, he said in 17 years time, in the year 1641 two or 3.[223] Mr
Cox was presented to this parsonage by my Kinsman George Huntley then
Lord of the Mannor and now at this present writing 'tis March the Eleventh
1681/2

Now as to Boxwell a little mile beneath Layterton[224] 'tis worth a man's sight
to go thither, for in England I know but one place more that may compare
with this, and that is Box-hill in Surry; as to the prospect of this ever Verdant
grove in respect of my kindsman's house which stands in a warm bottom it
groeth about the sixth part of a mile easterly from it, alongst the brow and
steep declivities of that hill, having above on the plain of the hill a stonewall,
surrounding this wood, and many acres beneath it, in which is a good warren
but the fat on the kidneys of many rabbets hath a yellowish tincture, gotten I
suppose by their eating box. Here also in this warren a little beneath the box
wood breaks forth a fountain of pure water which well with the box giveth
name to the place, then sliding a little way farther makes a fair fishpond wel
stor'd with Carp and Trout.

Here it may not be amisse to speake somewhat in generall of these Cotswould
or highland Countryes which contribute such pleasure to Travellers in length
and breadth stretching many miles, for we are long and steal up so gently e'er
we obtain their highest summets we cannot but wonder when we come there,
how we should get so much above another world, full of people and great
riches under us, such are the aluring prospects you find at Sir Gabriel Low's
house and at Simon's hall Tump hard by Mr Veal's house the highest land
about all these parts.[225]

*This section ends half-way down the page. It is all in much better handwriting than
earlier sections. In the bottom half of the page are 9 attempts at writing the names
Thomas Baskervile, M Thomas Baskervile, Mathew Thomas Baskervile (Thomas's
son).*

223 *See* Chapter 2 'Life and Kin' for TB's account of the relationships.
224 This indication of direction also shows that he has a map with east at the top - see
     St John's bridge above.
225 Sir Gabriel Lowe owned Newark in Ozleworth. Simon's Hall is in Wotton-under-
     Edge. Sir Robert Atkyns, *The Ancient and Present State of Glostershire (1712), 855
     noted* Thomas Veel Esq had a 'pleasant seat on very high ground from whence he
     has everyway a large Prospect'.

JOURNEY 7
TO STRATFORD-ON-AVON VIA CHELTENHAM, TEWKESBURY AND EVESHAM

The Bristol section (above) ends half-way down the page. Following it is a page of accounts, and then this journey in a different direction, which the HMC ran on with the Bristol text. It appears to have been written later than other accounts (in brown ink), and is rather untidy with exaggerated letters and alterations. There is no heading, although it starts on a new right-hand page.

Baskerville shows that he is working from memory in his comment about the date of this journey. The reference to the Evesham election suggests it was 1679.

There is a neatly-written and quite lengthy description of Tewkesbury abbey ruins and church in Oxford, Bodleian Libraries, MS. Rawl. D. 859, printed below.

In the year I think 1678 St James eve I went with Mr Stevenson from his house in Mooridge to Cheltnam[226] 18 or 20 miles thence and 5 miles beyond it to Tewkesbury a great Bayly town[227] in Glocestershire 34 miles from Oxford. This Town lyes in a confluence of waters 3 Rivers here about commixing their streames viz Severne, Avon, and Swillgate which in floody times makes an Iland of that part of the town where St Marys Church doth stand and in very high floods comes into the church.[228] In this great Abbey Church which is all they have in town are many Tombes of Eminent persons. The west window was broken by a violent Tempest. The people told Mr Wells formerly their Parson was suspended for speaking Words against the King in his Sermon.

The soyle about this Towne is good for gardening. I saw excellent Carrots of which and other garden goods they send store up Severne to Wocester[229] And Avon to other places.

Here they have an Act to make mustard seed into balls which may be carried with little trouble where you please and when you have occasion for

---

226 Mooridge or Moorage, Cheltenham. Mooridge was a house in Stanton Harcourt, possibly to the south of the village as Baskerville rode past some stones named by the Ordnance Survey as 'The Devil's Quoits', the remains of a stone circle.

227 Tewkesbury was a borough sending two members to the House of Commons; it had a Chief Bailiff not a mayor.

228 Severn, Avon and Swilgate.

229 Worcester, a little later spelled Woster.

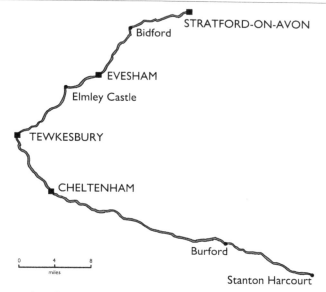

that sauce you dissolve it in vinegar or veriuce.[230] The usual price for balls not guilt with gold is 2d a piece.

Cole which comes from Shropshire down Severn 40 miles to Tewkesbury at the cheapest rate is sold for 7s 6d the chaldron.

The Town is populous hath some faire streets and seems to be bigger than Abingdon. <We dined at the *Swan* Mrs Read landlady.>

Tewkesbury may be 10 or 12 miles from Glocester 10 from Woster 7 long miles to Winchcombe 5 to Cheltnam and 10 to AEvesham or Esom in Worcester shier which chrisens or gives name [to] this famous Vale.

The country Parishes and Villages on the way thither are Hardwick Cammerton where is a hill with a brave prospect. Between that and Elmly is the remains of an Antient Castel and a Warren belonging to Captain Savage whose house is in the town of Elmly at the foot of the Hill. Upon this hill we had sight of Esom and with 2 or 3 miles Travail got thither.[231] The prospect of Evesham offers well at some distance for it hath 3 pretty handsome churches in it 2 of them in one church yard and a fair Tower built of hewen stone with six good Bells in it standing alone by it self at some distance from the churches to go into it.

230 Verjuice, a mild vinegar, was made usually from unripe crab-apples and in Italy from unripe grapes, hence 'green juice', and its use is being revived. Gammack, *Kitchen Garden Estate (2012), 17, 76.*

231 Elmstone Hardwick, Kemerton, Bredon Hill, Elmley Castle, Evesham.

Here is a stone bridge built over Avon full of Jack perch Roch Dace and other kinds. Here are some houses belonging (to) the Town on this side the Bridge. Esom is a maior Town and sends 2 burgeses to Parliament. The Competitors at present for the places were Sir James Rusher, Mr Parker Recorder of the Town and Mr Ridge.[232] Here they have great markets for the sale of Corne and Cattel. We lay at the *Crown* kept by the Widdow Bayley.

Esom is 10 miles from Tewkesbury 10 from Stratford and 5 from Broadway.

What look like aide memoire notes - Camdon Worcester Shipston Parsia

It is a pleasant Rode from Evesham to Stratford in Warwick shier[233] for part of the way lyes on the brow of a Hill overlooking Avon and its verdant meadowes.

We went through a Town called Bidford 5 miles from Stratford on the right hand of our way beyond Bidford toward Stratford, we saw the ruines of a great house burnt with fyre being the Lord Conways, who lives now near Oster.[234]

At Ridgely halfe a mile on this side Stratford Sir John Clapton[235] a gentleman of my acquaintance related to Sir William Kypt hath a faire house and good estate.

Stratford 4 miles from Henly and 7 from Shipston is a town for the bigness well built with faire streets and good Inns in it situate in a pleasant plain on the bankes of Avon made navigable for boates from Severen not long ago.[236] It hath 1 good Church in it and a long and well-built bridge to let people into town that come from Oxford and other places that way. Sergeant Rawleigh hath a faire house in this town.

232 Sir James Rushout, Mr Parker and Mr Ridge. This appears to have been the election of 16 August 1679.
233 Stratford-on-Avon.
234 Bidford-on-Avon, Alcester. Were the ruins those of Milcote manor (Milcote Castle) destroyed in the civil war? Edward Conway was created Earl of Conway in 1679 and occupied a manor house at Ragley, Alcester, where a new house, Ragley Hall, was built from 1680.
235 It appears that TB may have got confused between Ragley where the Earl of Conway was building, and Clopton near Stratford-on-Avon where Sir John Clopton, whose mother was a Keyte, was seated. HoP.
236 Which work included in 1638 building a lock at Tewkesbury where the Avon joins the Severn, previously blocked by the construction of a weir and the Mill Avon or canal. Anthea Jones, *Tewkesbury* (Phillimore, Chichester 2003), 88.

Thomas Baskerville
Thomas Baskervile
[*Several more signatures repeated 4 times beneath the one very bold one*]

A description of Tewkesbury Abbey and church

The account of Tewkesbury Abbey is written in a very child-like hand, almost like an exercise, though in typical Thomas Baskerville style. The edge of the paper is slightly torn.

Oxford, Bodleian Libraries, MS. Rawl. D. 859 f.98

Of the Abbey of Teukesburie

The ruines of this abbey are yet to be seene as a greate arched doore and som of the walles of a little rounde turret of free stone : som plumpe or water house. We vewed it upon the church leads and from thence likewise saw much of buildings of the abbey (towards the gate that lookes into the cittie) which are yet habitable. The church almost yet remaineth in her former perfection of beautie, only the monuments therin have bin somewhat defaced by puritants, and the leads that covered the little rotundoes, or round chappells, are taken from thence, and Tyle placed in the roome. This Church with the Adjoyninge Abbey was founded by one of the Erles of Warwicke not now knowne by anie other name then the greate Nevell, it is in forme from the greate Doores up to the bottom of the quire most resemblinge a crosse havinge for his head a stately quire Cloystred about it and havinge som Iles or little chappells adjoyninge to the same: it is built with many pillars and columes of Freestone beinge all vaulted over head, and of late playstred under foote with a Diamond worke at the expences of the whole cittie, but the quire is done with stone and so is the bodie of the church. After we had well vewed the inferior partes of the church we came into the quire which is seated round after the manner in Cathedrall churches being so done of oulde in the Abbotts times not any necessitie beinge now of it the whole assembly sittinge in the bodie of the church: round about this quire lie enterred many noble personages of which we will speake in order. The first we came unto on the right side was the Tombe of greate Nevell before named; it is built of stone of chappell wise, on the inside curiously painted, havinge overhead right upon the chappell, Nevells image kneelinge, aboout this monument there is nothing written, but the sexton told us, that his bowells were in Ierland his bodie lay under this cappell, and his hearte was at Rome: after we had well vewed it, we crossed to the other side where we saw a chappelle of like antiquitie builded by Isabell Ledespenser countess of Warwicke in honnor of Saint Mary Magdalen as appeered by the writinge round about, she died in London on St John the Evangelists day in the yeere of our Lord 1439, now this is a dubble chappell halfe way (for what purpose I could not learne) the lower was adorned with 4er or six little guilded pillars and at the upper end there is an excellent peece of worke well painted wherin is described the day of judgement, and underneath are many Types and Figures, as the Dove cominge to Noahs Arke with a branch of Olive, and the Angel salutinge the blessed Virgin. Sampson caryinge the gates of Azzah to the hill before Hebron, and Christ risinge from death the 3rd daye after he had broken the Gates of Hell. Adam sleepinge and Evah created out of his side, Christ dead upon the Crosse and the blood streaminge from his side. These with very many others are at the uper end, at the lower there is a more courser Worke and round aboute are drawen the twelve Apostles. The upper chappell extends it seal? from the lower end, above halfe way, which we could looke into because there is no entrance but by a Lader of which we were then unprovided. As touchinge the tombes in the quire or chancell I can say little because I tooke not the like notice as of the former, but was supposed that they were for som Noble men that ?died when the Feilde of Teuksburie was fought: from there we went againe downe the quire, and entred on the left hand into the Cloysters where we first founde ? Anotomie cut in Free-stone for an Abbot of that Church, then we came over the Duke of Clarence vault, which we could not have perceved but that it was so tould us, ?the entrance and all over beinge now covered with a playful worke, but not longe since any might have entred into the vault with the sexton who kept the key thereof : This Duke hath ?no monument for him in this church, but this vault lieth neere the foundation of the quire wall, round about a parte of which there lies som 5, or 6, Abbotts in Marble chests not otherwise fastened then thrust into the wall, which three or fower men with Leavers may easily take out and open at theyr pleasures.

JOURNEY 8
TO WINCHCOMBE VIA BURFORD, BOURTON-ON-THE-WATER AND SUDELEY; THEN SOUTHWARDS TO CHELTENHAM, PAINSWICK AND STROUD

This account is written in a hand similar to the description of Tewkesbury Abbey above, though larger, and generally offers a more 'modern' spelling and style. This journey was probably made in 1682.

A N ACCOUNT OF the way from Morage to Winchcome and other places -

As you ride through Stanton Harcourt fields to Beard mill where now lives our friend Mr William Parmee[237] you shall see yet standing a large stone but in our remembrance who live nere it, viz: in Tho: Baskerville, and Tho: Stephenson there was another standing bigger than that lately taken down by Mr Whitehall, and there is another now lying under ground in a land of Mr Stephensons, here is also part of a Burg hill some of it being lately cutt away by Mr Warcup, now Lord of More[238], these stones and verry probably many more in former dayes were sett up as people say in remembrance of a battle fought here.[239]

At Beardmill a mile in the way you forde over part of Windrush through the meadows and t'other part of Windrush to Hardwick where yet lives an ancient acquaintance of mine one Mr Franklin, and a little farther at Cockruph[240] our worthy friend Captain William Stonehouse; at Duckleton 3 miles on the road lives Justice Bayly, and at Curbridg 4 miles on the road did formerly live Captain Motleys father now defunct.[241] Captain Mottley a gentleman of my acquaintance has been a captain of foot in the Kings guards at London, and went to Virginia to quell the insurrections under Bacon.[242]

237 Beard Mill, apparently rebuilt *c.* 1575, was sold in 1607 with 1 ½ yardlands, various closes, and the fishery, to Richard Parmee of Eynsham; it was then a grist mill. It had two wheels in 1655 and 1698 and three in 1687. VCH (Oxon) 12.
238 Northmoor.
239 Named 'The Devil's Quoits' on the Ordnance survey map 1896. NLS maps.
240 Cokethorpe.
241 Ducklington, Curbridge.
242 An armed rebellion by Virginia settlers took place from 1676 to 1677, led by

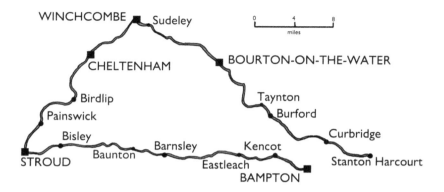

Between Curbidg and Burford is 4 miles, in the way thither a little above Curbidg you see Sir Francis Wainman's banquetting house and down in the bottom among trees in the parish of Breze norton stands his dwelling house,[243] upon the hill they digg good slatt and in the bottom on the right hand before you goe down to Burford you may see Swinbrook, where Sir Edmond Fettiplace has a good house and delicate gardens.[244] At Burford now lives our neighbour Mr William Lenthall who is now his father Sir John being lately dead Lord of the mannor, and is now makeing a fine garden a glymps of which wee saw as wee rodd by.[245] As for the Town of Burford tis seated by a river on the declivity of a hill in a delicate air, haveing such rare hills about it for hunting and raceing that it tempts gentlemen far and nere to come hither to take their pastime, these hills are adorned with many flowers and plants, amongst the rest the paschall or Pulsatilla flowers in the Easter time doe verry much adorne these downs.

From Burford to Winchcome is about 12 miles these country parrishes lye in and by the road.

    Tanton a mile from Burford where they digg good freestone and also at

    Nathaniel Bacon against Colonial Governor William Berkeley, after Berkeley refused to drive Native Americans out of Virginia.
243 Sir Francis Wenman of Caswell House, Curbridge, Brize Norton, was PM for Oxfordshire in 1664. HofP.
244 The Fettiplaces lie one above the other in threes in Swinbrook church. The manor house and gardens no longer exist.
245 'our' is largely blotted, as is 'who' further along the line, and 'these' at the end of the paragraph. William Lenthall's grandfather was the speaker of the House of Commons in 1640 and bought Burford Priory in 1637.

Barrinton. At Tanton now lives Mr Gascoigne, and at Barrinton Mr Bray who hath a fine house and park.[246]

Next great Risenton, where now Mr Hall is parson, 8 miles from Burford, here Mr Barnard has a good house, Little Risenton Lyes a mile from it on the side of the hill.[247]

Bourton on the waters lyes 2 miles farther in a bottome on a fine stream whose fountain or spring head beginns at a place calld Pinnok above Upper Guiting, about Windrush this stream of Bourton on the waters joyns with the waters that come from Sherbon, and there doe get the name of windrush river.[248]

Mr Virnum[249] is now parson of Bourton of the waters which parsonage is reported to be worth £300 per annum and Mr Trinder Lord of the mannor, they have for the generallity good houses here about haveing good stone to build with and John Rooke has built a neat house here.

Trouts breed in these waters and as high as Guiting.

Above this Town upon the hill on the left hand stands Clapton where Mr Woodman has a house bigger than the rest, and in the way on the hill above bourton you may see these country Towns. viz: Cold Aston upon the plain of a hill, Ailsworth and nonton in the Bottoms[250] but to proceed the next Town in the road is call'd Guiting where as you goe down the hill toward it you see a fair new built house in a square called the Grange, one Mr Gardner the present owner. At Lower Guiting you find an alehouse but at Bourton of the waters there was none, here also breaks forth a delicate spring much esteemed by the Towns people, and leaving this Town you now begin to goe up and mount the highest summets of these Cotswold hills, it being about 2 miles long before we got thither, leaving on the right hand great woods.

Here at the first glimps of casting our eyes into the bottoms under and large extents of the vale beyond it begatt in us a kind of pleasant horror to see what burly mountains did strut up here and there which by the intermedium of the

246 Burford, Winchcombe, Taynton, Great Barrington (illustrated by Kyp). The quarries are particularly famous, Taynton quarry being mentioned in Domesday Book. This road followed close to the river Windrush.

247 Great and Little Rissington. Edmund Hall (1661-1706) M.A. Pembroke College, Oxford; Rector of Great Rissington (1661-1686) CCEd.

248 Bourton-on-the-Water, Pinnock, Upper or Temple Guiting, Lower Guiting or Guiting Power, Sherborne.

249 George Vernon, Rector of Bourton-on-the-Water (1682-1693). CCEd.

250 Clapton, Cold Aston, Aylworth, Naunton, Guiting Power, Temple Guiting.

dusky air did make them look more strange and terrible. Before us the great Malvern hills did stretch themselves like a mighty bank, upon the right hand of these you may see the top of the famous Reaking[251] 8 miles from Shrewsbury and to the left the black mountain under which is the golden valley not far from Hereford, with a many more mountains in Wales <Shropshire and other places> unknown to mee, and soe having tired your eyes with stareing about, you see under you the ruins of a fine house call'd Shudly[252] Castle, and the now fam'd town of Winchcome because of their late planting tobacco and the souldiers comeing hither yearly to destroy it but now here is little or none planted.[253] The descent of this hill is verry steep till at length you come into a narrow lane full of rowling stones verry troublesome to horsmen, but in the way by a Farmers house a little above the Castle is a fountain or well whose springs doe bubble or boyl up like the water of a furnace with a strong fire under it, a little below this house is a passage for horsmen into the Castle yard, which hath adjoyning to it a large park encompass'd with a stone wall extending to the brow of the hill, here not far from the ruins of this house is the skeleton of a verry large barn, and then about a quarter of a mile rideing brings you into the Town of Winchcome through a purling brook strong enough to drive an overshot mill.

As to the town of Winchcome when the castle had its Lords, and the Abbey its Abbots and monks to spend the estates and incomes of both places here, then here was more to doe than at present, yet the Town for the bigness is very populous, and the people of it in their callings verry dilligent to get their livings.

Here in a morning at 4 a clock I saw many women of the older sort smokeing their pipes of tobacco, and yet lost noe time for their fingers were all the while busy at knitting, and women carr(y)ing their puddings and bread to the Beakhouse lose noe time but knitt by the way. Here also lives in this Town an ingenuous cooper or carpenter, who makes the best stoopers with a skrew to wind up the vessel gently, so that the liquor is little or nothing at all disturb'd by that motion. Wee lay at the sign of the *Bell* Mr Houlet a very respectfull man our landlord, and his wife who gave us verry good entertainment and seldom fail of good Ale for they have verry good water in their well. They keep

251 Wrekin. TB's route from Guiting Power is past Belas Knap and so to Sudeley. .
252 Sudeley, Winchcombe.
253 J. Thirsk, 'New crops and their diffusion: tobacco-growing in seventeenth-century England' *The Rural Economy of England: Collected Essays* (London, 1984), pp. 259–86.

market here on Saturdays, and have a fair on St Marks day and another on the 17 of July to which many good horses are brought to bee sold. Here is one fair Church; a small alms house and some ruins of the abbey yet remaining. <Mr Pits present owner of the castle and lands of Shudly.²⁵⁴>

On St. James's day 1682 wee went from Winchcombe to Cheltnum to see a fair there and soe wee began to ascend the hills again till we came to a famous Beacon above a small house of my Lord Coventrees in a warrin with a little chapel by it, which Lord as a countryman told us is a kinsman of Sir William Coventrees who now lives at Byberry.²⁵⁵ From the top of this high and aery becon hill the prospects are soe alluring and intermingled with soe much variety, that as a man may say it may be like that with which the devill did tempt Christ, a shew of the glory of the world and its riches. (viz:) great cities and Towns, and a plentifull country under you, for as you travell this ridg country way, here you see Glocester there Worcester, here Teuxbury and there Easome with many more eminent places. (but to proceed) As to Cheltnum, 4 miles from Winchcombe, 'tis seated in a plain encompassed with the hills like an amphitheatre, with these rich parrish towns about it. Cleve, Pressbury, Charlton Kings, and Lackington.²⁵⁶

Cheltnum hath one Church in it with a spire, as to any other buildings of the Town little else can be said of it save that there was a verry fine inn formerly a gentlemans house, but the Innkeeper being lately hang'd for coyning money it is now shut up.

It being St. James's day here was a great fair for lambs and other cattle, and abundance of horses for the cart and other drudging uses but few for the saddle, hither also do come some carts laden with fine white salt from the Whiches or salt pitts to sell. And country wenches have stockings hanging on their arms to sell to such as will buy them.

Leaving Cheltnum in our way towards Burlip we went by Sherrington and Collonel Norwoods house,²⁵⁷ where in the way is a curious spring with an iron dish chaind for travellers to drink. And soe getting up the downs, we

---

254 Sudeley passed from the Bridges family on the death of the sixth Baron Chandos to his widow, Lady Jane Savage, who married secondly George Pitt, and subsequently to their descendants. HoP.
255 Bibury. Postlip Manor house has a simple Norman chapel beside it. The Beacon is on Cleeve Hill. The road to Winchcombe ran over the hill.
256 Evesham, Bishop's Cleeve, Prestbury, Charlton Kings, Leckhampton.
257 Birdlip, Shurdington, Leckhampton Court.

had sight of 2 famous hills in the vale, (viz) Robinhoods hill, and Chosen hill, which stand opposite one against the other like great butts of earth for a mighty shooter, and here about 3 miles distance you have an alluring prospect of Glocester between them.

Burlip about 6 miles from Cheltnum is a throughfare village in the road from Glocester to London, tis built on the brow of these downs in a delicate air overlooking the vale country, and has some good Inns for entertainment.
 Hence in the way towards Stroud about 6 miles farther, you ride for 2 or 3 miles through high woods of beech, which muffle or hoodwink your eyes from the pleasant prospects of the vale and mountains of Wales beyond it.[258] Then being clear of these woods you see on the right hand a fine house in a warrin on the declivity of the hill under you,[259] and soe declining on the left hand you fall into a bourne, which leads by Paradise a little alehouse with the sign on the chimney, to Panswick a pretty neat market Town having in it one fair Church with a Spire, a Schoolehouse, and some good Inns for entertainment.

Here at this Town you beginn to enter the land of Clothiers who in these bourns building fair houses, because of the conveniency of water so usefull for their trade, do extend their countrey some miles, for they delight to live like the merry rooks and daws chattering and prating together, and if a man be able to purchase so much ground as will keep a horse or 2 yearly you shall have a house built there to spend £500 per ann: soe that he that hath land in such places may sell it at verry good rates and he that shall take a prospect of Wootton underedg, Croscombe in Somersetshire and other places where clothiers live, shall find the sides of the hills and country full of little grounds and paddocks.[260]

From Panswick to Stroud they acount it 2 miles

Change of handwriting here to one very difficult to read, squeezing material to the botton of the page

And Stroud is from Glocester 7 miles Newnam 9 Dursley 6 Berkley 10 Wotton under Edge 8 Stanley St Leonards 2 Tetbury 7 Hamton 2 Cyrincester 9 Norlidg

258 Cranham woods.
259 Painswick manor house and park.
260 Wotton-under-Edge, Croscombe.

12 Cheltnam 9 Winchcombe 13 Baunton 25 Stanton 30 Oxford 33[261]

As to the Town of Strowd it selfe little more can be said of it than that tis built on the declivity of a Hill having 1 church and a churchyard by it full enough of graves because the Parish is populous; Beesley[262] upon the hill was the mother church and to that formerly they did belong. Here is a ?hie a pretty large old market house and a small market place by it. For Inns they are of small concern save the *George* where we lay Mr Parre a very civill man the present master of it who hath lately built a faire Celler in which I told 29 vessels Hogsheads and Barrels with 3 or 4 kinderkins more, here you may likewise have wine and Coffe.

Here runs in the bottom under the Town a Bright streame called Stroudwater which passing by Stonhouse and Eastington doth not for aught I know ioyne the Severne till it hath washt Berkley[263] for there I saw a River which comes from these parts.

The way from Strowd to Oxford gos by Beesley to ?Beching bridge and Bybery.[264]

But from thenc to Baunton we went through Beesley to Edgworth in sight of Mr Daniele Rudlows house by the church[265] and then about a mile above Cirencester on the right hand in sight of it to Banton where we went over the water[266] and so to Barnsley. Then to Netherton next Eastlatch and Bouthrop then by Hathrowp in sight of Brodwell and Kincot town and then Alscot Blacke Bourton and Bamton.[267]

---

261 Gloucester, Newnham-on-Severn, Dursley, Berkeley, Minchinhampton, Cirencester, Northleach, Stanton Harcourt, Oxford.
262 Stroud, Bisley.
263 Stonehouse, Eastington.
264 Perhaps Bagendon bridge (at Perrotts Brook) near Baunton.
265 Could this be Edgeworth Manor built by Nathaniel Ridler in the late 17th century?
266 At Perrotts Brook. Above the line there are words inserted, illegible.
267 Netherton in and to the south of Hatherop, Eastleach (Turville), Eastleach Martin or Bouthrop, Southrop? Kencot, Alvescot, Black Bourton, Bampton. It seems possible that TB has confused Hatherop with Southrop.

JOURNEY 9
TO ST ALBANS FROM BAYWORTH VIA AMERSHAM, RICKMANSWORTH AND WATFORD, AND RETURN VIA ASHRIDGE AND TRING

The journey took place in 1671 and was written up in 1682.

AN ACCOUNT OF a Journy from Bayworth to St Albans vizt: <William Griffith then my man>

I Went from Bayworth to East Sandford where now lives Mr Daviss, 1682, thence to Brockington, Cookesome and so by Wattleton to Burton and Shirbourne, and so to Westerne Great Wickham.[268] Westwickham is remarkable for having their Church on a steep and high hill, but the parish or houses of West Wickham are in a bottome by a pleasant streame and so is the market town of Great Wickham in Buckingham shire.

    This stream is well planted with Mills to grind meal for London, and you may perhaps in two or 3 miles gate see 20 mills. Great Wickham layes in the Road between Oxford and London.

From Wickham we thwarted the Country to Amerstone[269] another thoroughfare Town in this shire from London to Buckingham and 'tis about 5 miles, from Wickham to Ammerstone, from hence 'tis two miles more to Chassom[270] another market Town in Buckingham shire of which my Lord Cavendish Earl of Devonshire was then Landlord 1671. Wee lay at the *Crowne* one Mr Terry the Earl of Devonshire's bayly being our Landlord; here also runs a nimble streame with mills on't to grind meal for London, and in a roome over the market house, people are much imploy'd to boult cleanse or sorte the flower from the brans.

    From this Town we went to Latmus where the Earl of Devonshire hath a fair house and thence to Cheyny where the Earl of Bedford hath another, and

268 Bayworth, Sandford(-on-Thames), Brookhampton, Cuxham, Watlington, Pyrton, Shirburn, West Wycombe.
269 Amersham.
270 Chesham

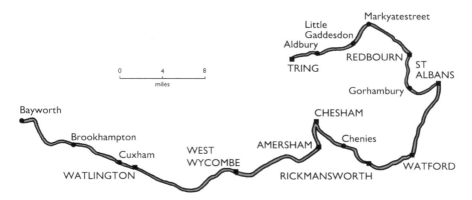

so through the pleasant bottomes of this Country, the hills being shaded with beech oak and birch to Rickmanstead a pretty little market Town, where upon a hill on t'other side the stream the Duke of Ormond hath a house and park called Moore Park, and in marching forward a mile or two more you come to Casabell a great house of the Earl of Essex, so that in this obscure Country their houses being as it were hidd in the bottomes you find in 4 or 5 miles travell four houses of the greatest Peeres in England.[271]

From Cassabell we went to Watford a market Town in Hartford shire, where the water was then so high September 24 1671, we could not well pass over without wetting our saddles for which reason we went another way to St Albons a great market Town about six miles from Watford and 20 miles from London, in Hartfordshire. St Albons is a great Town with many fair Inns in it, but the *Bull* Inn is the greatest that I have seen in England. It hath 4 Churches of these St Albons the Aby Church is biggest it being an ancient old fabrick and now much decayed, but as I heard this year '81 they are gathering money (by the incouragement of the present Bishop of London) to repair it, 'twas built as they told me by Offa King of Mersia in honor of that Saint martir'd by the Emperor Dioclesian.[272]

And in succeeding Ages he had here a rich shrine aequivolent to that of Thomas Becket's in the Cathedrall of Canterbury. But in the days when popery was turn'd out of this Land 'twas taken downe and carried to France as

271 Latimer House; Chenies Manor House; Moor Park, Rickmansworth; Cassiobury Park, Watford.

272 St Albans. The bishop of London in 1681 was Henry Compton (1676-1713), responsible for the 'Compton survey' of 1676 of Conformists, Nonconformists and Papists. Celia Fiennes also commented on the disrepair of the Abbey church. *The Illustrated Journeys* (1982) 118.

Mrs Selliors son told me of the *Lion* where I lay'd. But some unknown Author hath contributed these verses to his memory on the wall on the East end of the Church where his shrine stood

> *The verses written very large*
> Renowned Alban knight first martyr of this Land
> by Dioclesian Lost his life through bloudy hand.
> Who made him Sovraign Lord high Steward of this Ile
> and Prince of Brittaine Knights, to dignify his stile.
> He verity Imbrac'd and Verelam forsook
> and in this very place, his martyrdome he took
> Now hath he his reward, he lives with Christ above
> for he beyond all things, Christ and his trueth did Love.
> Here of a Mercian's king did Albans bones inshrine
> so all things there dispos'd by providence divine
> Naught but a marble stone of Albans shrine is left
> this work of all forme els hath changing time bereft.

Here also layes inter'd in the body of this Church an ancient English Traveller Sir John Mandevile,[273] having in the roofe of the Church over his body these verses for an Epitaph.

> Loe in this Inn of Travel doth Lye
> One rich in nothing but a Memorye

Here did live in the Town of St Albans in 71 one Mr Aris (Arris) a Parliament man and Doctor of Civill Law.[274]

Here is also in this Town a great deal of timber to be bought and sold, and gates for high ways ready made to be sold.

Here wee heard that the sea had verry lately made a breach into the fens of Lincolnshire drownd 4 or 5 parrishes and some thousands of sheep and other cattle, and that there were in the late tempestuous weather a hundred ships cast away on the coasts of Yarmouth and Norfolk.

Here is a small river running by the lower parts of the Town, but in the upper

---

273 It is appropriate for TB to notice the epitaph of a traveller who wrote *The Voyage and Travels of Sir John Mandeville, Knight* in the 14th century, though possibly not the author. Britannica. https://www.britannica.com/biography

274 Thomas Arris, MP for St Albans 1661. In 1651 he was said to be well-affected to the government, and so was a 'Parliament man' in the sense of being sympathetic to the Roundheads. HoP.

parts the wells are deep, my landlady told mee her well was 40 fathom deep.

Verrulam a village nere this Town from whence the Lord Bacon had his title was anciently a city, here was a great house but of late taken down and sold, and at present Sir Harbottle Grimstone is master of the land.[275]

These country Towns as well as I could hear country people name them to mee Lye in the way between St Albans and Tring a small market Town in Buckinghamshire; viz Radborne, Mucking, Street, little Gadden, little Aberry.[276]

Here I may not omitt to make mention of a place called Ashridge where the present Earl of Bridgewater hath a great house formerly some monastery which stands on the plain of the hill 4 miles above Tring. And because my loveing friend Mr Richard Blower since dead had been master of the horse a long time to the present Earl, as I came from Sturbridg fair with Mr John Hyde September 81 I went thither purposly to see him, and this ancient house grown more famous in the country by the present Lords great house keeping for which to help it he hath here a park for vallow and another for red deer, and in them especially nere his house such lofty groves of trees and soe thick set togather that the like is scarce anywhere els to be seen, which conspiring to keep out the sunn beams makes the grownd under them where they grow as bear as a barn flower without grass, and doubtless were it not for these trees, this would in the winter time be a verry sharp cold place, standing as it doth soe high and open to all the northern storms, and therefore it is good policy for such as live there to continue them as long as they can. Although the Lord Chancelor Hyde comeing hither one time to visit the present Earl found fault because it had soe much wood about it <here are squerrels plenty which leap and dance from tree to tree.>

As to the Fabrick or form of the house within the gatehouses, for it hath one fair gatehouse which gives entrance through a large court on the northern side of the house to the hall to which they ascend by steps on a terras walk which

275 The Roman town of Verulamium. Sir Harbottle Grimston (1603-85) was a Royalist, and MP for various Essex seats. Old Gorhambury House was built partly from bricks taken from the old Abbey buildings at St Albans, in 1563–68 by Sir Nicholas Bacon, Lord Keeper, and was visited a number of times by Queen Elizabeth I. It was sold to Grimston in 1652 but fell into ruin after New Gorhambury House was built in the 18th century.

276 Redbourn, Little Gaddesdon, Markyatestreet, Aldbury. (TB has inserted a comma between Mucking and Street as though they were separate places).

leads to the hall, and another gatehouse which leads to the stables, where Mr
Blower had his lodgings. It is a Square containing in it a small quadrangle,
and in that a little pond of water wald about with freestone, fed with the
water which first comes from a deep well drawn up by a horse in a great wheel
in 2 barrels or large buckets a man allways standing by as soon as the bucket
comes above the coller of the well to empty it into a ledden cistern, and here
the ingenuity of the horse must not be forgotten, for as soon as the man lays
hold on the bucket to empt it, the horse turns himself in the wheel without
bidding or forceing, and travels the other way to draw up the next bucket, and
soe this water after it hath served all the offices of the house runs into the pond
as aforesaid where doe live some few hungry carps, and this is all the fishpooles
that I saw about the house. Here doth also enclose this pool and quadrangle a
fine Cloyster, remarkable for this because my Lord will not have it blur'd out
for haveing in paint upon the walls some scripture and monkish stories.[277]

The hall is a noble roome, in which some good horses which my Lord hath
been owner of are drawn in full proportion, from hence at the lower end
you descend into the buttery or pantry, being a fair roome vaulted over and
adorned with many heads and hornes of stags or red deer which have been kil'd
out of my Lords own park and out of this roome the friendly gentleman of the
house led me <us?> into the cellars of wine ale and beere, in that for beer was
a range of vessels bound with iron hoops, each vessel containing the quantity
of 2 pipes, and in some peculiar rooms made on purpose for them <for this
was but one great vessel in a room> were some might vie with the Prince of
Hedleberg's tunn,[278] they look soe big upon you. They told me that to brew
one of the vessels of liquor they put in 6li worth of hops when hops were at 18
pence and 2 shillings or 2s 6d a pound. Here are fine gardens about the house
and the place took its name from a ridg of ashes, one of which being grown tall
and bulky my Lord lately cutt down and made a fair shuffle-board table in his
hall. Here is in the park a neat lodg house and a little without the park in the
way towards Tring a good country alehouse.

In the way as you goe to Tring a small market town in Buckinghamshire you

---

277 In 1604 Sir Thomas Egerton, created Earl of Bridgwater in 1617, acquired
    Ashridge in Little Gaddesdon, which had, as TB said, been a monastery. A new
    house was built in the early 19th century.
278 Supposedly an enormous wine vat in Heidelberg Castle, though rarely used to
    store wine. There have been four such and the current one was said to have been
    constructed from 130 oak trees in 1751.

goe by Sir Richard Anderson's house, whose son has married Mrs Spencer, Sir John Stonhouse's wife's daughter by her former husband.[279]

Tring is about 22 miles from Oxford.

The Earl of Bridgwater is now Lord Leftenant of Buckingame shire.[280] ann:1682.

JOURNEY 10
TO YORK FROM OXFORD VIA NORTHAMPTON, LEICESTER, NOTTINGHAM AND DONCASTER

There are seveeral changes of handwriting in this account, some rather untidy and possibly hastily written, and he refers to the lack of paper and pen to record an epitaph in Doncaster church. At the end he is doubtful of the names of places because his notebook was blotted. This journey takes him through a sweep of countryside where large-scale development would take place in the next two centuries.

A JOURNEY INTO THE North with my friend Mr Washborne Student of Ch. Ch. Oxon

ann: [1677]

From Oxford wee went through Bister to Brackly[281] in Northampton shire 7 miles from Bister and 17 from Oxford, in the way thither some miles on this side the Town you ride over a downy and delicate green carpet country excellent for hunting and raceing, here being posts set up for that purpose, but the Town lyes 2 miles below the raceing place in a bottom, in the which as I remember are 3 churches, but one of them at the end of the Town where my Lord Waynman[282] hath a good house, is but a ruinous heap.

From hence wee went through Torcester to Northampton about 30 miles from

---

279 The house, Pendley Manor, was at Tring; Richard Anderson bought the manor in 1606-7. Sir Richard Anderson died 1699. VCH (Herts) 2.

280 Originally entered as 'Hartfordshire', which was appropriate to Ashridge.

281 Bicester, Brackley.

282 Waynman or Wenman. Richard Wenman, son of Sir Francis Wenman, bt, was of 'The Tithe House', Brackley; created Visct. Wenman of Tuam 1686. HoP.

Oxford seated on the river Nine, which runs to Peterburough and so into the sea at Boston.[283]

Wee lay at the *Angel* one Friend master of the Inn who then had good wine and Beer in his cellars. To divert the time in the evening, wee sent for the

283 Towcester, River Nene, Peterborough.

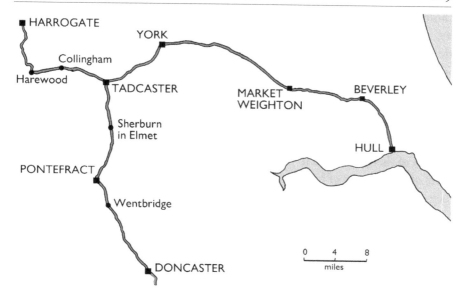

Town musick to hear them, but could not have them, but in the morning they came to plague us when we did not care for them.

Rising early on St. James' day, this Town beginning to fill apace with people that came to the fair wee got into the road, and after wee had turned off 12 long miles we came to Harburrough[284] another market Town as I think in Northampton shire, in the way hither joyning company with a verry curteous gentleman one Mr Hall a Londoner and a Lawyer going towards Lester where the assize was to be kept the next day.

These country towns or villages Lay in the rode between Northampton and Harburrough if the names be right as I had them from the country people. Kingston, Bowton, where the Lord of Banbury hath a house and park house, then Brixworth where Mr Sanders hath the biggest house, next Lamperd, where Sir Thomas Isham hath a fine house, and then Maydwell where Sir William Harley hath a fine garden and house.[285] At Harburrough wee dined with Mrs

284 Market Harborough was and is in Leicestershire.
285 Kingsthorpe, Boughton, Brixworth, Lamport, Maidwell in Scaldwell parish. An estate in Boughton belonged to Edward Vaux who died in 1661 without legitimate issue, having settled the manor on his stepson Nicholas Vaux or Knollys, sometimes called Earl of Banbury; his son Charles succeeded him, in 1674. The Isham family owned Lamport manor and Sir Thomas inherited in 1675 and died in 1681. VCH (Northants) 4. Maidwell Hall, a very large house, is now a school.

Lamb at the sign of the *Swan* who shewd us a bed where King Charles the 1st lay, and told us here is a fair kept on the 8th of October where good horses are sold. In the afternoon wee rodd towards Lester through these villages viz: Sibworth, Olim, Oleby.[286] And here as I may say I fell into the Land of Spires, for makeing prospects round about mee upon an indifferent hill for height, for all the country between Northampton and Nottingham except one hill 3 or 4 miles on this side Nottingham doth gently rise and fall, I told about 4 or 5 and twenty spires and towers but most of them spires or steeples, and yet the farthest of them did seem to be not much above 5 or 6 miles from mee, and yet none of the steeples of Lester came into this number although we were then as they said not much above 3 miles from it.

Leicester

A S TO LEICESTER, accounted 12 miles from Harborrough, 'tis now an old stinking Town situated upon a dull river inhabited for the most part by tradesmen viz: wosted combers, and clothiers, for the streets being then a sweeping and cleansing against the judges comeing in the next morning, the stinking puddles of piss and water being then stirr'd made mee goe spewing through all the streets as I went to see it yet it hath formerly been a Town of good remark for here is an ancient house or pallace call'd the Duke of Lancasters pallace, as also a large hospitall built by some of those dukes, and an old piece of building which they call Janus's temple.

Here is also a bridg over the river which they call Richard the 3ds bridge by which some say he was buried, and out of the town they goe over this bridg to Bosworth field where he was slain. Here are in the Town 5 churches of which 3 as I remember have hansome spires, and are to be seen a good distance from the Town. The *Red Lion* where wee lay is the best and greatest Inn of the Town and was then taken up by the Sheriff and his men. It hath in it a gallery or dineing room of great length with a long table in it to entertain people, the flower of it which was the first I saw of that kind being made of plaister like that of Paris. The stones of these parts especially those at Mount Sorrill being burn'd in a heap with wood almost to lime, when brought to the places where they use it as soon as it is slack'd and made into mortar they lay it while hot on the flower and smooth it immediately with their truells, and soe this flower when cold and dry becomes as hard as a rock, but such as intend to have such kind of flowers must be sure to timber it well, for in some places where I came the weight of the lime and stones had made the floor swagg soe that it was

286 Kibworth, ?Olim, Oadby.

lower at one end of the room than the other. This kind of flowering you shall find in eminent houses as far as from hence to York; the womans name at the house where wee lay was Newton, she had now good Clarret and our victualls was well dress'd. The next morning Mr Hall that courteous gentleman and companion brought us 2 miles on our way towards Nottingham, and then with many expressions of Love and civility parted from us for Lester again. About a mile without Lester in this rode was an Abbey which is now my Lord of Devonshire's house.[287]

From Lester to Nottingham is 20 miles.

These villages lay in the road as wee went to it: Mount Sorril, Burro, Prestwood, Houghton, Leinson, Lostock, or Costock, Bunny, Bradmore, and then Nottingham.[288] Here in a field near Gotham where the wise men were said to live[289] I saw many spires or steeples, I think I told 14 and the farthest not above 5 or 6 miles of and I was then in a plain or levell before I went up the hill towards Nottingham. A *change of pace in the writing - smaller and the lines closer together* But here by the way I must not forgett that wee fell acquainted on the road, with one Mrs Hodgkins an aldermans daughter of this Town, who when wee came to town directed us to one Mr Sullyes house master of the *White Lion*, who formerly had been Quartermaster in the army of King Charles the first this she did on the score of good ale and indeed wee found it soe, for he had a celler cut into the rock 46 stairs deep, by which means though it was then after St James tide and hott sulthry weather, the bear and ale was rarely good and drank excellently well, but you must conceve they were better maltmakers and brewers than at Oxford or Abingdon.

Nottingham

To give you a little character of Nottingham, it may be called, as a man may say paradise restored, for here you find large streets, fair built houses, fine women and many coaches rattling about and their shops full of all merchantable riches.

As to the cituation of it it is upon a pleasant rock of freestone in which

---

287 The mansion built on Leicester abbey site, outside the city of Leicester, was occupied first by the Hastings family and then the Cavendishes. It was in ruins by 1928. Historic England.

288 Mountsorrel, Barrow upon Soar, Prestwold, Hoton, ?Rempstone, Costock, Bunny, Bradmore.

289 The wise or cunning inhabitants of Gotham feigned madness to deter King John from creating a park for hunting there, fencing in a cuckoo - which flew over the fence.

every one that will may have sellers and that without the trouble of springs or moisture, soe that excepting Bridgenorth in Shropshire you cannot find such another Town in England.[290]

This town is devided into the upper and lower towns, for when you have a mind to leave the large and more spacious parts of this town on the plain of the hill, and will goe down to the lower streets nere the river, you must descend down right many stairs ere you gett to the bottome, and here you find as it were another town full of shops and people who have a convenience to cutt in the rock warehouses, stables or what rooms els they please for their own peculiar uses.

This town hath in the upper part of it a large and long market place.

For public buildings here are in in this 4 pillars with many stairs to ascend each of them and 3 churches one of them bigger than the rest in which they are now putting up an organ, ann: 1675, but that which will yet add a greater beauty and ornament to this Town, is the Duke of new castle's now building a sumptuous house in the ruins of old Nottingham castle, whose walls were demollish'd by the Parliamentarian and Oliverian people.

This house is seated on a rock extending it self towards the river soe far as the land will permitt where such as have a mind from this high precipice may tumble headlong into the river Trent many yards beneath it; they have gott up this building as high as the first story, haveing in it a noble staircase, each stair being made of one large entire stone brought hither from Mansfield, carried up as to form in a large square without any pillars to support it each stair geometrically depending one upon another.

For wine here is in this Town good clarret white wine and Rennish, but as to sack I cannot say much, and I believe here are about half a dozen taverns in town.

My landlord Mr Sully told me of 2 things that were remarkable on and in the river Trent, viz. 30 ancient manners *Change here to very untidy handwriting* by this River and 30 sortes of fish in this River, but both he and I had much ado to finde out that number but at length recconing al that I knew in Temes and those he knew besides in Trent we got to the number but some are so inconsiderable I doubt they will scarce pass muster.[291]

---

290 There is no account of a journey to Bridgenorth in this manuscript, but clearly TB had been there and seen the town on the rock above the river Severn.
291 The idea that the Trent is named because of the 30 fish in it was noted in Izaac Walton and Charles Cotton, *The Compleat Angler* (Oxford World Classics 2016),

The fish are numbered above each name

Salmon <1>, Flownders <2>, Sprats or young Herring <3>, Pike <4> Trout <5>
Chub <6> Barbel <7> Carp <8> Tench <9> Perch <10> Ele <11> Roach <12>
Dace <13> Roof or Pope <14> Blay <15> Gudgion <16> Minno <17> Cull
<18> Crawfish <19> Loach or Card <20>. In Trent he nam'd those that are not
in Tems viz Grayling <21> Bret <22> Burbout <23> Rud <24> Banstikel <25>
Lampurne which are young Camprey <26> Bream if it be not a Roch <27>
Muskel <28> a shell <29> smelt if it do come up so high in the river. Now what
to name for the 30 fish I cannot tell except you allow Grig which I could never
distinguish from an Eele although our fishermen have endeavor'd to shew me.

A neater and different hand for this para

From Notinggame to mansfielt is accounted 12 miles. The way leads through
Shirwood Forrest by a Forge driven by water where with weighty Hammers
bigger than men can handel they knok or beate out long bars of Iron when
they are made red-hot in that great Forge of Fire blown up by those mighty
bellows. *Back to hand as at top of previous page* In these damms or pooles of
water that forge the iron for here are many in this countrey are great store of
trouts, a gentleman that was in the Inn at Mansfield where I lay told mee he
had with angling taken 50 trouts in a day.

 As wee rode through this forest wee saw many old decay'd oaks of
which abundance were cutt down by the duke of Newcastles order to make
charcole, they told mee one Mr Jennings was the chief master or overseer of
these charcole works.

Mansfield a town made famous amongst country people by means of that
Ballad or song call'd Gelding of the devil[292] has one fair church in it, and little
more can be said of it, save that wee lay at the *Crown* a verry good Inn, where
wee had excellent Clarret, potted venison and other victualls well dressed, for
wee lay here Saturday and Sunday night; our Landlord and Landlady were
persons well bred, and had liv'd after a gentile manner before they kept this Inn,

---

151; Walton added that its name may also drive from 30 lesser rivers flowing into
it, but Charles Cotton pointed out this was not the case.

292 A 17th century ballad in which the baker's wife saves the baker from the same
fate he inflicted on the devil. University of Michigan Early English Texts https://
quod.lib.umich.edu

his name Hall, her maiden name Fretsville, they were allyed to one Mr Hugh Baskerville a gentleman of 200 pound per annum, with whome I contracted acquaintance, and since his sone an aturney at Chesterton in Darby shire hath been at Bayworth to see mee.

3 miles from Mansfield lyes Warsopp 5 from that Worsop, and 4 from that Blithe, then Harrow and Rossington and soe to Dancaster, a market Town in Yorkshire 20 miles from Mansfield in Nottingham shire.

When we came within 3 or 4 miles of Doncaster wee saw on the left hand a pretty bigg town with an old Castle in itt called Tickle.[293]

Doncaster a great town of Trade on the river Dunn[294] hath one fair church in it and the market is on Saturday.

Here they make excellent stockings for horsemen of verry fine yarn and variety of colours, and the woemen of the Town are soe importunate, for they goe with bundles of the stockings on their arms from Inn to Inn where travellers are that you can hardly evade layeing out money with them, for they will follow you up into your chamber and will not be denyed without a great deal of trouble, and they are to be commended for it, for this being the great rode between London Yorke and Scottland they doe by this means vend a great deal of goods. Here wee began to pay a groat a flaggon for ale, 14d a bottle for Clarret and white wine, and 2s 6d a quart for Sack, but their flaggons for ale were good measure, and larger than ours in Berks or Oxfordshire, and so it is in the city of Yorke, and as for such victualls as we had at the *3 Cranes* for there wee lay our Landlord had the grace to reckon enough for it, Hunt his name and as to behaviour he is a gentile man a jocky and one that loves to ride and talk of good horses. His ale being made of a brackish spring wee could not drink it, soe wee went to another house in Town where wee found verry good. Going in to see Doncaster church I saw at the east end of the wall this Epitaph,

> Ho ! Ho ! who is here?
> I Robin of Doncastere
> And Margret my fear
> That I spent that I had,
> That I gave that I have,
> That I lent that I lost

Quoth Roburtus Burx who in this world did rain 3 score years and 7 and yet lived not one.

---

293 Market Warsop and Worksop, Blyth, Harworth, Rossington, Doncaster, Tickhill.
294 Dun or don.

Thus my landlord Hunt writt this Epitaph in his house for I wanted a pen and paper to take it in the church.

Back to a previous very mannered hand

They account it 16 miles between Doncaster and Pumfret[295] but they were so long we thought them 16 in measure.

In the way between Doncaster and Wentbrig 3 of their miles we saw a fine spring with an Iron dish chained by, which they call Robin Hoods well.[296]

Passing Winbridg <Wentbrig> we went through BrotherWood. And here is another place called Fraterwood on tother side the River broad-Aire.

Pumfret is a fine town some 18 miles from Yorke hath in it 2 Churches the best impaired by the late wars as was also a stately Castel of which now only remaines the Platform and stump or bottome of the wall 2 or 3 yards above ground but yet it is handsom because imployed to fine gardens and a bowling Green where you may have for your money good wine march beer and fruites and at the Inn where we put our horses we had excellent beer. Here is about this town as also in Nottingam great store of Liquorish planted. The upper part of this town is rocky and I believe where the castel stood in which there is a staire case gos dow(n) a great depth for water.

Leaving Pumfret and going forward 6 miles towards York at night we found a poor Inn at a place called Shierbourne[297] but I must tell you going to see Pumfret let us out of the great rode between London and York. Shierborn is 10 miles from York: in the way to Tadcaster 4 miles nearer York: a market town is Hazelwood Hall, a great house Sir Walter Vavaster[298] owner. Here we had the first sight of Wharfe a great and Rapid River running by it as the name declares for there is no navigation against it Tis so full of great rowling beach stones by meanes of the nimble descent and fierce current.

---

295 Pontefract.

296 Wentbridge.

297 Sherburn in Elmet.

298 Vavasour was the Norman name for a vassal and Mauger the Vavasour was the vassal of William de Percy, whom he had accompanied on the Norman invasion. The Vavasour family remained at Hazlewood Hall, Stutton with Hazlewood, until the early 20th century. https://castrumtocastle.com/english-castles/north-yorkshire-leeds-hazlewood-castle/#History. TB's directions are confusing; Hazlewood is south of Tadcaster.

This River hath its originale among the high and great mountains of Cragwemb or Craven as they now call it, where the raines are so great and frequent and the floods so violent such bridges as ours with variety of Arches cannot stand against its fury for this reason where they build a bridge over this river they make but one intire arch from bank to bank. Nevertheless Broad Aire a river which runs like Tems (not far from Wharfe) in a level and plain Country <and I believe the springs rise in the plainer parts of Lancaster> hath bridges as on other streames. And to speak of Yorkshire in general, the greater part is a pleasant plain interlaced with good Rivers abounding in fish among which I here remember these names Dun Broad-Aire, Wharfe, The Ouse Ripple and Calder.[299]

York

YORKE A VERY Ancient Citty seems not to be so big as Bristol. From St. Peters the Cathedral great Tower the buildings old and streets narrow I told 19 Churches. The wall about it and a Castle where a Garrison is constantly kept is in good repairation; in this Castle is a large and spacious Hall new built where they keep the assizes for this great Shiere. This being the time of their assizes and I happening to go the first day of them to the castel in the morning when it began this forenoon was spent in calling and repeating the names of the nobility and gentry who were Justices of the Peace in this county.

The assizes for the Citty of Yorke is kept in another Hall in the town where the Lord maior sits Judge: and in doubtfull matter of Law dos ask the Judges advice, who sit by him.

This makes me remember an old Prophesie :
Winchester was
London is
York shall be.

As to the Cathedral or minster at Yorke it is the greatest now standing in England but never finished it being covered or Ceiled with wood lower than the vaulting of stone was intended which takes from the beauty of the Roofe of the body and Cross to the westward of the Quire and this Ceiling of wood is beneath those two orbicular windows in the north ,and south of the abovesaid Cross.

In the vestrey of this Church they have a well to which they have stone stairs to go down and they brought up water for me to tast, called St. Peters well.

The Tower of this Cathedral like Winchester is plain without Pinacles

299 Don, Aire, Wharfe, Ouse, Ribble, Calder.

and the stairs so high to get up and down that it made my thighes ake very much and I fell that night into a feaver but to asscend the Piller at London the labour is not much because those staires are not above a 3d part the height of these at Yorke.

As to the situation of this town it lyes on both sides the River Ouse navigable from Hull of which I shall speak when I come thither for vessels of neer a 100 tuns burthen by the help of Spring tydes. The bridg which joyns both parts of the town beside lesser Arches hath one very large and high Arch like one I have seen over the river in Bilbo in Biscay so that a vessel of 40 or 50 tuns may sayle under.

The largest street of the town is that on this side the bridge as you enter from London Rode but the greatest part of the Citty is on tother side the river in which part Wine street winding about like an Arch hath most esteem but in general the whole town is old timber building and must have a purgation by fyre if ever it arise in beauty like Northampton or London.

Here is near the Castel and that part of the town dead standing water which corrupt the Aire of which they make a strong heavy slugish Ale so that I could not well digest it at the *Talbot* where we lay near the church Mr Bell master but we went to quench our thirst to a barbers house where wee had good China Ale 6d a quart bottle and after 2 or 3 times coming theirther for 4d. Here my Landlord did Aske us whether we would bite? I asking what he meant he told me if people had a mind to eat when they came to drinke at his house they should have cold rost beef and such like victuals for nothing and indeed at one town on the rode between Skipton and Leeds we had our dinner of cold meat for nothing paying for our Ale 4d the bottel.

This town is pretty well served with fish fres Cod plenty but oysters in their season deare halfe a Crown a hundred and are brought hither in shipes from Scotland for they had none in the sea near the mouth of Humber till of late as a man in Hul told me for a Scottish ship laden with oysters being there cast away they now begin to breed there so that as the Proverb saith 'tis a bad winde which blows nobody good, but that which will much disgust a South Country man when he comes to Yorke is the bad bread he shall finde there a hungry raw tasted manchet and if you call for household Household bread they have none but what is made of Rye and that so coarse and blak you will care not to eate any of it.

Now as to fruites the Appels are good for little else save to quadel so that here you finde in those parts quadlings and Quadling Tarts all the Summer long as soon as they are good to eate which I believe are not till August, and Cherryes which with us are ripe in great plenty at midsummer here were cry'd up and down the streets to sell at Lammas faire[300]; their Astichooks[301] are small in respect ours at Oxford

The Tole of this Faire for 2 days is paid to the Archbishop of Yorke a person with whome formerly I had acquaintance when at London he lay at my worthy friends Dr Jones house and here I met his eldest son at a treat of musik which a Knight of this Citty gave such people as came to his house to hear it, but Bishop Sternes house is at a place called Bishopthorpe 3 miles from York where he hath a stately Pallace seated by the river Ouse.[302] I saw it at a distan(c)e but my friend Mr Charles Washborne went thither to the bishop to have Institution of Induction for Long Preston[303] and John Stannyman went with him but my travailes to the top of the Tower did so far discompose me I could not go my self.

The edge of this page is damaged Here we got the acquaintance of Mr ?Oldand who is related to Mr Blakaller of Abingdon, Mr Mace and Mr Harrison and here is in Town a famous midwife who got so much money by her trade that she keeps a Coach and a good house, whose maiden name was Baskervile but now Hodgkin. This woman hearing of my name was very desirous to see me upon which I went to her house where she bid me welcome and told me a sad story of the evils which befell her after the death of her Husband in the late wars.

She told me after her Husbands death she was so poor she had scarce a smock to Breech. And that shee had 2 sons, lusty men who had been soldiers for the late king but his party being deprest they were driven to such extremity they were faine to rob on the high way, and being taken they were both brought to York goal in the Castel and being arraign'd for their lives were both condemned to be Hanged and executed. Accordingly some told her if she would beg the youngest son she might have him but had a mind to the oldest which would

---

300 1 August.
301 artichokes.
302 Richard Sterne archbishop of York 1664-83. CCEd.
303 Charles Washbourne, son of Thomas, of Dumbleton; vicar of Long Preston, Yorks, 1677, until his death in 1703. CCEd.

not be granted and so both went to the grave together. Those sad disasters begat in this Citty such a commisseration of her condition that they advised her to turn midwife and in that trad(e) she has been so fortunate that she keeps a good house a Coach and is grown wealthy. She hath one daughter who is maried to a townsman of York and they live with her.

They have good wine in York especially Clarret and Sack and one Tavern has a fair room built over the River Ouse.

Towards Long Preston, detouring first to Hull and Harrogate

HULL IS BUT 30 little miles from York and the way good so we went thither to so see it, this and Portsmouth being the only Towns which in England they do always keep Garrisons as those had before the late wars; when in their beginning Hotham shut the gates against King Charles the first.[304]

Barnbe[305] is 8 miles in the Road from York toward Hull upon Kingstown or Humber for so the River is named when the other rivers unite viz Ouse Wharfe Broad Aire Dun Trent and others.[306]

In Barnbe at the signe of the *George* lives Mrs Tomms and her son.

Next Wighton[307] 5 miles further and then Beverley a large market Town 7 miles more. The way theether over fine Carpit downs called the Woalds. In this town we saw many shops shut up which are used by the Londonners when they come heither to a faire. Here are 2 Churches one large with a body and the Quire as Cathedralls. Here is inter'd in this church as the Clark told us the so famed Earle Percy who as the ballad sings was met <in Cheve Chase[308]> by Douglass a Scottish Earle upon which insu'd a Hot Hunting match soe both the Earles with many more gallants were leaft dead on the spot. <(Between the downs and Beverley the Lord Burlington hath a great house).[309]> Here runs by

---

304 Sir John Hotham MP (married 5 times) was governor of Hull in 1642 and controlled the store of ammunition. He plotted to surrender Hull to the King and was arrested and eventually condemned to death by parliament. *See also* Chapter 6 'Miscellaneous Writings'. HoP.

305 Barnby on the Moor.

306 TB appears to be confused about Kingston upon Hull on the Humber.

307 Market Weighton.

308 The ballad of Chevy Chase or Cheviot Chase may refer to a battle in the 15th century; it was printed several times in the first half of the 17th century. University of Michigan, Early English Texts https://quod.lib.umich.edu

309 In 1643 Londesborough (between York and Beverley) passed by marriage to Richard Boyle, Earl of Cork (created Earl of Burlington in 1664) for whom Robert

this Town a river called Hangwater. And Hull is 6 miles.

Hence the way thitheir for the most part seems to be a forsaken country by the sea large meadowes full of grass hay and cattel but backward in respect of us because of the cold clime and Aire from the sea for we were got into August and they here had but newly begun Hay Harvest the first crop.

As to Hull the great Garrison of the north as Porchmouth in the South, tis seated in a level on the Banks of the Humber no hills being neer it. Being now got to it and ready to enter we saw a drawbridge and a broad and deep moat full of water surrounding this part of the Town. Leaving this behind us we came to another deep moat of water with a draw-bridge over it where is a strong Gate-House Gates and Purcullis and a strong wall on the inner bank surrounding this moate. Then allowing room for defence where men may stand and use their Armes we came at length to another strong Gate which let us into the Town, with a wall surrounding their houses both walls and gate-Houses being well stored with guns to annoy the enimy whenever he shall come to attacke it. Now as to the Town it lyes round and close compact together with some pretty large streets and may be something bigger than Abingdon but very populous because of the great resort of Shipping.

It hath 2 churches one a large and well built Church to which the Governour went on Sunday Attended with a band of men who stay there in the churchyard and Porch till prayers and Sermon are ended and then they waite upon him backe again to his lodging who quartered at the In where we lay. The Governors name is Gilby[310] who hath the repute in this town of a very honest gentleman, my landladie where we lay and whose name and signe I have forgotton keeps an ordinary every Sunday for such as will dine there. Collonel Gilby being to dine here this day she would have had us to dine with him but my lipps being then very sore and broaken out I was loth to Ingage his Company.

He took an account of our names the first night we came theither and so he dos of all stranger(s).

In our Inn we had good sound stale bere and good Clarret, but we could get no Hull Ale.

The weomen of this Town have dutches faces for they are not so clear complexon'd as in the upper parts at farther distance from the sea.

Hooke (1635-1703) laid out gardens c 1660-80. Boyle reintroduced deer to the park c 1650. Historic England.

310 Lieutenant-Colonel Anthony Gilby was MP for Kington upon Hull elected 1660, and captain of the Hull garrison 1660 to ?81. HoP.

Oysters are here 2s the Hundred for al they begin to Increase at the mouth of Humber.

The river here like Severene at Ast passage[311] and lower is very muddy of a reddish colour and never cleare because of the intermingling of tydes with the Rivers Current.

Upon the northern side of the Town lyes the Haven in which a great many ships may ride, at the entrance is a great Chaine to keep out intruders when they please and on the other side this Haven here is a strong wall and at the end to seaward a good Castele wel planted with Guns and another fort some halfe a mile of for the defence of the other side of the town.

On the shore of the sea or Humber without Hull I had a prospect of these Parishes viz Pann, Marfleet, Barton I think are the names for they were something botted in my note booke, some of these if not al are in Lincoln Shier on the farther side of Humber.[312]

From Hull we went back again to York another way and came into our former Rode at Whighton.[313]

In a Common here about I found fine flowers of blew colour much in form like the Jancenella but their blew was not so deep. I took up some of their roots and brought them to Mooridge and set them in our garden but they never came up again. Mr Bobert said it was the Calathian violet.

In that part of Yorkshire called Craven is a strong Tree as to us in these parts called the Within Tree, it hath leaves somwhat like an Ash and bears beautifull Clusters of red berrys as big as a muskadine grape. In Wales some tell me they make a good liquor to drinke which cleanseth the blood. I brought home some of these berry and set them in my Garden at Bayworth and after 2 yeers they came up so now I have halfe a score young plants, these berrys grow on a tree neer Mr Washborns Vicaridge house in long Preston.

Having now satisfied our selves with the sight and pleasures of York, Hull, and these parts we set forward on a Journey toward Long Preston whether Mr Washbourn was to go to be their Vicar or Parson. This town lyes in Craven one

---

311 Aust.
312 Paull, Marfleet, Barton-upon-Humber. Barton-on-Humber was in Lincolnshire as TB surmised, the other two places were in the East Riding of Yorkshire.
313 Market Weighton.

of the 4 Ridings in York Shier.[314] On our way we went back again to Tadcaster and there Struck of on the right hand to Collingame and Harwood a small market town and a ruinous Castel by it.[315]

Here we went out of our Rode to Long Preston which went through Otley and Crossed Wharfe again. To see the Spaw Waters at Harricate a village in Knarsbrow Forest by a town of that name a mile or more distant from the Wells.[316]

As to Harricate a village made good by reason of the resort of peopel to the Wells it stands in a delicate place for pleasure in the Summer time on a plain neer a gentle brow of a hill overlooking Knarsbrow where you have also a noble prospect over the large Vale of Yorkshier, and it being then a faire day we saw the minster in the Citty of York at 18 miles distance.

At your first coming hether you shall meet with a troublesome delight an Importunity among the weomen here almost as eager as that of the water men at London who shall be your servant to fill water to you when you go to the Wells or bring it to your lodging when you do not. This clamour we were faine to indure <because we were not resolved to drink the water> this evening and next morning (for they got into our Chambers before we got out of our beds) with pots of water one cries out I am pretty Betty pray let me serve you another cries Kate and coz doe let we tend you but to tell you the truth they fell short of that.

For their faces did shine
like Bacon Rine.
And for beauty may vie with an old Bath guide's Arse
The Sulphur Waters had so foul'd their Pristine Complexions.

TRAVELS TO SURVEY BRIDGES ON THE THAMES

BRIDGES WERE CRUCIAL markers on a road. During the course of his journey to Long Preston in the Craven district of Yorkshire, Baskerville observed that bridges over the river Wharfe for example were built in one great arch because piers in the river could not withstand the force of water when

314 TB counts Craven as a 4th Riding.
315 Collingham, Harewood.
316 Harrogate, Knaresborough.

the river was in flood. In his home county of Berkshire and in neighbouring Oxfordshire and Gloucestershire the problem for the bridge-builder was the opposite one of crossing the flood plain. His interest in bridge design led him to investigate in more detail a number of bridges over the Thames, and the Harleian manuscript contains several pages devoted to this study. He started with Cricklade, also writing about the market town. Cricklade was within a 50-mile distance of his home at Bayworth, and he commented that this was a possible length of journey in a day given good horses.[317] Cricklade was also, as he noted, the highest navigable point on the Thames for boats. He went specially to look at Hannington bridge, noting when listing the bridges in order that he had not seen it, and subsequently inserting an extra piece (or scantling) of paper in the folio with his detailed description.

~~~

A Description of Cricklade bridge and of Lechlade and St John's bridge
British Library, MS Harl. 4716

Unusually these extracts, and the verse descriptions, are divided into short sections with headings supplied by Baskerville. He tried to write about bridges over the Thames on several occasions, the last one in 1692.

Cricklad Bridge f.4

ON WILTSHIRE SIDE, begins hard by 7 bridge houses, where is a foot Bridge built of wood for people to go over in time of floods, which has 22 Passes for water between the Postes. Then the Casway on which horses travail in time of floods hath 9 passses for water.

But 2 passes are small and then you enter into Creekelad[318] on this side.

3 streams of water run through these Passes viz. Those Passes of the timber bridge,

and those 9 Passes for water in the Stone Casway.

The biggest streame is called the River Rey.[319]

Its top springs rise at Wroughton commonly called Roughton.[320]

317 See Chapter 3 'Oxford' page 36: 'allowing 50 miles to that stretch of way, which men with good Horses doe easily performe in a day'.
318 TB uses a variety of spellings for Cricklade.
319 River Ray.
320 A nice example of the difficulty TB had with being told the names of places.

Thence it descends on the West side of Swindon to Shaw, Rodborne,[321] and then to Cricklad.

The 2d streame rises in Bradon-Forrest[322] and thence descending by Purton runs to Cricklade, or Crekelad.

The 3d not fur or else a dead stream.

Cricklade stands on Wiltshire ground.

The Bridges and Casway to go into Glocestershier from Cricklade are 580 paces or yards long, to the further side of the Bridge over that stream which comes from Cyrencester.

The other stream which runs by Ashton-Canes[323] comes in by Cricklad Town.

The 2d Bridges viz. That Bridge over Ashton Canes stream, and that bridge over Tems or Cyrencester stream and the Casway between, have 12 Arches for water to pass. But the Casway which leads from Tem's Bridge to Latton in Glowstershire (a mile from Cricklad Town) has no Arches.

At Drifelde and down; springs arise which run on the East side of Latton and force their waters into Tems West of Isey.[324]

On a Tombstone in the little Church-yard of Creeklade, I read this Epitaph,

> Underneath this Tomb, alas lyes twain
> Who lived in one, and so shall rise again.

A short description of Cricklade in verse follows, see Chapter 5 'An exploration in verse'

Hannington Bridge *f.4b*

I AM TOLD HANNINGTON Bridge is the next, below Crecklad of any note, built of Timber, for horse and foot people, to go over the River, and there is a foord by it, for Carts, Wagons, and Coaches, to go through the Water. Mr Freak lives at Hannington.

Baskerville returns to Hannington Bridge, number 3 in his list of Thames bridges, later in the volume (see below). His description of Lechlade leads on to St John's bridge nearby.

---

321 Rodbourne.
322 Braydon, Purton.
323 Ashton Keynes.
324 Driffield, Eisey.

Leach-lade

ff.8-8b

Is a small market Town in Glocester shire in the Rode to Cyrencester and Glocester.

The way hence leads through Fairford to these places.

Leach-lade Market is kept on Tuesday.[325]

I can not yet learn whether they have any fairs there. < 'A fair the 10 August'.>

But St Johns Bridge-fair about half a mile from it, is one the most eminent in England.

This town has good Inns, and brave Medows by it,

And here is fine Angling in dry Summers for fish.

They have 1 fair Church with a steeple seen a great way from Hills over this pleasant place interlac'd with watry Meanders.

Here stands a good house by the Church which Sir Edward Battars or Bathers was Master. <Bathurst>

Some tell me Sir Thomas Cutler has married a Daughter of his <and Mr Coxeter another who lives in that house> And I am told Mr Loader and Mr Oatridge are gentlemen who now live in town 1692.

Many boats come hither to lade and unlade goods, I have seen 6 or 8 boats togeither at their Wharfe.

For besides Corn of all sorts which they lade to go down stream. Here comes from Severn and Avon landed at Teuxbery where both these Rivers do unite and elswere, on horses and in Carts and Wagons by land great weights of Cheese especially that sort gos by the name of Chesshier Cheese, for here about The Boates Masters have Warehouses to secure their goods; and Hops in time of scarcity, and other goods comes from London-ward hether and are sent as aforesaid by land to Severn and thence in Boats to Bristol and elswere; and in ships to Ireland.

St John's Bridge

The next below Hannington bridge is about 140 yards in length thwarting the River between Glocestershier and Berks, It has 11 Arches to vent water in time of floods but 2 of these arches are great, built over the Main stream where loaden boats go through.

Two Inns are by this bridge viz. the *Bear* opening upon the bridge where now Mors lives 1692. And the *Baptist* or *St Johns head*, the best Inn, a little

---

325 Lechlade. Saturday first written then crossed out.

from the bridge in Glocestershier where Master and Miss Baker did formerly live, but now they have let it [to] Dame Hodson[326] and her son.

St John Bridge fair, is kept on the 29 day of August in the Meadow below the bridge on Glocestershier side, to which Oxford boats and others resort to sell Ale, Beef and Carrots, and to carry goods from this fair down stream, And here at a Mill below this Meadow, Leach flu runs into Tems.

which stream I suppose divides Glocester shier from Oxford shier.

It is a great fair for Cattle and Cheese, and here you meet with brave sage Cheese no place elswere in England shows the like, much diversified in figures, green and white, as to round chees, and some in shape of Dolphins and Mermaids as Countrey Carvers display them in Chees fats.

Some little sage Chees of late has been sold at Newbridge fair, which fair since Sir Edmond Warcope[327] got the Charter is not above 20 yeers standing Anno Domini 1693

A list of Thames bridges and ferry boats

(ff. 16-17)

AN ACCOUNT OF Bridges over the famous River Tems beginning at Cricklad the highest navigable place for Boats with the names of Bridges on this River, the number of Arches in each bridge and the measure of yards according to my paces which is nigh the same measure from hence to London Bridge.

1st Cricklad Bridges in Glocester shier side are 580 paces or yards over see more at large at the beginning of this Book[328]

2 Hannington Bridge I have not yet seen

Castle Eaton bridge was inserted here. It meant the description of Hannington bridge on a small piece of paper added in to the folio at this point became number 3.

[2] Castel Eaton bridge is built with timber and stone Peers and plank and

---

326 Bodson written first and crossed out.
327 'Edward' written first. Sir Edmund Warcup, Lord of Northmoor, secured the grant of two annual fairs in 1675; they were held in an inclosed meadow of c. 10 a. adjoining the Standlake road north-east of Newbridge. VCH (Oxon) 13 pt 1.
328 *f.4* above.

railes tis about 73 yards over

34 arches for water to pass and at the end of a long stone casway a bridge of 2 arches Postes between them makes 8 arches. And here are

<3 Hannington Bridge is about 120 yards over the river and is built of partly stone peers partly timber posts between. 4 great stone Peeres and 4 timber 8 arches besides to vent water in time of Floods 16 in all. Covered with timber Plankes and some o'm are pitch'd with stone upon the plankes. Horse and foot people go over the bridge. Carts wagons and coaches goe through the water by the bridge out of Wiltshire to Kempford[329] in Glowster shier. On Wiltshier side are 2 planks for foot voak to pass in time of floods before they come to the Arches. Tis about 3 miles from Highworth town. Sanders Alehouse is in Wilts, hard by the bridge.>

4 St Johns Bridge is 140 paces or yards over and has 11 Arches.

5 Radcot Bridge, the maine streame where boats pass through is about 22 yards over and has 3 great Arches;

The second streame has a bridge with two Arches which leads to Wyer,[330]

The 3d streame has a bridge over with 4 Archies but not for great boats to go through see more in a sheet of paper,[331]

6 New bridge on Barksheir side has 17 Arches to the main bridge,

The Main bridge has 6 Arches and is about 53 pace or yards over

On Oxford sheir side beyond the maine bridge are 28 Arches

The Causway on Oxfordshire side is about 300 yards and the Causway on Barkshire side are 373.

And in all over Causways and Bridge about 726 yards, over 51 Arches, to vent water in great flouds;

Bablock Hythe has a great boat to carry over Carts and Coaches

Ensham[332] has a great boat to bear horses over

between Witam and Woolvercot[333] is a stone bridge that has two Arches

329 Kempsford.
330 Could this be Friar's Court?
331 The sheet of paper seems not to be bound in with the folio.
332 Eynsham.
333 Wytham, Wolvercote.

through which laden boats do pass, and here by the help of foards and their bridges both horse and foot do pass into each County viz. Barks and Oxford shire see more in a sheet of paper.[334]

Oxford Bridges

Hinksey Bridge containes 18 Arches from the foot path which come from Hincksey ascending by stone steps into the horse Casway viz. from the place to the South side of Fryer Bacon's study are 20 Arches, North of Fryer Bacon study are 3 Arches and 1 over Grampond stream which makes 4 Arches on that side[335]

The whole number amounting to 42 Arches

The bridge is about 100 yards over beginning at the South side of the Arch south of the Study and so paceing through the Gate way as far as the Quine of the wall which turns into the Wharfyard

The whole length of these Bridges and Causway may be a mile and 1/2

Maudlen Bridge[336]

Is about 220 yards over, and it has 20 Archies for the waters of Charwell[337] to pass

So that reckoning all these passes for waters and the length of causeways it may measure a great deal of the length of Essex bridge in Hungary which some say is 3 miles over the Danube

At Sandfoard[338] Ferry when the water is high, is a boat to carry horse and man over

Collome Bridge[339] is about 100 yards over and has 6 Arches

Hart Bridge[340] is about 270 yards over and hath 17 Arches

---

334 Similarly not present.

335 Friar Bacon's Study was a gateway at the north end of Folly Bridge; it was so named because it was supposed it was used as an observatory by Roger Bacon. It was demolished in 1779. 'Folly' was the name of a mid-seventeenth-century tenant. 'Grampound' is presumably part of the 'Grandpont', the long causeway and bridges over the Thames to the south of Oxford. Grandpont tithing was in Berkshire. VCH (Oxon) 4; Thacker, *The Thames Highway* (1920), 118.

336 Magdalen.

337 Cherwell.

338 Sandford-on-Thames.

339 Culham.

340 Hart bridge near Appleton, a short distance below Newbridge.

at Cliffton Ferry[341] is a great boat to carry horse and man over,

Dorchester Bridge in London roade thwarts Thame River neer its entrance into Tems. It is about 220 yards over and vents water through 11 arches in floody times

At Shilling Ford[342] ferry is a great boat to waft over Carts Coaches horse and man.

Wallingford bridge is 310 yards over and has 19 Arches
    15 is a number cut on a stone of the Bridge
    it was in the year 1692 when we saw this Bridge and some say it was built so many years before this date of the Lord viz. 1692

341 Clifton Hampden.
342 Shillingford.

Radcot Bridge and Coxwell Barn, Oxfordshire, both fourteenth century in origin, were features of the scene near Bayworth described by Thomas Baskerville.

5
AN EXPLORATION IN VERSE OF COUNTRYSIDE AND RIVERS
within a day's horse-ride from Oxford

T HE NARROW FOLIO in the Harleian collection of manuscripts in the British Library (Harleian 4716) contains a very mixed selection of Thomas Baskerville's writings. It consists of paper pages which have been mounted to conserve them, and the folios have been numbered. His son, Matthew Thomas Baskerville, later wrote his name in the book but was too young to have written the characteristic descriptions of rivers, bridges and countryside which it contains, one of which is dated 1692 and another 1693; Baskerville was then 63 years old.

Inserted at the beginning of the folio is a page headed 'No 1', a tantalising indication that there were probably more writings than have been collected together here. It appears to be one small section of a verse account of the Deal area, another about Hinton Waldrist and Longworth, a third about ladies and ladies' hats, and a fourth about a river or sea trip where there is good air compared with London smoke, another indication of Baskerville's keen awareness of air quality. The last verse was written on the page when it was the other way up. Folio 3 is a draft of an account of his friends Mr Coward and Mr Stedman, having as he said 'room in this scantling of paper',[1] which was copied more neatly into the Rawlinson volume (*see* Chapter 3 'Oxford'). On the verso are some accounts. The main verse narrative set out below follows a description of Cricklade and its bridge, and occupies folios 4 to 11b. There is then a list of people put to death as a result of the civil war (*see* Chapter 6 'Miscellaneous Writings'), and a note of trees at Bayworth and Sunningwell (*see* Chapter 2 'Family and Kin'). On folios 16 to 17 are more descriptions of some bridges; these and the prose description of Cricklade are presented in Chapter 4. A

---

1 'Scantling' is more usually applied to structural elements in a ship, of which TB had a seaman's knowledge.

separate booklet listing the taverns in London and 10 miles round London is bound in at the end, and is set out in Chapter 7 'London Taverns'. A last page in this composite folio volume contains miscellaneous notes in and about Bampton church which have not been transcribed.

A major component of the volume is the verse narrative of journeys in the area to the west of Bayworth and Stanton Harcourt, mainly in Gloucestershire, and was based largely on the prose accounts of his travels which are in a different manuscript (*see* Chapter 4 'Journeys in Industrious England'). He specifically refers to earlier journeys, and repeats some of the observations and anecdotes. The verse was carefully written, making use of lines ruled on the pages, with very few alterations or corrections. With his usual tendency to be stimulated by a place-name to write about matters loosely connected, there are occasional prose interruptions to the verse, or perhaps he had not yet managed to work those observations into verse.

Descriptions of the countryside in verse were fashionable in the seventeenth century. Michael Drayton's Poly-Olbion (1612, 1622) a 15,000-line poem, navigates the nation county by county; it was a more ambitious and literary project than Baskerville's, whose verse is rather more everyday.[2] John Taylor, the water poet, also wrote much about his travels in verse, and like Baskerville did interrup the verse with prose interludes. Baskerville's verse starts with a boat trip on the Thames or Isis, almost an imitation of Taylor's journeying, and there is a definite theme of tracing the rivers flowing into the Thames, and of noting their value to the fisherman; but the boat trip could not be continued up smaller rivers and once more Baskerville is 'jogging on', on horseback. He notes good inns and inn-keepers, and his exploration of rivers does take him into some territory not covered in the prose travels, at least not as far as accounts of them have survived. Some of the verse works well, but he was defeated in his attempts to express some of his observations in that form. Nonetheless, there are insights into seventeenth-century English life, and his own character shines through.

~~~

British Library, MS Harl. 4716

The first page of the booklet, headed 'No.1', contains four different, apparently hastily-written drafts in verse.

2 https://poly-olbion.exeter.ac.uk/

No. 1.

Deal and Dover in Kent

Nor dry ground at Deal by Dover
Nor other places which the sea did cover
For on our side sea did cover
Many thousands acres of land
Which now are grown a pleasant strand
But below Dover tis other wise
For there the sea did higher rise
So that by Chichester Selsy steeple
Is now scarse seen by any people[3]
And the needels or rockes so white
Standing by the Iland of Wheght
Shewes once you joyn'd to Old England
But now Hurst forts built on that strand
And tydes stir twixt the Ile and fort
And ships sayl there and fish do sport.

Hinton Waldrist and Longworth in the Vale of the White Horse, historically in Berkshire now in Oxfordshire

now from Hinton over a fine down
you may walk on to Longworth town
where ninty tow lives for certain
ParsonBlagrove[4] and Mr Martin
but maister Sanders he good man
hath leaft his house is dead and gone
Adams can make boots without fault
Aunt C...oway makes pure good malt
that dame Weston she yet sels Ale
And gardenners set goods to sale
for peopel here do get renown
by laboring in their garden grounde
to raise carrots Turnips and gather peese

---

3 While there is erosion of the coast at Selsey, there appears no basis for the folk tale of Selsey church steeple being under the sea, and bells being heard in storms. VCH (Sussex) 4; https://www.eastbournearchaeology.org.uk/?page_id=171.
4 Jonathan Blagrove MA Oxford, Magdelen Hall; rector Oddington 1679-1699 and rector Longworth in diocese of Salisbury 1681-1699 (death). CCEd; Foster.

your Oxford cittizens to please
And sometimes a bouncing cabbage
fills the Chops of ranting baggage

The dangers of entangling with women when dressed up

Our little mathers are pretty things
when tied about wth silken strings
But when in stature they arise
Advanceing Towers toward the skyes[5]
and glistring linnen do put on
as if they would out vie the sunn
with high forheads and loafty lookes
And thoughts streacth'd on Tenter hooks
The man whos quivers full of them
They'l make him stare abroad for men
or else to live therafter
drink small beer and good spring water
that happy he may be hereafter
when good men mingle with his daters
or from betwixt their pleasing thighs
a lasting Issue may arise
God who gives us nightly songs
Joynes peopel every where in throngs
but if hasty death who oft does rage
should drive poor mankind of the stage
the divel may crawl out of's hell
and march about without controwl

Written upside down on the same page

now some voaks toes perhaps may itch
to give mine arse a kick o're the britch
because I gave 'um so much ramble
at sea to make their guts to wamble
but Ile tell them that London smoak
as suddenly again will choak
so therefore breath a while this aire

---

5 Compare the headdresses of women in Newbury Chapter 4.

in time youl see another faire
where voak do ramble about so thick
that you may stir them with a stick

~ ~ ~

A few lines of verse conclude the Cricklade material, and introduce the main verse.
Baskerville wrote the headings to each separate incident or waterway.

Two Churches, Creekelade Town dos grace;
And one faire street, their Market place
Their Markets kept on Saturdays,

As people here about do say,
And 4 fairs they do keep here,
In the Compas of a yeer:
First   The 3rd Tuesday after Easter
            The 2nd St Matthewes day (Tuesday in April for the fair)
            The 3rd <in our Almanak I noted the 2nd>
            The 4.

                                                        Rey Flu:

Here Roughton river called Ree[6]
Joynes with the Tems as you may see,
So farwell Cricklad, come off that ground,
We'el sail in Boats, towards London Town,
For this now is, the highest station,
Up famous Tems for Navigation,
But when th 'tis joyn'd with Bath Avon,
Then row your wherrys farther on,
For Baskervile, Matthews were Projectors,
How to do it since Lords Protectors,[7]
Who did conclude, Sixty Thousand Pounds,
Would throughly open, each river ground,
For by power of Lockes, Rains, and Fountains,
They'll make Boats to dance, upon the mountains,
But further yet, to ease your mindes,
How these great works, were then design'd,
Here read their Book, there you will see,
'Twas possible, such things might be.

Interruption concerning Hannington Bridge see Chapter 4

But I'le return, our Boats move on,
We're come to bridge of Hannington
So, here if any are now dry

6 Wroughton and the river Ray; *flu: fluvius.* The Ordnance Survey marks the land as
   liable to flooding.
7 Four bills were introduced into parliament after the Civil War to join the Avon and
   the Thames but were defeated; the first stage of the link was made in the early 18th
   century. VCH (Wilts) 4.

Here's Ale to quench your thirst hard by,
In sixteen hundred ninety tow,
Sanders made Ale, to serve the Crew,
Ingolsom[8] is on Wiltshier side,
Is here about 'tis not deni'd,
Where my friend Loader, has some land,
As people there, do understand,
And the Amneys Ise bear in hand,
Are all on Gloster-sheir land,
At Holy-Rood Amney Pledwell's alive,
And Dunce, at Down Amney, before he wiv'd.[9]
Kempford is now Lord Weymouths land,[10]
Is built upon the Gloster strand,
At a distance brave Parks appear,
For ought I know, well stokt with deer,
The famous Thinn, of Long Leet Park,
Was a kind kinsman to this spark,
Which in the days of pleasant yore,
Treated great Monmouth o're and o're.
Ten days at least that Duke did stay,
And feast'd at Longleet, every day.
Fourteen Tables were dayly spread,
With brave victualls, and good bread,
At the lowest Tables, as some say.
Your farmers din'd every day,
I rode one day by that great house,
While they were merry and did carouse,
That house so big to me did appeer,
There's scarce a bigger in any shier,
But it was the unhappy fate,
Of this rich man, in Coach too late,
In a street nigh White Hall-Pallace,
There devills did show their Malice,

8 Inglesham. See below for references to Ampney Crucis.
9 Ampney Crucis; Robert Pleydell owned the estate when Sir Robert Atkyns was writing (1712). Down Ampney was owned by Edmond Dunch; one Edmond Dunch married the Hungerford heiress. HoP.
10 Kempsford was owned by Sir Thomas Thynne, and he inherited Longleat in 1682. Thomas Thynne (died 1682) was a friend of the Duke of Monmouth but in 1686 the family declined to support his attempted rebellion. VCH (Glos) 7.

For from a Blunderbus a sore blow,
Did lay this Gallant very low,[11]
Great Monmouth Duke, a while before,
Leaft that Coach, where Thin lay in's gore,
And the Moon that night, Amaz'd with horror,
Did shine upon us with bloody Colour,
And his griev'd sister Madadam Hall,
Died quickly after, her brothers fall,
She was wife to one, of good renown,
A Grave Justice, in Bradford Town.

Red Pool

But while these sad stories disturb your minds,
Wee'r got by the help of water, and winds,
Down the Isis into Red Pool,
So here wee'l stop a while and cool,
For Boats do oft come hither to lade,
Malt, Barly, and other good to trade,
Down to Oxford, and Abingdon,
And thence in Barges to London,
For wharfingers, a house provides,
To keep goods dry, on Wiltshire side.[12]

Coln flu:

Here conjunctions, famous prove,
On the score of united love,
For here about Cown River wends,[13]
Its water into little Temes,
And so these pleasing Banks they wash,
And help the Boats, down with a flash.

---

11 A journey to Longleat which was not included in TB's written accounts. An inscription on the monument to Thomas Thynne in Westminster Abbey records that he was shot in the Haymarket, London, on 12 February 1681/2. TB was aware of the news.
https://www.westminster-abbey.org/abbey-commemorations/commemorations/thomas-thynne

12 Fred Thacker 'after much enquiry' concluded that Red Pool was at the elbow in the river at Inglesham; the river was part of the Wiltshire boundary. Thacker, *The Thames Highway (1920), 31.*

13 Thacker noted that 'An aged deaf man at Denham, in Middlesex, once spoke to me of his river as the 'Cown', to rhyme with 'own'.' Thacker, *The Thames Highway (1920), 36.*

Cown stream is like Collaterall line,
Ile trace its Banks, I hope to finde,
Something besides Earth and Water,
Here's fish, and fowl, prepar'd for slaughter,
Brave Troutes do prime and Caper at flies,
And then they'l vanish in a trice,
And now I see where the houses stand,
Built on these banks to shelter man.

Castle Eaton

'Tis Castleaton saith my friend,
That's up next stream, as Coln dos wend,
But my friend he is mistaken,
In Wiltshire stand Castleaton,
And there I think Sir Steven Fox,[14]
Has land so rich 'twill fat an Ox.
For soyle in these parts are so rare,
It gives Beasts delicious fare.

Ferfat or Fairford

So next upstream, is Ferfat town,
A place for Inns, of good renown,
Barker they say's Lord of this place,
Whose house hard by, adds a grace,[15]
And now remember ere you pass,
Go into Church and see that glass,
There you'll find, in Glaziers paint,
The figures of some Ancient Saints,
A wonder 'tis be it spoaken,
Roundheads leaft it so unbroken.
Hathorp is pretty nigh this Town,
'Tis also seated hard by Cown.[16]

Cown Allen[17]

14 Castle Eaton. Stephen Fox, knighted in 1665 for considerable services to Charles II in exile. In his own words 'a wonderful child of providence', Fox rose to immense wealth and public prominence from genuinely humble origins. Elected to parliament for various Wiltshire constituencies. HoP.

15 Samuel Barker's big square house and the glass in the church was referred to in TB's journey to Bristol (Chapter 4).

16 Hatherop.

17 Coln St Aldwyn. Several generations of the Fettiplace family were lessees of the

And so much for this watry town,
I'le now fish upward on the Cown,
And try my skill to catch some Trouts,
And bring the matter so about,
If I can catch some fish to eat,
At Bybery[18] Inn, there I'le treat,
For I hope, Mr Fetiplace,
Will give me leave to tread on's grass,
For he has now in Cown Allen,
The best house there for to dwell in.

>   Bybery

So now I've fish the Sun's nigh down,
Let's jog away to Bybery Town,
And seize on beds at Crawford's house,
And then wee'l tipple and Carouse,
For this Ale is of their brewing,
You'l digest it without spewing.
A dish of trouts is meat sublime,
Had we here but some good Wine,
Taken in the dry Month of July,
Then they are best to eat, truely.

>   I read this Epitaph in
>   Bybery Churchyard.

Your glass doth run, time will not stay,
Make use of time, now whilst you may.

Here Sir William Coventry
Delighted to live and dye,
Reputed a good housekeeper,
Allways free of his good liquor,
In Sacvills house he did quarter,[19]
For poor Sackvile is a Martyre
Troubled with distracted thoughts

manor from the Dean and Chapter of Gloucester. Giles Fettiplace (died 1702) was
a prominent Quaker. VCH (Glos) 7.

18 Bibury.

19 Sir Thomas Sackville acquired Bibury manor in 1625. His grandson who succeeded
to the manor was a lunatic. VCH (Glos) 7. Sir William Coventry of Whitehalll and
Bampton was knighted in 1665; died 1686. HoP.

I wish to sence he may be brought.
Frank Coventry I'le here bewayle
For rich Kindred was his Jayle
They died, and Lands tumbled so fast
On Frank, to grave he went at last
The mournfull view of his lost friend
Was that which brought him to his end
    He was for Conversation
    A man beloved in this Nation.

                Bybery Inn

Now as to Inn of Bybery
How the Rode by it doth lye,
Oxford Coaches to Bath go bye,
And sometimes where they stop and lye,[20]
For Crawford was an Oxford man,
Tho now from hence he's dead and gone,
Yet in remembrance of his life,
He leaft Ten Children and a wife,
The woman look'd so maiden like,
As if again sh'd touch and strike,
And so she did, for Gafer Scuse,
Has again broake open her sluce,
And he now is the very man,
that lives Inkeeper at the *Swan*,
And his wife is still as fruitfull.
As if she would be ever youthfull.

                Bybery Wells

Here do these famous springs arise,
Which makes your Trouts to live and thrive[21]
The Springs so hot from earth do flow
They do not freeze in frost or snow
And some say, if they do not flatter,
Horses are cur'd by this water,

---

20 Francis Crawford was assessed on 3 hearths in Bibury in 1672, and this is presumed
    to be the coaching inn called *The Swan* opposite Arlington Mill. TB is referenced
    for the fact that it was occupied by a widow at the end of the 17th century. VCH
    (Glos) 7.
21 In the early 20th century a trout farm was established next to Arlington mill. VCH
    (Glos) 7.

So if you'l know, how to apply it
You may go thither and try it

One Solus lives in Bybery Town
And the Parson's brave house stands nigh Cown
Solus is a man that is Kin
To Thomas Sure my loving friend
Who from his observations
Help'd me me in these relations,
He is a man who understands
Learning, both on Sea and Land
Has skill in Phisick Phlebbotomy
And in the Artes of Fishery,
Birding and other Artes also
As those at Hinton and Duxford know,
He brought his wife from Bybery
I wish them both, felicity.
   Chidworth. Coln Rogers. Coln Dean.
Up staires againe, we must venture
And into brisker Aire enter,
E're wee shall find, the highest springs
Contributors to these good things,
'Tis Cown Rogers and Cown Dean
That you'l find next up the great stream.
But if you'l follow a lesser spray
That water leads another way.
        Chidworth.
Up to Chidworth[22] to a fountaine
Which there breakes out, from that mountaine
Just above Master Howes find house[23]
And to his Pool where fish Carrouse
This Pool is in a Garden sweet,
Where Maidens may wash and cleanse their feet,

---

22 Chedworth.
23 Sir Richard Howe owned Little Compton or Cassey Compton before 1701; it had
  come to John Howe by 1636. Johannes Kip illustrated the house, garden and park
  showing the River Coln canalised close to the house. The spring, now pouring
  through a stone crocodile's mouth, rises in Compton Abdale and joins the Coln at
  Cassey Compton. Jones, *Johannes Kip;* VCH (Glos) 9.

And here in town once Ale I bought
To wash my mouth, and cleanse my throat[24]

Chidworth Beacon on a
Mountain of Cotswoald,

But yet to add to your desire
Get up staires a little higher,
And there you'l find on top that plain
A Beacon which dos yet remain,[25]
So here you may if you please
See Welch Mountains beyond the Sea
Whose tops I think if day be clear,
To Barkshire Woodton do appear
For looking thence both wayes with eyes
The hills in two shires I espye
Viz, Woodton-hills of which wee'r prowd
And Monmouth Mountains as high as clouds
So from our Hills as doth appear
We may pry into Ten shiers,
The like I think, is no where found
In any place on English ground[26]

The Shires visible, on
Sunningwell and Wootton
hills, are

Bucks, Berks, Wilts, and Gloster shire,
On Woodton hills do plain appear,
And Monmouth Mountains on Chidworth downs
May be seen above Woodton Town,
And hills in Hants peeps through a glade
Which rains and River Tems hath made,
So hence, if hills to us appear
They are Easterly from Kings-Clear,
North-Hamton, Bedford shire and Herts[27]
I have seen on our hills in Berks,

---

24 See Chapter 4 and the verse below for a description of when TB and six other
   men rode through Chedworth on their way to Withington and were handsomely
   accommodated at the inn.
25 Chedworth beacon SP0440 1232.
26 Boar's Hill in Wootton is 143 m (468ft).
27 Kingsclere in Hampshire, Northampton, Hertfordshire.

And Oxfordshier, is our next County
We dayly feed upon its bounty.
                              Withington
Now you have view'd this Countrey over
Lets jog on further to discover
What we can above Cown-dean
Of other town, upon Coln stream,
So once again I do espye
Sweet Withington 'tis in my eye,
And now Im'e got into't again
Here's our kind Dame and goodman Pain
At the *George Inn*, they'r both alive,
I wish u'm health and both to thrive
For 17. 7 horse and men
Were fed at night and morn agen,
Good meat, Methegline, Ale and Brandy
Here we had as good as can be
And to fulfill each mans desire
In cold season we had good fire,
So God be with these honest people
Wee'l gang to yonder Tower or Steeple[28]
                              Combton of the hole
This they call Comton of the hole[29]
Where springs break forth, without controwl
                              Frogmill
Nex(t) above this you'l find Frogmill,
The water makes a currant still,
Here Dame Powell[30] had a being
But now she has leaft of seeing,
She kept good Cyder, Wine, and Beer
And good meats, to make good Cheere
This about 3 miles off doth lye
From springs that rise at Cubberly.
                    Shipton-Olife, Shipton Sallis,

28 As TB implies, the *George Inn* was close to the church, and the building, partly
   medieval, is now divided into a house and cottage; from the end of the 18th
   century it was denied a licence. VCH (Glos) 9.
29 Compton in the hole now called Compton Abdale.
30 See Chapter 4 on Dame Powell and the two Shipton parishes.

Whittington

Next up stream lyes Shipton Olife
And then you come to Shipton Sallis
Where Mirs Heydon[31] had a being
If she had not leaft of seeing
But highest springs, rise at Whittington[32]
and so from hence I'le get me gon.

Northleidge

The Downs are brave, the Aire is sweet
I'le therefore travail on my feet,
From Whittington cause pathes are beat
'Tis not 5 miles unto Hamnet,[33]
So here I find a watry veine
That's something more then heavenly raine
Descending into Norleidg town,
South from the Rode, on that brave Down,
Here if you have a mind to stay
You may have drink, and your horse hay
Both very good of Master Stone
At *Kingshead* if he be not gone,[34]
Here is a great Church and Tower
And good Almes-houses for the poor.
Spinster I think, is here best trade
Stockings and cloath, of yarn are made
Markets they have and fairs also,
But when those days are, I don't know.[35]

Stowell, Alesworth and
Burford Downs,

31 Mistress Heydon; Susanna Heydon inherited Shipton Solers manor from her husband Robert but passed it to her son Robert (died 1668) from whom it came to his young daughter Susanna. A number of members of the Heydon family held the manor from the mid-16th century. VCH (Glos) 9.
32 Powerful springs rise at Syreford in Whittington parish. Jones, *The Cotswolds* (1994), 32-33.
33 Northleach, Hampnett.
34 The King's Head, now Walton House, was the principal coaching inn in Northleach. It was kept until mid-18th century by a prosperous Northleach family called Stone. It ceased to be an inn soon after 1859. VCH (Glos) 9.
35 In the margin there is a note added in brown ink 'market on Wensd - faires St Peters day'.

When waters congregate together
Then they asume the name of River
So below Northleidge as I'm true
These waters are called Leach flu
And at Northleidge I'le swear on book,
Their waters is called Leach brook
Which trills away to Stowell town[36]
And by Aldworth[37] nigh Burford Downs
Here take your pleasure in florid May
And you will find these Downs are gay.
Bestride your horse and cast of care,
And gently breath this fragrant Aire
For this may cure your foggy lungs
And make you breath out pleasant songs
Then pray you alight from of your horse
And walk upon this verdant grasse
And then some mountain plants you'l spye
Very beautious to your eye,
Here is small Burnet brave in wine
For to refresh and cheere the mind.
Wine you need not ride fur for't
Good wine is always at Burford
Many beautifull plants here be
As Simplers in their Monthes do see
But that which makes these Downs so gay
Is Pulsitilla in Month of May,
Though for its name if you ask all
Some will call it flower Pascal,
Of all the flowers in my eye
Its most like the Emonie,[38]
Who's colour is of darkish blew
And so I'le leave them to your view.

Racing

Next for the glory of this place

36 Brown ink correction to Stowell - 'Eastington', the farming settlement close to
   Northleach town.
37 Aldsworth.
38 Anemone Pulsatilla or Pasque flower, now known as Pulsatilla vulgaris though
   related to the anemone.

Here has been rode many a race
Such Aparitions here apeer
As are not seen every where,
King Charles the 2d I saw here
But I've forgotten in what year
The Duke of Monmouth here also
Made his horse to swet and blow,
Lovelace, Penbrook and other gallants
Have been ventring here their tallents
And Nicholas Bainton on black Sloven
Got silver plate, by labor and drudging
Sutlers bring Ale, Tobacco, Wine,
And this present have a fine time
So at last a golden shower,
Into Burford town dos power
And there, such as will spend may stay
For I must jog another way.

East Leach, Bothorp, Sowthorp.

Down hill to Eastleach and Bothorp
And down Leach flu to Sowthorp,[39]

Faringdon Parvva

Faringdon Parva is in sight,
Of Leachlade where I'le lye this night[40]
At the *White Hart* which Ange my friend
Without any sinister ends
But love, to thank him for that book
The same before on which you lookt
For here 'twas lodg'd by Baskervile
And here it lay with Ange a while,
But my names sake has since that
Gee'n me the books and River-Plat

Account of Lechlade in prose here and St John's Bridge, see Chapter 4 section 12.

Highworth River,

39 Eastleach Turville, Eastleach Martin (also called Eastleach Bouthrop or Botherop), Southrop. VCH (Glos) 7.
40 Little Faringdon is to the north of Lechlade whereas Faringdon is well to the south-east.

The fair is done, each maid kist
So I crave leave to be dismist,
Away they ride, trot run and go
As fast as in the Morn they flo
So over bridge I'le gallop after
And search about for other water
And here I find a stream divides
Sweet Barkshier from the Wiltshire side
Which makes an Ile or watry Ham
between Buscot and Inglesham
And in Buscot I understand
Dwells a captain of our train bands
Master Loveden is his name
A person of good worth and fame
Long may he live in wealth and honour
With a kind lass to tumble on her[41]

Lord Chief Justice John Holt, son of my ancient acquaintance Sir Thomas Holt defunct, I am told has meanes in this Town.

Colshull and Hyworth

Colshull[42] and Highworth both apeer
I find I'me come to either, neer
On Colts-hill bridge I rode o're water
and so I went to Highworth after,
But mine eyes cauld not forbear
To gaze and see whats here and there
Highworth Town, houses tree and Towers
Made me gaze on't half an houre
But Coltshill buildings[43] being rare
Made me again that way to stare,
So asking about this and that
Some did mention Sir George Prat
And said, he was that worthy wight
Which built this house so brave and tyte,
And I suppose his honored wife

41 Walter Loveden and his wife Dorothy acquired Buscot manor in 1557. Edward
   Loveden was the owner when TB was writing his verse. Distant relatives retained
   Buscot until the mid-19th century. VCH (Berks) 4.
42 Coleshill.
43 See Chapter 4 Journey 7, also TB's prose description of Highworth.

Dos now live there, is yet alive,
Who keeps her gardens very neat
And buildings too, very compleat,
The prospect oft so well doth lye
'Tis very alluring to the eye
Alderman Prat some say did poure
Upon Sir George a golden shower
And this made Masons go to wars
Fight, raze, and cut the free stone quars
And men of Mettal stirr'd about
In every quarter to find out
Fit materialls for to grace,
And beautify, this pleasant place
So farwell Coltshill, as from thee I went,
My mind did run on Adams banishment

Highworth Rode

The way to Highworth town is lowly
So horses here, moves hoofs but slowly
But as you get up higher ground
And mount again toward Highworth town
You shall to gratify your sight
Come in the Land, of Shitton come shite
For Cow turds stick on many places
And are to walls, shitten cases
This shows that wood is pretty deer
As they find who buy it there
For Cole a great way of dos come
And also deere bought by the Tun.

Highworth

Highworth is a good Market town
Where beasts are sold to stock your grounds
On Wednesdays, they come up hether
To sell in fair and fowl weather,
Two fairs they keep yeerly I say
Lamas and on Michaelmas day
At Lamas day brave lambs are sold
Worth many pounds of glistring gold
And here, if I'me not mistaken
Is a Cheap place, to buy bacon

A Baylife is their Chief Commander
To Chastise tongues, that do slander,
Their Church stands high in the weather
8 bells in Towr call Voak hither
Durham was a Minister here,[44]
But when, I did not note the yeer
He must not be a person mean
It must be Salisbury Dean
That injoyes the Parsonage here
Worth 500 pounds each year

Sinnington

The Warmfords of Sinnington[45]
Bury their dead when life is gone
In the south Ile of Highworth Church
By daylight, or in night by torch.

There I read this epitaph bestow'd on the father of the present Sir
Edmond Warnford

Buried in May 1650

His Epitaph

Sleep sweetly elect dust, under his care
That made thee breath, more holy thoughts than aire
When that blest soul dwell in thee, in whome grace
So soon thrust sin and death out of their place
To let in Christ, to whom hee's gon and stays
Combust a while, under God's own bright rays
But yet you both shall meet again, and shine
Sunlike beyond expression Death and time.

The Instability and Fickleness
of Human life

How fickel is our human life
Nature and Death always at strife,
One way there is we all come here
But more to go then days in yeer
Easter Six hundred Ninety tow
Old Hartwell was alive as you

---

44 Thomas Derham, vicar of Highworth with Sevenhampton 1662 until death in
   1702. TB is correct that Highworth was a prebend of the Dean of Salisbury. CCEd.
45 Warneford of Sevenhampton, a chapelry in Highworth parish. Sir Edmund
   Warneford of Warneford Place, Highworth (died 1700). HoP.

I merry was with him at *Crown*
That Inn was his, in Highworth town
But such his fate a few days after
I heard how he was Choak'd by water
Such was the fate of 'tother frind
'Twas water brought him to his end
Honest John Hearns some yeers before
And I, did vange to young Blower
Both were my friends, breath'd on such ground
They both did live in Abbey town[46]
Therefore since breath may cease tomorrow
Let's sing this song to vent out sorrow.
The Poets Allusion in this song
Shewing the ficklenes of human life,

1

The gloryes of Birth and State
Are shadows, not substantiall things[47]
There is no Armour 'gainst our fate
Death layes his Icey hands on Kings
Septers and Crowns must turmble down
And in the dust be aequall laid
With the poor Crooked sithe and spade.

2

Some men with swords may reap the fields
And plant fresh Lawrells where they kill
Yet proud Nerves at last must yeeld
They tame but one another still
Early and late we bend to fate
And must give up our lingring breath
Whil'st the pale Captive Creeps to death

3

The Garland withers on your brow
Then boast not of your mighty deeds
But on deaths purple Altars Mow[48]

46 Abingdon.
47 The first two lines are written at the bottom of the previous page, and the number
'1' for the first stanza was entered at the top of the next page.
48 James Shirley, poet and playwright (1596-1666); Mow in TB's script should be

See how the Victors Victim bleeds
All heads must come to the cold Tombe
Onely the Actions of the Just
Smells sweet, and blossoms in the dust.

End

Highworth town and Villages make a great
Parish, these be their names.
East Throp, West Throp, Frusson, Maggot Mill
Sinnington, Marson, Blundon, Cevel Hamton
Berriton,[49]   Gentry in Hyworth

Parish

Sir Edmond Warnford at Sinnington,
Sir John Earnly at Berriton,
Mr Cleane at Blundon,
Mr Husse at the same town,
Mr Bond at Maggot Mill,
Mr Southby at Marson, brother to Mr Southby of Caswell.
Mr Glide, Mr James, Mr Batson, also at Marson,

Cole diggers

As in Cole Countryes under ground
So I move slowly in my bounds
Yet I go on early or late
By sight heresay and musing Pate[50]

Coxwell

So then since I must name a Text
'Tis Coxwell, that shall be the next
This is now the Lady Prat's land
As those lives there, do understand[51]
And here if drye, you may have Ale,
From such as offer it to sale.   1693.
This by our River East doth ly

'Now'. The wording of the poem is not quite the same as in the version printed in the *Oxford Book of English Verse* (1949) 304-5; it may suggest TB had learnt it by heart, or there were variants published.

49 An early minster church, Highworth retained a large parish. Eastrop, Westrop, Fresdon, Maggot Mill, Sevenhampton, Blunsdon, Marston, Hampton, Burytown.
50 Which seems to be a description of his personal rate of progress in his travels.
51 Lady Pratt died in 1697? Her will separated the manor house from the manor. VCH (Berks) 4.

And here's is a Barn built brave[52] and high
So big and great it doth appeere
Scarce a bigger in any Shiere,
Excepting Chols Well mighty Hulk
May said to be, the greater bulk,[53]
But that with this, may not compare
For Coxwell Barn is built so rare
That when Chiefe Builder away did fly
On the score of some faults he should dye
This work stood still, like to diminish
'Cause non but this man, the barn could finish
Yet at length some strange Magnetick power
Drew the man back to indure a shower,
Yet not till this Barn was built brave, and high
And then poor man, he was forc'd to dye,
This Barn for length is little lesse
Then 63 yards I do guess
With Pillars and Rafters all of main Trees
No saw touch them as you may see
I viewed this brave Barn, upright and all thorow
And could find, no fault save a Porch too narrow.

Fi Harris Barn, Comner Barn[54]

Of tow barns more brave Berks may boast
So big, they'l contain a small King's host
Fi-Harris is the third for glory
Like Westminstr Hall built without story

---

52 'very' written at first to be replaced with 'brave and'. Great Coxwell was in Berkshire but is now Oxfordshire. The barn was built in the 14th century, next to the manor house, while Beaulieu Abbey owned the manor. VCH (Berks) 4. TB probably paced the length externally (199 ft), which compares with the internal measurment of 48 yards (144 ft).

53 The great barn at Cholsey, Berkshire, 303 ft long and the longest known in medieval England, was built by Reading Abbey, and demolished in 1815; the engraving in the *Gentleman's Magazine* vol 86 (February 1816) shows its enormous length and huge roof. Bond, *Monastic Landscapes* (2204); VCH (Berks) 3.

54 Fitzharris in Abingdon, Cumnor. Both were Abingdon Abbey estates. Fitzharris Farm is just north of Abingdon, and was one of the three central Abingdon abbey granges. A little of the fabric of Cumnor barn survives. Bond, 'The Reconstruction of the Medieval Landscape', *Landscape History*, 182 (1979–80), 64; Impey & Belford, 'The lost medieval barn of Abingdon Abbey at Cumnor', *Oxoniensis* (2017).

or beams, to trouble the sturdy Pitcher
By over working to spoyl his liquor
The fourth's at Comner neer that Church
I can not tell where it has a Porch,
But as to length in days of yore
'Tis now much shorter then before
                        The foundation of this Barn
                        is about 65 yards in length
These Barns stood up so stiff and stout
No winds did hurl these 4 about
In year of Charles Restauration
A dreadfull wind did grieve this Nation
It fell out in a Lenten time
When Voak at Abingdon drink wine
First Munday in Clean Lent a faire
made many to go there for Aire
But Aire and winds were in such rage
None but God could them aswage
for in our poor Sunningwell Town
five Barns were hurled on the ground
And Thousands more were turned over
As winds blew thwart from seas to Dover
So many Trees on ground did fall
As if the winds would blow down all
God grant again such winds may'nt come
Whilst I have eyes to this sun
            Soninghamton and Shrineham[55]
Here yet this River is a bound
To Berks shire and your Wiltshire ground
And here about waters invade
Lands, so that Meadows are made
And the fish prepare'd for slaughter
are very good in this fat water
Which are inrich'd by Various hills
When great showers from them do trill
This Sinning people do know
And those at Shrineham say 'tis so
Sinnington is on Wiltshire side

---

55 Sevenhampton and Shrivenham are north and south of the river Cole.

Shrineham doth in Berks abide
Shrineham is a fertile Soyle
Better then in many a mile
Declining towards the warm South
And so drawes heat from the Suns mouth
For blustring Winds and nipping colds
Are kept from hence by hills so bold
And Ashbery[56] stream dos run down
to mello Medows nigh this Town
And quench the thirst of man and beast
And melliorate winds from Northeast
So here if any where, fruits will thrive
Grass, Corn, roots, herbs, to keep's alive
But hempe so mighty high doth grow
I never saw it elsewhere so
Some stalkes big as Coulstaves for water
Which green may bear a weight thereafter
And to conclude here's rocky ground
Where Samphoyne-grass, dos now abound
All these occurring blessing stir
To make folke happy without demur.
Therefore next we will discover
What people here abouts do hower
And what Transaction have been here
for now I'm come to't very neer
So now I see 'tis no mean place
For 2 good Inns, their streets doth grace
And here's a Church built neer the rode
Different from the Ancient mode
Erected by a Judge called Martin[57]
Who was the builder on't for certaine
In days of peace before our wars
And sad bloody intestine jars
But Judge Martin is dead and gon

---

56 Ashbury.
57 Henry Marten was a judge in the High Court of Admiralty 1617-1641, and served
   several times as an MP for different constituencies. He was knighted 1616; died
   1641. He bought an estate at Longworth and rebuilt Longworth church, but held
   the presentation of Ashbury church, which was a sinecure. VCH (Berks) 4.

To him there did succeed a son
Who was a man of wit and sense
Good nature, learning, wit and Eloquence
He breathed his last in Chepsto Castle
There troubles and death with him did wrestle
His soul is free'd, his body lyes low
In Chepsto Church as Tombe doth show
And there upon't these words you'l finde
To shew to others what was his minde
     September the 9th 1680[58]
Was buried a true English man
Who in Barkshire was well known
To love his Countrey's freedome above his own
Who being immur'd full 40 yeers
Had time to write as doth appeer
     His Epitah[59]
Here or elswhere all's one to you to me
Earth Air or water grips my Gostles dust
None knowes how soone to be by fire set free
Reader if you an oft tri'd Rule will trust
You'l gladly do, and suffer what you must
My life was spent in serving you and you
And deaths my pay it seems, and welcome to
Revenge destroying but it self which I
To birds of pray leave my old cage and fly
E(x)amples preach to the eye care then mine says
Not how you end, but how you spend your days.
     end

Hardwick, Fettern are gentry here
And Blagrove to as 'twill apeere
Lancston at Bourton and his wife
Holloways sister both alive
Charles Holloway is his name
A man at Oxford of good fame

---

58 These words on Marten written larger than the rest of the verses.
59 The story of Henry Marten and his imprisonment in Chepstow Castle and the
    epitaph on his tomb were set out in one of TB's longer interruptions of his Oxford
    narrative and clearly impressed him. (See Chapter 6).

All 3 friends of ancient standing
Love and kindred, are commanding
Make me pay duty as here you see
To their present future memory
But he who bore the greatest sway
Was Major Wildman as they say
A happy Politician
Who here reaps pleas'd fruition.
Here Beccot house when rent and tore
He builds again nigh place before
Improves the Lands makes people stir
And worke for money without demur
There's scarse a Change or turne in State
That he had not his share in pate
Still happpy in old Age we see
Alderman Wildman now is he
In the famous City London[60]
Where a many have been undone
A many in these Revolutions
Have not made such good conclusion
For there be some Politick Pates
Keep watch and ward or'e City gates.

Brave Gardens are by Beccot house[61]
And lovely Pools where fish Carrouse
And Banket house is built so neat
Nothing can be more compleat
This Vission house was built by Martin
It stood when tother was tore for certain
Fair Thorne is a Gentleman here
So now I hope I shall get cleere

60 John Wildman was a leader of the Levellers and was critical of Cromwell.
   Frequently imprisoned, he lived for some years in Holland until 1688; he became
   a freeman of the City of London, an alderman as TB said, and was knighted in
   1692. He died in 1693.
61 Beckett Park in Shrivenham, sold by Henry Marten to John Wildman, who
   bought a number of royalist estates. Part of the manor house was burnt down
   during the Civil War. In the grounds are a large sheet of water and a rectangular
   summer-house or Banqueting House of 17th-century date locally ascribed to Inigo
   Jones. VCH (Berks) 4.

And take a flight to yonder downs
Westerly from Ashbery Town

The next folios list people put to death in the Civil Wars, followed by Bridges and Taverns.

6
MISCELLANEOUS WRITINGS

I
CAVALIER OR ROUNDHEAD?

Thomas Baskerville was too young to be taking sides in the years when Charles I was ruling without calling a parliament; when in 1640 the King was forced by financial necessities to call one, he was 10 years old. However, by 1649 and the execution of the King on 30 January 1648/9, he was 19 years old. He quite often dates a description or comment by reference to the execution of the King, but more often by the Restoration of Charles II in 1660, two exceptional events.

The civil war permeated memory of the past, as in his account referring to three Deans of Wells, where incidentally the date of his birth is recorded. (*See also* Chapter 2 on Thomas Baskerville's life and Chapter 3 on Oxford). In writing about some Deans of Wells, he referred to Walter Raleigh, Dean during the years of the wars 'being very hot', who was stabbed presumably because of his royalist allegiance. When describing St John's College, Baskerville recounted the efforts of the fellows to protect their plate from being taken by Charles I and melted down to make coins. His account of his journey through Essex in 1662 (*see* Chapter 4) contains a description of an event in the second civil war in the summer of 1648, when a Royalist army attempting to raise support for the King took refuge in Colchester from Sir Thomas Fairfax's pursuing Parliamentarian army, and withstood an eleven weeks seige.

References to other events in the Civil War were scattered through Baskerville's writings. He recounted that Sir William Waller's soldiers threw down four crosses near the church or in the churchyard in his description of 'Bayworth, Sunningwell, Hills and Rivers for fishing' (*see* Chapter 2). The soldiers also destroyed the glass in the chapel at Bayworth which Hannibal had probably created, it being 'cut in pieces'; this was mentioned in his lengthy writing on Oxford University (*see* Chapter 3) a propos Christ Church cathedral glass being taken down, which had been painted by the same Dutchman Van Linge.[1] He observed that the buildings in Faringdon were largely rebuilt after their destruction in the civil war.

There is no direct hint in his writings about his father's political sympathies or his own, but in 1649 the realities of the civil war came close to both: a group of Levellers, revolutionary members of the parliamentary army, arrived in Sunningwell, and some quartered at Bayworth. The Baskervilles were apprehensive that their finest pastures would be spoilt. Although there is no direct evidence, it could be that the two men quartered at Bayworth manor had been told that they would meet with a pleasant reception by Henry Marten, or perhaps that the Baskervilles, like many gentry, were not committed to either side. Marten was a neighbour, a Berkshire man, committed to the parliamentary cause. The Baskervilles were happy to spend at least one evening drinking with some Levellers. There is another, briefer account of the encounter with the Levellers in the List of those put to death after the Restoration. Typically, Baskerville recounts his and his father's experiences with the Levellers in the course of his history of Balliol College, written some 30 years after the event. The reminiscence was stimulated by mention of an erudite and significant member of the college in the 14th century, John Wycliffe ('John Wickles'). It is set out below.

~ ~ ~

(i) The Lollards, and the Levellers in Sunningwell and Burford, 1649
Bodleian Library MS Rawlinson D810 *(ff.36b-37)*

John Wickles

There were two of the name Masters of this house [Balliol] the latter is he of whome we now write; he was first Fellow hereof, then Master[2], and was he that gave the name to the Wicklevites. His letter written to the Pope is to be seen in Foxes Acts and monuments whom Balaeus Commends as liberally as Pitsaeus spends his black mouth upon. He was Publicque Reader in divinity in

---

1   Chapter 3 'Oxford'. Abraham van Linge's windows painted in 1630 to 1640 for Christ Church Cathedral at Oxford are an excellent example of the destruction of the lead line-method, the usage of <u>vitreous enamels</u> on glass as a blank canvas and then fired. Lead lining is used to hold together pieces of glass. The duration and intensity of the firing determined the final colour along with the colour and type of enamel. van Linge must have been born in 1604–5, as he was aged 29 when he matriculated at the University of Oxford as a privileged person on 4 July 1634, with his profession given as "Artis Peritus" (art expert).

2   Master of Balliol 1361.

the University mentioned in 5 severall writings in Abbots fly box by a publick Notary April. 9. 1361. He set up the doctrine of the Waldenses, who were called Lollards in England, who being also written Lolleards seem to be so called quasi Low Lords that is Levellers.

But here a word be the bye, since there was an Apparition of them in my time.

In Parlamentary days when Sir Tho: Fairfax was Generall and Cromwell Liuetenant Generall of the Armyes then afoot in England, some of them did mutiny and began to set up for Levelling.

This I here incert because their Randevouz or chief place of meeting was in Blagrove Lease near Sunningwell of which I was Spectator, where met about 10 or 12 Troops of horse in expectation of many more, who spent the best part of a Summers day in debates what to do, while we were expecting when these Gallants like a flight of Locusts would settle their horse in our best growing grass and eat all bare to the ground.

Now here quartered in Bayworth and Sunningwell a Fortnight or more before this meeting a Troop of horse who had for officers to overlook them one Perkins a Corporal and Searle a Quartermaster, who lay at my fathers house. These officers being in the Confederacy the Troop mounted a horseback this morning to meet the rest, but their hearts failing them, they stood Loyteringa good while in our upper Field whilst Corporall Perkins no doubt used the best Retorick he had to get them along wth him, but to no purpose for they slunk away over Sandford Ferry and the Corporall I think was faine to go alone to these Levellers, as being one of the Chief'st who was to head them. He was a big fat man, and had Redish haire which with his good nature bespake him to be Collerick as my Father and I found when we did sometimes Tipple good Ale wth Searle and him at dame Richardson's house. Here sometimes being elevated wth the great thoughts of what he might arive at, such like words would drop from him - you will see some sport e're it be long. But the wary Generals quickly put an end to those rash actions, for scarse were these hot spurs got from Blagrove-lease over new Bridge, but the Generals with their Army entring Abingdon and without stay marching forward took these Gallants a bed at Burford. Lieutenant Green anoth(er) Chieftains among them got a horsback and made his escape, but poor Perkins was taken and shot to death.[3] The rest upon their submission were pardoned and received into the Army again.

3 *Burford buildings and people in a Cotswold Town* (A Catchpole, D Clark, R Peberdy, England's Past for Everyone) ed S Townley, (Phillimore 2008) 93.

(ii) Some notes of those punished for participation in the Civil Wars

IT IS NOT CLEAR what exactly was in his mind when Baskerville prepared a list of people put to death in the Civil Wars. Whereas the verse account of an exploration of rivers in the same manuscript was a finished item and well-written, the list of deaths was not a finished production, containing corrections and indications of where the order of items should be different. It starts with one man hanged in 1640, and then a longer account of some involved in the Leveller movement, adding details not in the Rawlinson manscript version above. The list then continues with a number of other men punished for their involvement in the Civil War and subsequent unrest. He did describe Venner's accomplices as a 'bloody crew', and listed many more who were against monarchy than for it. However, compare the comments on Henry Marten in the verse account of his travels along the rivers to the west of Sunningwell, quoted below on page 247.

quoted below on page 247.

~~~

British Library Harleian 4716 *(ff.12b-14b)*

A List of people put to death in the Civill warrs in and about London
In King Charles 1rsts time
1640 One Bensted a seaman was apprehend(ed) and hanged in St Georges Fields in May being one of the Crew that came to plunder Bishop Lawd's Palace in the night, but being forewarn'd prevented them.[4]

<div align="center">1649</div>

Lieutenant Col: Lilborn head of the faction called Levellers was seised for a book of his called *England's new change-discovery*[5] which was the bottome and

---

4   On May 11th, 1640, a 500-strong horde of artisans and apprentices assaulted Lambeth Palace, home to William Laud, Archbishop of Canterbury. On the night of the attack the Archbishop fled across the river Thames to Whitehall. Thomas Benstead, who was around 16 years of age, was found to have fueled the protest by means of drumming. This warlike activity meant he would be accused of treason, before he was hanged, drawn and quartered. To serve as example, his limbs were "distributed on London Bridge". Young Benstead is thought to have haunted the Archbishop's nights for a while. Layers of London, https://www.layersoflondon. org/map/records/attack-on-lambeth-palace quoting P Griffiths, *Lost Londons: Change, Crime and Control in the Capital City, 1550-1660* (Cambridge: Cambridge University Press, 2011).

5   The title was *England's new chains discovered.* Or The serious apprehensions

foundation of the Levellers design. And one Lockier[6] a trouper for promoting of the like modell and two others now sentenced by a Court Martiall and Lockier was shot to death accordingly and most sumptuously and in great state a footman leading his horse in black after his hers [hearse] attended by 1000s in black and seagreen ribbonds all of his party some men of note and estates carried to his grave in the new Church yard London.

After the death of Lockier at the later end of May twelve troups of Levellers met in Blagrave-leaz neer Abington where the Author of this history saw them, from thence they went to Burford but before they got over the river, Generall Fairfax and Lieutenant Generall Cromwell were come to Abingdon, the Levellers got to Burford and took their quarters there where they were for the most part took prisoners[7] 3 were shot to death viz. one Tomkins and Corporall Perkins a man whome the Author of this history knew because he did quarter some days before at my fathers house at Bayworth.[8]

1649

Marston a notable Agitator who had escaped from Burford defeat was then taken into custody the messengers accordingly came to his lodging in Aldergates Street and sending him word to come down, he with a stiletta killed two of them outright and sorely wounded the 3d and escaped but being retaken and terribly cut in his endevouring to make another escape was araign'd at the Old-Bayly and condem'd to be hang'd in the street and accordingly executed.

1644

+ + + place Sir Alexander before the Hothams.

About the end of Octtober Sir Alexander Carew who was Governor of St Nicolas Iland at Plimouth was tried by a Court Martiall for endevouring to deliver up the Iland to the King and sentenced to be beheaded which sentence was executed upon him on Tower hill, and by the same Court Martiall Sir

---

of a part of the People, on behalf of the Commonwealth; (being Presenters, Promoters, and Approvers of the Large Petition of September 11. 1648.) Presented to the Supreme Authority of England, the Representers of the people in Parliament assembled. By Lieut. Col. John Lilburn, and divers other citizens of London, and Borough of Southwark; February 26. 1649 whereunto his speech delivered at the bar is annexed. TB omitted the word 'chains' and then inserted 'changes', and 'discovery' was nearly right.

6   Robert Lockyer (sometimes spelled Lockier) (1625 – 27 April 1649) was a soldier in Oliver Cromwell's New Model Army. He was the only soldier executed for his involvement in the Bishopsgate mutiny.

7   In Burford church where Anthony Sedley scratched his name in the lead of the font. TB has not named Private Church, the third man shot on May 16th 1649.

8   The inconsistency of reference to the author and 'my father' suggests TB was himself writing this.

John Hotham and his son were in like manner areign'd and found guilty and executed for designing to quitt their partie.

Sufferers on the Kings side
On the 8th of May 1641 the Earl of Straford was brought to the scaffold and beheaded on Tower hill.

1643

Some Caveliers had a design to seise London for the King.
Mr Challener, Mr Hasael, Mr Blinkhorn and Mr White these 4 was condemn'd of which two of them were executed.

+ + + 1644

January Sir John Hotham his son was put to death.
the 2d of January Sir John Hotham the father, was put to death;

1644

January the 10th William Laud Arch-Bishop of Canterbury was beheaded on Tower-Hill.

1644

The Lord Macquire and one Coll: Macmahan were seised in Dublin the night before the breaking forth of the rebellion in Ireland and had been prisoners in the Tower till 1644 and some before broke out from thence wading over the mote escaped away, being found in Drury lane were condemn'd at the Kings Bench to be hang'd draw'd and quartered and suffered accordingly.[9]

1647

Captain Burley for beating up a drum in the Ile of Weight endevouring to free King Charles the 1st then a prisoner in Causebroock Castle[10] was condemn'd and executed at Winchester February the 10th 1647

1648

King Charles was beheaded on Tower-Hill.
on January the 30th 1648.

Duke Hamilton, Earl of Holland, and Lord Capel these 3 were beheaded in the Palace yard March the 9th 1648.

1650

Dr Levens Dr of Civil-Law who had all along served the King was apprehended by the state spies and severall Commissions from the King's found with him, he was brought before a Court Martiall and there sentensed to be hang'd and

9 MacMahon, Hugh Óg and Conor, Lord Maguire, 2nd baron of Enniskillin (*Dictionary of Irish Biography*).
10 Carisbrooke Castle.

accordingly executed against the old Exchange in Cornhill on July 13

1650

Eusebeus Andrews a Royalist and formerly the notary to my Lord Capell was tirpp (?) and sentens'd as a traitor was beheaded on Tower hill August 22

1650

Benson[11] a Royalist was executed at Tiburn 7 October

1651

On the 15 day of August Mr Love a Presbiterian minister[12] was beheaded for conspiring to bring in the King.

August 22 1651

Potter and Gibbins were put to death on Tower Hill for conspiring to bring in King Charles 2d

1654 July 10th

Mr Vowell[13] was hang'd at Charing Cross and Coll: Gerard was beheaded on Tower hill both lovers of the King.

June the 8th 1658

Sir Henry Slingsby and Dr Hewit[14] were beheaded on Tower hill sufferers for the King.

About the same time Ashton, Betilly and Stacy[15] were hang'd drawn and Quartered in Tower street in Cheapside; sufferers for the King

November 27 1661

John James was hang'd and quartered being one of Venner's bloody Crew.[16]

11 Benson was involved with Colonel Eusebius Andrews, secretary to Lord Capel, in plotting a rising in the Isle of Ely.

12 Christopher Love (1618, Cardiff, Wales – 22 August 1651, London) was a Welsh Presbyterian preacher and activist during the English Civil War. In 1651, he was executed by the English government for plotting with the exiled Stuart court.

13 Peter Vowell plotted to assassinate Oliver Cromwell.

14 Revd John Hewett (or Hewitt) D.D., onetime chaplain to King Charles I, plotted to restore Charles II.

15 Colonels Edward Ashton, Mr John Bettely and Mr Edmund Stacy were fellow conspirators with Slingsby and Rev J Hewett. Granger *Biographical History of England* (1824) 11.

16 John James a weaver and seller of small coal around London and a Baptist. The Fifth Monarchist uprising in London in January 1661, led by Thomas Venner and members of his Swan Alley congregation, was the last, desperate outburst of the revolutionary fervour generated by the English Revolution. Over forty people were killed in street fighting, with many others wounded. Venner was subsequently hanged, drawn and quartered, and twelve of his surviving companions were also put to death.: Capp, Bernard, 'A door of hope Re-opened: The Fifth Monarchy, King Charles and King Jesus' (2008). http://go.warwick.ac.uk/wrap

April the 2 1662

Miles Corbet, Coll: Oaky and Col: Barkstead were executed at Tiburn, 3 of their high Court of Justice who did condemn King Charles 1st to be beheaded.

June the 14: 1662

Sir Henry Vane one of the Kings Judges was beheaded on Tower hill

December 22 1662

Philips, Tongue, Gibbs, and Stubs were executed for conspiring against the Goverment.

(iii) A stay in Chepstow and a boat trip up the Wye to Tintern

B ASKERVILLE'S ACCOUNT of Chepstow and his journey up the Wye was an interlude in the history of Oriel College, Oxford, with relevance to the Civil War period. It was touched off by mention of 'Thomas Cornish Byshop Tinensis', one of the past fellows of Oriel. Intrigued by the notion that 'Tinensis' might be Tintern, it seems he jumped on his horse and rode to Chepstow. In fact, the see of Tinensis was a suffragan episcopate of Wells Cathedral.[17] While Baskerville was astray in this suggestion, it did lead him to a description of the mills along the Wye and a tributary river. He was not much interested in the ruins of Tintern. The journey up the Wye was not dated, but Baskerville must have been writing this account after 1684. It is an example of his irrepressible desire to describe what he observed and to follow ideas as they occurred to him. Johannes Kip in his engraving of Chepstow Castle for Robert Atkyns' *Ancient and Present State of Glostershire*, drew the bridge which Baskerville described.[18]

While he was staying in Chepstow with a very distant family connection (*see* Chapter 2 'Family and Kin'), Baskerville visited the church and copied down Henry Marten's epitaph. Marten was famous as a Regicide who signed the death warrant for Charles I, but he was not executed, possibly because his innate sense of fairness led him to defend some of the Royalists, earning him the respect of Charles II.[19] Consequently he was exiled within the country, and after some other places of imprisonment, was sent to Chepstow Castle, where he spent the rest of his life.

Marten's house in Berkshire is referred to in the verse account of

---

17 *Handbook to the Cathedrals of England southern division Winchester, Salisbury Exeter, Wells* (John Murray 1861) 242. Thomas Cornish, died 1513, " Tinensis Episcopus," titular bishop of Tenos [Tinus], a Greek island, and suffragan of Bath and Wells from 1486 to 1513.

18 *Johannes Kip: The Gloucestershire Engravings* Jones ed. (2021).

19 ODNB.

*Kip drew the unusual bridge linking Chepstow and Tidenham over the River Wye
quite soon after Baskerville visited the bridge and measured its height above the water
(Johannes Kip artist and engraver)*

Baskerville's travels based on the rivers to the west of Sunningwell (*see* Chapter
5) and he copied out the epitaph again, prefaced by his own 'epitaph' on Henry
Marten which was complimentary. He wrote a comment on Shivenham church
built by Judge Martin, and then continued

> To him there did succeed a son
> Who was a man of wit and sense
> Good nature, learning, wit and Eloquence
> He breathed his last in Chepsto Castle
> There troubles and death which him did wrestle
> His soul is free'd, his body lyes lone
> In Chepsto Church as Tombe doth show ...'[20]

~~~

Bodleian Library MS Rawlinson D810 *(ff.28b-29b)*

As touching this Bishoprick of Tinensis, of which Thomas Cornish sometime
a scholler in Oriel was Bishop (if the word be not mistaken in the Copie) I

20 Quoted here from British Library, MS Harl. 4714, f.11.

have sough(t) for it in Heylin's Geography, and cannot find there any see of
that name.

In the English dominions Taviensis I find, now Landaffe two miles
from Chardiffe a seaport Town in Glamorgan shier, which Church I saw anno
dmi 1684 and in it a custome remarkable continued by those people to their
deceased friend for sometime after their death, which is, that on Saturday night
or Sunday morning they dress their graves with the best flowers they can get.
But to returne in our search of Tinensis, being at Chepsto in Monmouthshier
where I had a hearty welcome from my worthy friend Mr Alde, he told me,
that 4 miles thence by land and by water up the River Wie was a place called
Tintern which name hath some Analogy with Tinensis worth a Journey thither
to see it.

So having a Boat prepared by Mr Alde, who overlooks the Kings
Customes in the River, with good Company in't accordingly we went and
landed by the ruines of a great Church in bigness equivalent to some Cathedralls
and by it some old walls they said of an Abbey.

Now perhaps upon the dissolution of Religious houses this might be
made a Bishop's See some time and after being cast into the Bishoprick [of]
Lan Tave or Landaff, This famous Church (for they [were] Lord Abbots) for
want of means to repair it fell to decay.

Here also upon a small streame which come(s) out of the mountains
into Wie by this Church for variety of Mills contributing toward the
manufacture of Trade you may travel many miles before you finde the like. For
here you see Mills or wheels driven by water which makes the great bellows
blow the fire to melt Iron. Here is a Mill to forge Iron, A mill to draw Wire,
where many men do work in swinging seats wth Pincers tugging. And in the
water a soaking to make it tough, you see many round bundels of Forged iron
for to make wire, here is a mill to grind Rape and Linseed, Engines to present
the Oyl of which they can make a Barrel full in a day.

And here is a mill to mingle Red and Yellow Oaker wth kinds of Earth
they lay in great Cisterns of water to soak and prepare it, and then having
passed the mills to mingle and incorporate it, 'tis laid in dabs of 3 or 4 Pounds
weight to dry on shelves of Rods in stories one above another.

Here also on the Banks of the River, as we went back again, We saw
a heap of reddish Oare wch yeeld Led digg'd out of these mountains but
at Mendip and other places 'tis of a bluish colour. And to conclude, your
wandring eyes in this pass by water are caught with much variety: vizt a flight
of Salmon Wires, men a fishing in Curricles or leathern boats, high mountains,
beautifull woods, steep Rocks and dangerous precipies, and so being now got

back safe to Chepsto again, for the wind was boysterous, Take here an account of some remarkable things before we returne to Oriel.[21] Chepsto has a very strong Castle to guard it on the bank of Y.

Captain Woolsley is the present Governour under the duke of Beaufort A man beloved in this Country.

In this Castle the famous Mr Henry Martin was a prisoner 'till his death, who made his own Epitaph and lyes inter'd in Chepsto Church, now being made accquainted with it by my Co: Alde (he being my Countryman, and his son my loving friend) we went thither to see it And read theese lines on his Tombstone. September. the. 9. 1680

> Was buried a true Englishman
> Who in Barkshier was well known
> To love his Countrys freedom 'bove his own
> But living Immur'd full 40 years
> Had time to write as doth appear

His Epitaph

> Here or elswhere all's one to you to me
> Earth Aire or water gripes my ghostless dust
> None knows how soon to be by Fire set free
> reader if you an oft try'd Rule will trust
> Yould gladly do and suffer what you must
> My life was spent in serving you and you
> And death's my pay it seems and welcome to
> Revenge destroying but itself which I
> To birds of Prey leave my old Cage and fly.
> Example preach to the Eye, care then mynd sayes
> Not how you end, but how you spend your dayes.

Chepsto besides the Castle hath strong walls about the Town.

I mention this on the schore of an Eccho which gives so many repeats to your voyce, sure England can not afford the like, 3 or 4 times you hear your notes or words return'd again after you have done speaking, Now the place where you find this Eccho is in the way as you go down the hill from Hardwick my Cosen Alde's house towards the town

The next remarkable thing is their draggs instead of Carts to bring Faggots and other Carriage to the Town, much used in Wales where the wayes are narrow, and to make an end, Chepsto Bridge may pass for one of the

---

21 This sentence reads as though it was a note made while composing the text, copied out accidentally in a neat copy.

highest in England. It is built of Timber, having a strong Peer of stone in the middst of the River to support the sleepers from each side of the shore.

One day Mr Alde and I went with a Plummet and Park twine to prove the hight, and found, from the top of the Raile on the Bridge side 'twas 18 yards 1/2 to the ground under water.

2
ST HUGH, ST WINNIFRED AND THE SHOEMAKER

P ROMPTED BY WRITING about St Hugh, bishop of Lincoln, Baskerville copied from a pamphlet a long poem about another St Hugh and St Winnifred.[22] The editor of *Collectanea* omitted the poem because it appeared that it was already printed in the seventeenth century, but it is of some interest not only for the picture of medieval life but for the topographical relevance to St Winnifred's well, and is not readily available to a modern reader.

~~~

Bodleian Library MS Rawlinson D810 *(ff.31b to f32b)*

I must again to St Hugh, the venerable esteeme the gentle Craft has still for his memory will not let him dye, so what lately I got in a Pamphlet, here you have it.

I

When Cupid with his gold Bow
Had Shot St. Hugh unto the heart
Then he a lovers grief did know
For wounds of love do inward smart
But that which did increase his pain,
Was fair Winifreds disdain.

---

22 TB has confused St Hugh the bishop of Lincoln with another St Hugh who loved St Winifred.

2

For often times he sought her love
And by fairest means assaid
If that her fancy he might move
Who was resolve'd to live a maid
To gain her love St Hugh did try
But Winifred did still deny.

3

Who having but some years before,
Receiv'd the Christian faith of late:
Her former sins she did deplore,
Forsaking all her fathers state,
And to her Beads and prayers fell,
Living by a springing Well.

4

Which when once Sir Hugh did hear,
Unto the well he did repair,
And found his Winifred sitting there,
Like an Angell bright and fair:
Whom with these words he did salute,
And thus began to urge his sute.

5

All health to fairest Winifred,
Have pitty on me dearest love,
Restore my Joys which now are fled:
And of my service now approve,
Let me not dye thus unregarded
Love with Love should be rewarded.

6

But Winifred with angry look,
From chiding him could scarce refrain,
And having in her hand a booke,
She mildly thus replied again:
Sir Hugh, leave off to seeke my love,
Which I have place'd on things above.

7

And take this answer once for all:
With this Sir Hugh to weep began,
And like a living funerall,
He went from thence both pale and wan,
Unto the sea resolves to go.

8

And quickly he arriv'd in France,
Where travelling on to Italy,
Fair Ladies did begin to glance,
Upon Sir Hugh with wanton eye,
But yet he thought their beauty rare,
Could not with Winifred compare.

9

And to Venice once he came,
The Curtesans much love did show,
To raise in him an amorous flame,
But they in vain the fire did blow,
For sitting like a male content,
On Winifred his thoughts he bent.

10

Nor could they win him with their Art,
Which only brought into his mind
The love of her to whom his heart,
Like to a Prisoner was confined,
For still those flames did freshly burn,
Which made him back again return.

11

And being now for England bound,
The ship did sail with gentle wind,
Till by and by they quickly found
That raging Neptune was inclin'd
To cast the ship and all away,
Which made Sir Hugh devoutly pray.

12

And at the last his prayers were heard,
For now the day began to clear,
And Englands chaulky shore appear'd
So that the ship did anchor there,
And here Sir Hugh did come to shore,
At Harwich, very weake and poor.

13

For all his money being gone,
You may suppose his heart was sad,
And to himself he made great moan
Untill he met a merry lad,
Who was a shoo-maker by trade,
Who bid him not to be dismaid.

14

With him Sir Hugh had soon agreed
Into the Countrey for to go,
That he might supply his need
For he was loath, himelf to show,
Or in his tattered cloaths appear,
Unto his Winifred so dear.

15

Who now in Prison did remain,
For Dioclesian in those days
Did like a cruel Tyrant reign,
And sought by divers bloody wayes,
The Christian faith how to suppress,
Which fair Winifred did profess.

16

Which when once Sit Hugh did hear,
That with a shoomaker then wrought,
He tooke his wages for that year,
And therewithall new cloth he bought,

And so to Flint-shire back he went,
Where Winifred was resident.

17

Where being come he heard by fame
How Winifred inprison'd was:
And, 'cause he did extoll by name
Her Virgin faith which did surpass,
Sir Hugh with this beautious maid
In a prison strong was laid.

18

And condemn'd was to die,
With Winifred to sufffer death
Who both did shew much constancy,
Meaning to resign their breath
Like loving Martyrs, that their love
Might be Crown'd in heaven above.

19

And while these faithfull lovers lay,
In the prison both togeither,
The shoomakers came every day,
And in kindness did present,
Yeilding them so great reliefe,
As did much aswage their griefe.

20

The shoomakers most faithfully,
Did come unto him in distress,
And while he did in prison lye,
Much kindness to him did profess.
Thus the shoomakers were true
And faithfull ever to Sir Hugh.

21

Who their kindness to requite
Gentle men did name them all,
And their trade to do the right,

He the Gentle craft did call,
And in this song before his end,
The shoomakers he did commend.

1

The Shoemakers I needs
   must praise,
who ready were
   at all assayes,
To help me at my want and need
Such fri(e)nds are true friends indeed.

2

For when I was most
   cast down,
And fortune seem'd on me
   to frown
The Gentle craft I tooke in hand
And thereby I my living gain'd

3

Our shooes we sowed and
   merry were
Our landlords rent we did
   not fear;
And now to raise the shoomakers fame,
The Gentle craft I will it name.

1

And this same title they keep still,
Which unto them Sir Hugh then gave,
And evermore continue will:
For in their minds they did engrave
The memory of good Sir Hugh:
Who to the trade much love did shew.

2

But now the dysmal day was come,
That Winifred and Sir Hugh must dye,
Who like to Lambs receiv'd their doom

The Tyrant's thirst to satisfie.
And so unto that Spring they came,
Which retaineth still her name.

3

There a scaffold raised was,
On which these prisoners mounted were,
She in beauty did surpass,
He with a countenance most clear
Nothing could their hearts dismay:
It seem'd to them a marriage day.

4

Kindly then they did embrace,
Being full of chast desires;
Fear could never them deface,
While their love to Heaven aspires,
And having so with earth made even,
They kist in hope to meet in Heaven.

5

Then Winifred her love to shew,
Desired that She first might dye,
And did desire her friend Sir Hugh,
To learn of her true constancy,
And learn how to resign his breath,
Who like a lamb there bled to death.

6

Tyrant, saith She, I Sacrifice
My blood to wash away my sinns
And I see even with these eyes
When life doth end, then Joy begins.
And as she did, begin to faint,
And as she liv'd, dy'd like a Saint.

7

And all the while that she did bleed,
Her blood in basons they did keep,

And with it poison, with all speed
Was mixt, to bring aeternall sleep
Unto Sir Hugh, who there did dye,
Like to a Maryr constantly

8

And greedily he drank a cup
Of Winifrreds sweet crison blood,
And then another he drank up,
Untill he reel'd whereas he stood:
For now the poison did enflame,
And cruelly burns in each vein.

9

Thou cruel tyrant then sayes he.
To Winifred I sacrifice
My life by thy fell cruelty:
And with those words forth with he dye
And they are cal'd being dead
Saint Hugh and Saint Winifred,

10

But Sir Hugh's body did remain,
Hanging up even in that place,
Which the shoomakers did claim,
And finding him in so brave a case,
The shoomakers without delay
Did steal Saint Hughes bones away.

11

And all of them to shew their love
His bones from thence they did remove
Which he to them before did give
And their tooles they for his sake,
Of Saint Hugh's bones did make.

12

And now when they do go abroad,
Into the Countrey to and fro,

They travel with a little load,
For Saint Hugh's bones must with them go,
And if you would their number know
Read these verses here below.

A drawer, a dresser, two wedges and a heelblock
Squar'd like a dye whereon we may knock,
A hand-leather, and thumb-leather to pull out shoes
Of needle and thimble we must to be sped,
The pincers, the pricking-aule, and rubbing stone
The aule, steele, and tackets, and sow-hairs well grown,
The whetstone, stopping-stick, and paring-knife
Do all belong to a journamans life,
And in our Apron made of Lambs leather
Wee shrowd St Hugh's bones from all wether.

Now he a forfeiture doth pay,
That can not reckon his tooles in rhime:
Sir Hughes bones unto this day
The shoomakers do still enshrine
In their aprons, thereby to shew
Their faithfull love unto Sir Hugh.

4
MEMOIR OF TOM HYDE

A FTER QUOTING THE words of a song at the end of Baskerville's account
of Corpus Christi College, Oxford (*see* Chapter 3) he wrote this long
account of Tom Hyde's life. It is Baskerville's most fluent piece of writing. As
with the letters of Thomas Newe from Carolina, he perhaps sought to give
himself and Tom Hyde's father, both his close friends, a measure of consolation
and a lasting memorial. There are glimpses into the life of a gentry family.
George Hyde did not scorn to bind his sons apprentice, and there are other
examples in Baskerville's writings. There is also a long section about Tom
Hyde's brother George and his adventurous life, in which Baskerville tells us
more about his own visit to Barbados and conditions there. He leaves George

being sent back to Jamaica, which he had been one of the party to seize, taking Tom with him, and another brother, Humphrey, being sent to the East Indies. There are interesting sidelights on English colonists' experiences.

George reached Jamaica but Tom Hyde endured some difficult conditions as a prisoner of the Spanish in Cuba. After working for some years, Tom Hyde was shipped back to Spain to be tried. He escaped, and eventually found an English ship sailing from the Groyne, a bay sheltered by a long peninsula, now known as Corunna. The ship was an unusual one, designed by Sir William Petty with two keels. Petty was a member of the newly-created Royal Society, formerly The Royal Society of London for Improving Natural Knowledge, founded in 1660. He reported on his new design, and the Society holds a model and also illustrations of the ship. Baskerville was generally interested in ships and in August 1663 he had reported to his father the trial run of the 2-keeled ship from Dublin to Holyhead. (*see* Chapter 2 Letter no 45.) Tom Hyde was fortunate, and left the ship near the Isle of Wight, before it sank close to Portsmouth. Accounts of the ship's voyage suggest it sank in the Bay of Biscay.[23]

~ ~ ~

Bodleian Library MS Rawlinson D810 ff.60-61

Tis a Common Saying that Sorrowes
are Drye
Therefore Ile wash u'm away with honest
Tom Hyde's good health

Here is a Carowsing Cup, unto the best of men
And when that this is drunk all out, then wee'll begin agen
For here is nothing constant in this world to be found
And so drink up your liquor, and let this health go round.
2
Each man his can all in hand, and cap upon the ground
Each man unto his liquor stand, and let this health go round
Then take your Cups and turn them and what you do not drink
Put in your Caps and burn them, whatever you say or think.

23   https://www.liverpool.ac.uk/~cmi/books/miscWr/experiment.html

Tom Hydes Memoires

Tom Hyde had a noble soul full of Courage and Loyalty, he was the 4th son of my Loving friend Old George Hyde Lord of Blagrove and Wootton in Berks joyning to my estate in Sunningwell and Bayworth, he was given to Hospitality, a bountifull housekeeper, in his days I was at the eating of many good Feastes in Blagrove house.

He had a numerous Issue, he had 16 or 18 Sons and Daughters by Elizabeth his wife.

Now as to Mr Thomas Hyde he was my Companion at Bayworth House a good while, and then did spend the remainder of his days with Old Sir John Packington at West-Wood in Worcestershire,[24] and at Ebrington in Glocester-shire with my worthy friend Sir William Kypt,[25] Tom's Mother being Sir Williams Aunt, so at Eberton my beloved namesake did breath his last; but his valour and the various Providence of God to him in the progress of his life compells me to write more.

After he had learnt to read and write at home, his father bound him an aprentice in Cow-lane London in Parliamentary days, where my namesake did Couragiously weather his time, but to little purpose, for his Master poor broak, and Tom obtaining no money from his friends did never set up his trade. Yet at a hard rate he did pick up a living about town, ready to ingage in plots to restore the King and did not come home to trouble his friends, but at long run King Charles the 2nd came hither peaceably and was made King of England. And then Tom Hyde was one while a Trooper, and when the war brake out between us and the Dutch, as it did twice in his days of Manhood, then he went to sea, his busines was in times of ingagement to attend a gun, to which work they did alow 6 men in that Ship. And after the dangers of war were over, and peace was concluded between the Nations, he found a leasure time to go to Bishop Stafford[26] where he got acquaintance with a Widdow who kept an Inn and spent some time there with her. There he learnt the art to pickell Turneps to serve for sauce to eat with rost meats instead of Capers.

Thus as you have heard he spent his time till at long run the Noble Soul George Hyde his brother 2nd son to old George Hyde and Elizabeth his wife one of the Gallants that took Jamaica after a tedious exile found the means to

---

24 Sir John Packington, 2nd baronet died in 1680. Westwood House, in Westwood Park near Droitwich, is a splendid extended Elizabethan hunting lodge.

25 Members of the Keyt family lived in Ebrington and owned Hidcote Bois. The house at Norton was burnt down in 1741. Sir William Keyt, baronet, died in 1702.

26 Bishops Stortford?

come again into England to refresh his tir'd Sunburnt Body.

The section on George Hyde written very small and in close lines, into the gutter of the page. It was clearly fitted with difficulty into a space left for it.

George Hyde in his youthy days was a brisk spritfull lad, and his Father to set him in a way to get a livelyhood bound him aprentice to a Woollen Draper in Pauls Church Yard London. But George would not indure this confine but went away from his Master idling and scampering about, and when 2 of my brothers viz Nicholas and William 3rd and 4th Sons of our father Hannibal Baskervile went a voiage to Greenland to catch and make oyle of Whales, George Hyde would fain a gone with u'm, but being a slender lad not strong enough for hard work, the Commanders of the Ship did refuse him, so vexing because he could not bear my brothers company to sea, he came loytering home againe to Blagrove where his friends not knowing what to do with him, at length to be rid of him bound him a servant to Captain Blithe a Barbados Planter for 4 years, and thither he went with his Master.

It was not long ere Blith growing poor stole out of the Iland leaving poor George to shift for himself, so at a hard rate in great want of bone meat, he was forced to stay in Barbados some yeers before our Fleet under Admirall Pen came hether in their way to raise more men to take Sancto Domingo.[27]

Now I, and my Brother Henry Baskervile, first and second sons of our father Hanibal and Mary Baskervile our Mother were bound to go that yeer to Barbados when our foresaid Fleet did saile for the West Indies, so George Hyde's Parents did desire us to bring their Son at our returne into England again.[28]

To be brief our meeting of George Hyde in Barbados was very Providentiall we made no inquiry after him so it came to pass after we had moored our ship in Carlile Bay laden with brave Sack from the Ile of Palma, next day Henry and I had leasure to set our feet on this Sugarlike Strand, where viewing Coll: Hallys house and the brave Springs which there brake out, and run into the Sea (the water is of a pleasant soft tast like milk and no heat will corrupt it at Sea], we had a miles march through trees and bushes, all different from those of Temperate Zones, so at length we got into the Bridge Town. It was not long ere a Negro came by with a bag on his back offering sugar to sell, so we fell a Chaffering about the price, being minded to have some to put in

27 Admiral Sir William Penn (1644-1718).
28 Thomas Baskerville's mother was first married to John Morgan and so he distinguished his brothers from three step-brothers and sisters.

our wine, for Palm Sack you are to understand is wroffer in tast then that which comes from Teneriffe to England, nor will those lushous wines indure a voiage in the Torrid Zone. Now while we were debating the price for the Negro would have 3d a pound for Muskavador or sugar, our army now here made all victuals dearer. A brisk man steps in among us commending the Negros goods. Various thoughts did then possess my minde and phisiognomy made u'm labour briskly at last resolved in my self that twas such a man I went aside with my brother and privatly told him that was George Hyde. Henry upon this gazing solemly on him said no. But being then fully resolved to know who the man was I stept to him and clasping his middle said, George how doest doe? George upon this sudden imbrace brake out of my arms, but redubling my words to him said, I '?don't you know me? So after a pause George said no. At last in conclusion I told him our names, and so with great joy we did inbrace each other, but not without mingles of sorrow. For he gave us to understand that my brother William Baskervile was then in the Iland who after a dangerous sicknes

> By the love of God to spare
> And true relation that took care

was got well again. But our dear Brother Robert Baskervile 5th son of Hannibal and Mary, and Richard Westley whose father was Vickar of St Cuthberts Wells and Robins Godfather were both dead and buried under water one 4, tother 5 dayes before our fleet saw Barbados.

> Thus Death doth seize and take away
> Some Friend some Foes every day.

So night coming on we parted with George Hyde almost as man may say with dry lips for good liquor is deer in Barbados, and money scarce in poor seamens pockets, but with hopes to meet again speedily as we did in feaw days after.

At the 2nd meeting, having time, by the fore top George led us out of town to see the Country and tast a Dragm of killdivell which was so strong and firey, I was afraid it would have burnt a hole in my throat before it fell in my stomack. This liquor is also called Rum.

'Tis distille'd from the pure juice of sugar canes when brought from the fields and ground in their Mills, or Ingenios as they calls them.

We had opportunity after this to meet divers times, when I did acquaint him with his Parents desire to see him again in England, but George had a noble soul and said he would not go home with us, when so many Gallants were in motion to advance the honour of England.

To be short he went of with the Fleet, did escape with life in Hispaniola, where 1500 Planters were killed and the design of taking St Domingo lost by not following Admirall Pen's advice which was to land imediatly before that

Town, but the contrary was put in practice.[29] So failing there they fell upon Jamaica and took it. Here George Hyde among Thousands that went to the grave stood with life above ground, for he could digest alligators flesh as easy as we do heifer beefe. The death of Oliver Lord Protector and the troubles in England presently after, did retard the sending timely supplyes to Jamaica, so that this Colony was reduced to great extremityes they had but 1500 men left alive, but after King Charles restauration they began to thrive a pace.

> From Jamaica now Ile fly
> To Berks with George Hyde by u'm by

Where at Blagrove he found a kinde reception from his parents, but these good voak had Children more than they knew well how to dispose of, for Humphrey their 6th son had now worn out his aprentiship in London, but money being wanting could not set up his trade. So George was advis'd to go back again to Jamaica and take his brothers with him, George took Tom but would not admit Humphrey, so Humphrey went to the East Indies and was put ashore on an Iland cal'd Angedeva where he is still dead or alive for ought we here. The bruit was then when Queen Catherine came to King Charles for a wife, that wee should have Tangier and Goa for a Portion with her, so Humphrey and others went theither to take Possession for the English.[30] Tangier we had, but they would not permit the English to enter Goa on such account.

Reverts to much larger writing at this point

So leaving Humphrey Hyde in the East Indies among the Portuguzes I returne to George and Tom Hyde in England who beng provided of necessaries, and a ship to sail in, went off for the West Indies.

I gather from Tom Hydes words, they went a Privatering by the way to Jamaica to get some Purvant. For Tom Hyde told me, he had a girdle of gold dust about his middle upon his bare skin where he kept it to help him in all extremities of want. This showes the Spaniards were not over eager to strip the poor men of which more anon.

But to return, spending some weeks at Sea they came at length into the Gulph of Florida. All things went well before, but here a sad disaster befell our Gallants. Their Ship stuck fast on the ground, which you may be sure, put u'm all in a sad consternation Grim-Pale Fac'd death the King of Terrors staring at present upon u'm all, and by Computation they were far from land.

29 These events were in 1655.
30 Catherine od Braganza married Charles II in 1662.

How many hours they staid togeither in this wofull condition I have forgot, and now Tom Hyde is dead 'tis too late to aske, But Mr Smallbon, their Chyrurgion at that time in the Ship did confirme the truth of Tom Hydes story who told my loving friend Mr Thomas Ellis at Foxcomb Hill, he flung a Bag of pease to Tom Hyde in the boat at parting.

Tom Hyde was gone but e're now from Foxcomb when Smalbone came theither to quench his thirst, who having not seen him since their parting at sea, would gladly have spent some minuits with him.

But pardon this diversion Ile now go on with the Storie

The Ships Crew had no other prospect of safety but to lighten her: so in order to that, as many men as the Long boat would carry with some provision to sustaine them, went into her and so they parted with sorrowfull hearts.

Those in Ship and those in Boat imploring God's mercy to preserve them, which indeed was good and great, none of them perishing in the Sea. For not long after the Boats Crew was gone out of sight, the Ship was a float, so George Hyde with the rest of his company got safe to Jamaica. But Tom Hide with his Gallants had a share of more sorrow and trouble. For they poor souls were bogeing in the Sea some dayes and nights, in which space of time their victuals was almost spent, yet at last God gave them Comfort also, they got a sight of Land and so made in with the shore where they saw a fishing-boat. This apparition did revive their heavy hearts, so they made what hast they could to her to know what land it was, and who were the Masters of it.

But instead of an answer the fishermen when they came neer let fly a gun at u'm dreading they were Buckaneers and so made what sayle they could to land and Tom Hyde and his Comrades, as fast as they could after them and so to Land they got at last where the Spaniards made them Prisoners.

The Countrey on which they landed is called Cuba the greatest Ile for length in the West Indian seas, but Hispaniola in breadth has greater extent.

Its farthest Northern Latitude lyes under the Tropique of Cancer, viz. 23 degr 1/2 Southward in Breadth it streach almost to 20 Degrees. The Chiefest Citie in't is the Havana. A place to which the Plate-Fleet dos resort and they bear their treasure to Old Spain. To this Town Tom Hyde and his Comrades were brought, where they lived under Confine, and were dayly sent to work at the fortifications of this strong place for which they had some wages to buy themselves victualls.

Thus they spent their time 'till the Plate-Fleet was ready to sayle.

Now it is the Custome of these Partes under the Spanish Dominions to send their Criminals to be try'd in Old Spain, so in order to that, they were shipte and came to St Lucars.[31]

Here my friend Tomas began to forecast how he might escape this dreadfull Tribunall: So thus by the good providence of God, it came to pass.

While their ship was a moring some boats from the shore came aboard to see and ask how their friends did, and some to slide away goods uncustomed which Tom perceiving found the means to slip into one and lye close. So these Voak loath to [be] seen with what they had there made hast to get ashore and hide it.

So Here Thomas stept forth and had no trouble to answer questions; for none did ask him what he did there.

Now having learn'd to speak Spanish in Cuba he pass'd about town for one of them, but seeing no English ships here to ship into dreading a second sezure he march'd out of Town in hast. So now having leaft St Lucars, and ships out of sight behinde him, you may be sure his thoughts and heart were more easye. And now Toms girdle of golden dust was a Cordial to him to bear his Charges in this Country.

As a man may say the desire Voak have to see their Native Soyle and friends there, will make u'm project and stir how to accomplish such desires, so in order to this Tom Hyde did foot it along the Spanish Shore from town to town in search of an English ship to get home, but saw none till he came to the Groine[32], but long look't for came at last as the Proverb has it. Here he found one where he had leave to sayl for England, but it was such a one, the like was never seen before nor since.

I saw the cut of this vessel in print to be sold at the Royall Exchange London. It was built as they say with two Keeles and it had 2 holdes or bodyes for stowage of goods, but above they were united in one broad Deck and the Masts as I remember were proiected to stand in the middle between them.[33] Now great wager being laid on this vessel, some that she would founder at sea in a storme, others that she would work well in it, She was to decide who should winn to perform a voiage from Plimouth to the Groin and back again thither.

So all things being provided to sayle, to Sea she went, and came well to the Groine. Now to come hither, she is to thwart the Biscane Bay where dreadfull stormes do arise, as I found by experience in twice sayling over it. The like overtook this vessel which mounting her aloaf on the seas were ready to split the 2 hulls asunder, and the breach of waves between u'm made a terrible

31 San Lucas, part of Cadiz.
32 The Groine is in Galicia, Spain, now known as Corunna.
33 See also his letter to his father about the ship, Bodleian Library, MS Rawl. D. 859.

noise like Claps of thunder which struck such amazement in the saylors, they were loath to go back again in her, for these reasons she staid a good while at the Groine.

Mony is a powerfull Commander, great wages did prevaile with a pack of Seamen to bring her back again to Plimouth, so amongst this Jove Crew Tom Hyde went into the double-Keel'd ship.

I heard some say by a wind in fair weather this Double-Keeled vessel would lye neerer than any other vessell or ship by point but I hast to set Tom Hyde ashore, that I may conclude my History of Corpus Christi.

The weather was so fair while these Gallants were at Sea, that they came in sight of the hills about Plimouth, and there as if Providence had a peculiar regard to Tom Hyde a Coasting vessel sayling by u'm he stept into her and they landed him in the Ile of Wight, where having a Sister married to Mr Boreman he went to their house to be merry with them. But it was the bad fate of the Double-Keel'd Ship by a storm before they got in to Plimouth to be sunk and the men drown'd.

So Farwell George, and Tom, God save
Their Souls, their bones lye in the Grave
They both do rest in English ground
Their deeds have gotten them renowne.

7
LONDON TAVERNS

'If it be true that good wine needs no bush, 'tis true that a good play needs no epilogue; yet to good wine they do use good bushes; and good plays prove the better by the help of good epilogues'.

Rosalind's words at the end of *As You Like It* might have been echoed by Thomas Baskerville. He spent time in London and was acquainted with a number of taverns and the 'bush' or sign each displayed, while in the towns visited on his travels, he frequently commented on where there was good wine to be had, whether in an inn or tavern, and the particular varieties, though not always naming the taverns; occasionally he had to admit he had forgotten the 'signe of the house'.[1] He was also inclined to comment on the quality of the beer, ale and cider, sometimes noting the water used in the brewing; in Gloucester 'the people are wise and brew their own ale not permitting publick brewers.'[2]

A traditional way of indicating a house where wine was sold was to hang a bunch of ivy leaves outside, which stay green for quite some time, rather than part of a grape vine. Both John Taylor, who published a list of London taverns, and Thomas Baskerville, whose list is published here, noted a small number of taverns where the sign was still a bush - probably no longer a bunch of ivy leaves or other greenery but a painting of a bush.[3] Most inns and taverns, however, had signs displaying a fairly standard variety of names which continue in use today. There were 17 taverns called the *Ship* in London in Baskerville's list, 16 called the *Crown* and 14 the *Swan*. The origins of inn and tavern signs appear to have been in chivalric heraldry. They provided a way of indicating ownership, perhaps by the lord of the manor, or, like the *Three Tuns*,

1   Chapter 4, Journey 1.
2   Chapter 4, Journey 5.
3   Taylor noted two with the sign of a bush, *Travels* 390, and Baskerville three, with another two 'the Bush and Grapes'.

A fearsome sign in Eastcheap to encourage wine-drinkers, one of four Boar's Heads amongst the taverns listed in Baskerville's manuscript. He also described the ancient Boar's Head ceremony in Queen's College on Christmas Day (Walker Art Library / Alamy Stock Photo).

ownership by a member of the Vintners' company; freemen of the Company were able to open a tavern without a licence.[4] Baskerville noted 14 London taverns called the *Three Tuns*.

Inns and taverns displayed similar signs, although there was a difference in their function; one inn visited by Baskerville had an adjoining tavern. Inns were generally larger establishments, with ample stabling, and offered residential accommodation. Houses of prominent families had sometimes been called Inns, and had signs hanging or fixed on them; the Paston family moved their sign from the Prince Inn in Norwich to a different house in King Street in the fifteenth century. Gray's Inn and Lincoln's Inn in London show that 'inn' was an appropriate name for a corporate residence. The town houses of the gentry sometimes became inns, as Baskerville noted after the fire in

4   Cox, *English Inn and Tavern Names* (1994), 21; Clark, *The English Alehouse* (1983) 12.

Northampton.[5] Taverns, on the other hand, were more modest establishments, specialising in selling wine and sometimes food, but not accommodation. Like urban inns, taverns were also meeting places where business could be transacted.[6] The Levellers met in a tavern near the Guildhall, in one of four in London called the *Nag's Head*. Baskerville collected his list of the taverns before they began to decline in popularity through competition from the new coffee houses; in Gloucester he noted 'the *Fountain* a tavern and coffee-house Mr Vaughan master'.[7]

Samuel Pepys's *Diary* contains notes of 164 visits to 80 different London taverns in the post-Restoration period 1660-70, probably a decade before Baskerville compiled his list. Approximately sixty percent are also named in Baskerville's list. Some taverns had unique names, like the *Hercules Pillars* or the *Grange* named by Pepys and Baskerville, but Pepys only visited one or two out of the sixteen called the *Crown*, twelve called the *Bull*, or ten called the *Fountain*, and he had a big choice of venues called the *Swan* or *Sun;* he doesn't seem to have patronised the several taverns named after English monarchs recorded by Baskerville, but perhaps these represent a very recent fashion. Many heraldic tavern names were long-lasting, while at the same time new tavern names were being adopted, like the *Hercules Pillars* which gave name to an alley and reflects knowledge of the Straits of Gibralter.[8] The variety is fascinating.

Baskerville's list of taverns is at the back of MS Harleian 4716 in the British Library. It may have been compiled in the 1680s when he was writing up his journeys through England and was thinking about publication, but it is not dated, except for two entries added in later, with 1690 and 1698 noted against them. He named the sign for nearly every tavern, apart from a few towards the end where he had to admit the name was unknown. A picture had to be put into words, not a written name displayed outside the house, and the spelling in the manscript is phonetic, for example 'fleas' for *Fleece*, 'bare' for *Bear*, and even the word 'tavern' itself is generally written 'tavren'.

The hand-writing of the list is not good, perhaps as Baskerville hastily jotted down the names as he walked round the streets of London; a debt is recorded at one tavern, there is a note that he usually stayed at the *Rose* and the *Ship* in Westminster, and a select number of taverns were marked with a

---

5   Larwood and Camden Hotten, *English Inn Signs (1985) 2-3;* Clark, *The English Alehouse (1983), chapter 1.*

6   Everitt, 'The English Urban Inn', *Perspectives* (1973), 104-9.

7   Chapter 4, Journey 5. Clark, *The English Alehouse (1983), 10.*

8   Cox, *English Inn and Tavern Names* (1994), 99-105.

symbol 'I+I' perhaps indicating exceptional value. It is possible, however, that he commissioned someone else to prepare the list for him; the handwriting of a few later additions in a brown ink suggest he was adding to another's work, as does the fact that in his accounts of his travels, Baskerville wrote the names of the signs more accurately.

The poor handwriting as well as the spelling make the list difficult to read. There were no boards carrying street names, but knowledge of London streets today helps in interpreting Baskerville's manuscript.[9] Printed maps were srarting to standardise the spelling of more important place-names, but Norden's map of London of 1653 contains variations and there have been changes since Baskerville's list was written. For example Piccadilly was spelled with a 'k', 'Pickadilly', on William Morgan's map of 'The City of London, Westminster and Southwark' of 1682; it had not been listed in 1653. Baskerville or his helper wrote 'puckedely'.

To publish a list of London tavern names was to follow in Taylor's footsteps. Taylor published three pamphlets in 1636/7: 'Travels and Circular Perambulations' listed taverns in 'central' London; a second publication, 'Honourable and Memorable Foundations', listed taverns in ten counties round London and Taylor also produced the 'Carrier's Cosmographie', a record of the inns where carriers arrived and departed, and the towns from whence they came. Taylor arranged the first list by tavern names, all the Swans grouped together, and the Kings Heads and Bears and so on, and against each he noted the name of the street in which it was to be found. The second publication, covering ten counties round London, was arranged by county and place, and named the master or mistress of each tavern. The third publication, the Carrier's Cosmography, added more names to the lists.

Baskerville probably knew Taylor's works and he followed the scheme of separating taverns in London, as then defined, and those in the 10-mile area around (but not ten counties - Taylor's more ambitious project). The gates into the city were important markers, with a few taverns noted by Baskerville as 'without' the gate. Perhaps he saw himself as updating Taylor's popular works. But the interesting and distinguishing character of Baskerville's list is that it is arranged by area and road. He (or another) appears to have made a tour of most major and some minor thoroughfares, endeavouring to list the taverns in order, and indicating where in the list a tavern name added later should go. Page numbers were used in five places to indicate where the order of the streets should be altered and were marked also with an asterisk.

9   Taylor's lists and the inn names and streets or places in Larwood and Hotton helped interpretation in a number of cases.

The scribe's journey started 'by Westminster ferry', which placed him at Westminster stairs, at the side of New Palace Yard. From there he covered streets in some sort of geographical order, moving gradually eastwards and then crossing the river and again moving from west to east in Lambeth and Southwark. Well-known streets today include Whitehall, Piccadilly, Pall Mall, Strand, Fleet Street, streets near St Paul's cathedral which was then newly rebuilt after the Great Fire of 1666, Threadneedle Street, Tower Street, Lincoln's Inn fields, Holborn. Altogether he named 124 streets within London, and at least 386 taverns. Taylor had named 398. Taverns were not necessarily long-lasting and their names might also change. The Stillyard where Rhenish wine was sold was noted by Baskerville, but Taylor had noted three others, all patronised solely by Dutchmen, a fact which Baskerville does not record.

It is not surprising to find 17 taverns in Holborn; this was a main road into London from the west, and travellers would look for refreshment as soon as they arrived. There were 19 taverns in Fleet Street and 20 in the Strand which were the main east-west roads parallel to the Thames, close to the many landing places. Similarly refreshment for travellers could be found in the 11 taverns on the eastern approach to London along Whitechapel.

In the section on the ten-mile radius of London, Baskerville named 49 places without specifying any street names: Deptford, Battersea, Hampton Court, Highgate, Hampstead, Bow, Chelsea, Hammersmith, Kensington, give a flavour of the boundaries of late seventeenth-century London; here he noted 128 taverns. At the end of the taverns list, he suggested he had named 485 altogether, and guessed there might be 500, but in practice there are at least 514. The difference is largely accounted for by later additions to the list, and possibly where two names on the same line not linked by 'and' were interpreted as one tavern.

Despite the civil war and the great fire of London some 20 years before Baskerville's list, London had been substantially rebuilt, and indeed had expanded, particularly in the suburbs in Essex, Surrey and Middlesex, which 'were growing inexorably during the late sixteenth and seventeenth centuries'.[10] There were new streets like Piccadilly, which were not named by Taylor. A second great destruction of London in the Second World War has altered some of the street patterns and the narrow alleys that once existed have mainly gone. Nonetheless many of the principal streets exist today.

10 Clark, *The English Alehouse (1983)* 49.

SUMMARY OF THE STREETS WITH NUMBERS OF TAVERNS

STREET OR AREA	No.
[Cheapside] Market st market	1
Aldermanbury	1
Barnaby st	2
Bartholomew Lane	2
Bedford st	1
Bishopsgate st	3
Bishopsgate without	8
Blackwall	2
Bloomsbury market	4
Blowbladder st	1
Broad st	1
Bucklesbury	1
Burching Lane	1
by Westminster ferry	2
Cannon st	1
Carter Lane	1
Cateaten st	1
Catherine st	2
Chancery Lane	6
Charles st	1
Cheapside	8
Clare Market	1
Clare st	2
Clerkenwell Green	2
Coleman st	2
Corkehill st	1
Cornhill	11
Coventry st	1
Dowgate	1
Drury Lane	4
Fenchurch st	3
Fetter Lane	2

Fleet St	19
Friday St	1
from Hungerford market east in the Strand	15
Globe Alley	1
Grace Church st	11
Grays Inn Lane	4
Great Eastcheap	1
Horleydown	1
Horton st	2
Hungerford market	3
Hurt st	1
Islington	2
Jermyn st	1
just without Aldgate	1
Katherine st	4
King St	3
King St, Westminster	10
Knightrider st	2
Knightsbridge	4
Lad Lane	1
Lambeth	8
Lanehouse Causeway	1
Leadenhall st	4
Leathbury	1
Leicester Fields	2
Lichfield st	1
Lions st	1
Little Lincolns Inn Field	2
Lombard st	2
Long Aker	2
Ludgate st	5
Luton st Hatton Garden	1
Marylebone?	1
Michels? Lane	1
Milk st	1
Mill st	2

Minories	2
Moorgate	1
Narrow-wall st	1
Newgate st	6
Newgate to Holborn	4
Newington church to London Bridge	10
Old Bailey	2
Old Fish st	3
Oxenden st	1
Pall Mall	3
Panton st	1
Paternoster Row	2
Paul's Chain London to Paul's wharf	3
Paul's churchyard	1
Paul's yard	4
Petty France, Westminster	1
Piccadilly	7
Poultry	3
Primrose st Soho	1
Pye Corner	2
Queen st	1
Ratcliffe Cross st	1
Ratcliffe Highway	2
Red Cross st	2
Red Lion Fields	2
Redcliff	2
Shad Thames st.	?
Shadwell Dock st	1
Smithfield	4
St Alban's st St James's Market	1
St Giles's church to Holborn Conduit	17
St James's Square	1
St John st	3
St Martin Legrand	2
St Martin's Lane	2
St Tole's st [Tooley?]	4

Stepney	3
Stocks Market	2
Strand to Hungerford market	5
Thames st from Puddle dock to London bridge	10
Threadneedle st	6
Tottenham Court	2
Tower st	3
Upon Garlic [?hill]	2
Vere st	1
Wapping	8
Wapping & Spring Hund?	1
Wapping Wall st	2
Warwick Lane	1
Water Lane in Blackfriars	3
Watling st	2
Westminster	2
Whitechapel	11
Whitecross st	1
Whitehall nr Charing Cross St	9
Wish st	2
without Cripplegate	2
Wood St	4

Taverns in the country 10 miles round London (ff.25-27)	
Acton	2
Barnes	1
Barnet	5
Battersea	2
Between Hammersmith & Kensington?	2
Blackheath	2
Bow	3
Bristol Causeway	1
Bromley	2
Camberwell	3
Charlton	1
Carshalton	2
Chelsea	7
Chiswick	2
Clapham	1
Croydon	4
Deptford	5
Dulwich	3
Edmonton	1
Enfield	1
Fulham	2
Greenwich	4
Hammersmith	4
Hampstead	3
Hampton Court	3
Highgate	3
Hounslow	2
Ilford	2
Kensington	4
Kingsbury?	1
Kingston	8
Merton	1
Mile End to Romford	2

Mitcham	2
[Stoke] Newington	1
Putney	2
Richmond	3
Romford	5
Stratford	3
Tooting	2
Tottenham	2
Turnham Green	2
Turnham Green (Brentford?)	4
Turnham Green (Old Brentford)	2
Waltham Abbey	1
Waltham? Cross	1
Wandsworth	6
Welling	2
Wimbledon	1

British Library, MS Harl. 4716
Additions in brown ink apparently made after the list of taverns was compiled, are indicated with brackets < > as is the practice adopted elsewhere for Baskerville's text. 'The' is entered at the beginning of each group of tavern names, implying that it should be understood as preceding each tavern name, but is here omitted. Capital letters for proper names have been used throughout in the modern version.

The pages of the central London section of this booklet were originally numbered, but the numbers are crossed out and the series of folio numbers in the manuscript are continued: ff.18-27. The page numbers are given below because relevant to the re-orderings Baskerville indicated.

TAVERNS IN LONDON
(page 1)

by Westminster ferry	*bie Westmenster fery*
Hart	*hart*
Bear	*bare*
in Paul's yard	*in pullis yard 1690*
Dog	*doge*
Greyhound	*greyhound*
Fleece	*fleas*
Castle	*Castell*
Petty France, Westminster	*pety france westminester*
Globe	*globe*
King st, Westminster	*Kingstreet wesmint.*
Feathers	*fethers <Shepherd 1698 Sheapperd 1698>*
Fountain	*fountain*
Bull	*bull - I+I*
Bell	*bell*
Sun	*sunne*
King's Arms	*Kings armes*
Swan	*swane*
Mitre	*miter*
Angel	*Aingell*
Whitehall nr Charing Cross st	*whithall nr Chearin Cros streat*
Goat	*goert?*
Red Cross	*Red Crose*
Rummer	*Rumer*
King's Head	*Kings head*
Thistle & Crown	*Thisell and Crowne*
Crown	*Croune*
Three Tuns	*3 Tunns*
Bull's Head	*Bulls head*
Golden Lion	*golden Lion*
Piccadilly	*Tavrens in puckedely*
Blue Post	*blew pos*

Cross Keys	*Cros keys*
Hart	*hart <to pay * y>*
Fountain	*fountain*
Three Kings	*3 Kings I+I*
Sun	*Sunn*
Duke of Grafton's Head	*ducke of graftens head*
Strand to Hungerford market	*in the strand to hungerford market*
Chequer	*Chequer*
Rose	*Rose*
Cock	*Cock*
Greyhound	*greyhound*
King's Armes	*Kings Armes*
Hungerford market	*in Hungerford market*
Three Tuns	*3 Tuns*
and another	*and another*
Castle	*Castell*
from Hungerford market eastwards in the Strand	
	from Hungerford market ?Est.. in the strand
Golden Tun a ?pipe tavern	*golden tunne a ?pipe tavern*
Sun	*Sunn*
Bear	*Bare*
Half Moon	*half mone*
Goat	*Goate*
Bush and Grapes	*Bush and grapes*
Fountain	*fountaine*
Feathers	*feathers*
Vine	*Vinie*
Swan	*Swane*
Five Bells	*5 bells*
Mitre	*miter*
Greyhound	*Grayhound*
White Horse	*whithors*
Kings Arms over against St Clements Church	*Kings Arms over against St Clements Church*
Westminster	
Rose	*?we heare tennet ofe and begin at*
Ship	*I goe to the rose and the Shipe at Wmt*
(page 2)	
within Temple Bar	*Within Tempell bare*
Taverns in Fleet St	*Taverens in fleat street*
Three Tunns	*3 Tunns*
Queen's head	*queans head*
?Thepenyell	*thepenyell*
Golden Fleece	*golden fleas*
Bugle Horn	*Bugell horne*
Half Moon	*halef mone*
Henry the Eighth	*henerey the eight*

Star	*stare*
Green Dragon	*Green dragon*
Sun	*Sunne*
Globe	*Globe*
Bulls Head	*bulls head*
Gold Ring	*Gold ring*
Crown	*Crowne*
Greyhound	*Grayhound*
Castle	*Casell*
Five Bells	*5 Bells*
Feathers	*fethers*
Old and Young Dunstons or the Two Devells Taverens	
	old and young dunstons or the 2 devells Taverens
Chancery Lane	*Chanser Lane*
Pope's Head	*popes head*
Rose? & Crown	*Roles & Croune*
Horn	*horn*
Horseshoe and Horn	*Horshue and horn*
Globe	*globe*
St John's head	*St Johns head*
Fetter Lane	*in Fetter Lane*
Red Hart	*Red hart*
Cross Keys	*Crose Keys*
from Fleet bridge to Ludgate	*from fleat brige to Ludgeat*
Three Tuns	*3 Tunns*
George	*Geoarge*
Ludgate st	*Luggeat street*
Swan	*swane*
Wonder?	*Wonder?*
Old Dog	*old doge*
Paul's churchyard	*pauls Churchyard*
Mitre	*mitter*
Water Lane in Blackfriars	*water Lane in Blackfreyers*
Dragon	*dragon*
Bunch of Grapes	*Bunch of graps*
Red Cross	*Red Cross*
Carter Lane	*Carter Lane*
Feathers	*fethers*
Paul's Chain London to Paul's wharf	*Pauls Chain London to pauls wharf*
Castle	*Casell*
Buglehorn	*Bugellhorn*
St Paul	*St paull*
Knightrider st	
Castle	*Casttel*
Charles II's Head	*Charles the 2nd hed*
(page 3)	

Thames st from Puddle dock to London bridge

	Thames street from Pudell docke to London brige
Queen's Head	*queen head*
Three Cranes	*3 Cranes*
The Rhenish winehouse in the Stillyard	*the Renish winehous in the stillyard*

Thames st from London Bridge to the Tower of London

	in Thams street from London brig to the Tower of London
Horse	*horse*
Salutation	*Salutation*
Swan	*Swanne*
Gun	*Gunn*
2nd Salutation	*2nd Salutation*
Ship	*Ship*
Crown	*Crown*
Vine	*Vine*
Old Fish st	*old fish street*
Sun	*sunn*
Feathers	*fethers*
Swan	*swane*
Upon Garlic	*upon garlicke*
Dog	*is the Dog*
Golden Fleece	*the golden fleas*
in Michaels? Lane	*in Mikels Lane*
Hoop & Grapes	*the Whope and graps*
Great Eastcheap	*great Eas Cheap*
Boar's Head	*the Bores head*
Cannon st	*Cannon street*
Jacob's Well	*the Jacobes well*
Friday St	*freyday street*
Bell	*the Bell*
Watling st	*watling street*
Salutation	*the Salitation*
Nag's Head	*Nages head*
Bucklesbury	*Bucklesbury*
Fountain	*fountaine*
Dowgate	*dowgeat ainchantly dungeat hill*
Swan	*swane*
Queen st	*queen street*
Rummer	*the Rummer*
King St	*Kingstreet*
King's Head	*Kinshead*
Mitre	*miter*
Golden Boy & Tun or Backs	*golden boy and Tunne or backes*
(page 4)	
The Old Bailey	*the old Bayle*

King Charles II's Head	*King Charles the 2nd hed*
Half Moon	*halfe mone*
Warwick Lane	*Warwicke Lane*
Feathers	*fethers*
Paternoster Row	*paternoster Row*
Castle	*Castell*
Crown	*Crowne*
Newgate st	*new geat street*
Newgate	*new geat taveren*
Black Dog	*Black doge*
Three Tuns	*3 Tunns*
Sun	*Sunn*
Queen's Head	*quens head*
Queen's Arms	*quens Armes*
Blowbladder st	*Blowbladerstrete*
Spotted Dog	*spottd goge*
Cheapside	*Cheapside*
Half Moon	*half mone*
Mitre	*miter*
Fleece	*fleas*
Nag's Head	*nages head*
Shepppard	*Shepppard*
Fountain	*fountain*
Feathers	*fethers*
Bull's head	*bullshead*
Milk st market	*milck stret market*
Sun	*Sune*
The Poultry	*the poultry*
Rose	*Rose*
Ship	*Shipe*
Three Cranes	*3 Crane*
The Stocks Market	*the Stocks markett*
Mitre	*miter*
Bush Grapes	*Bush graps*
Lombard st	*Lomber street*
Kings Arms	*Kings Arms*
Salutation	*Salitaton*
Cornhill	*Cornhill*
Globe	*globe*
Crowned Swan	*Crouned Swan*
Pope's Head	*Popes head*
Swan	*Swan*
Bear	*Bare*
King's Head	*Kings head*
Golden Flour	*Golden fleur*
Mermaid	*mermaid*

White Lion	*whit Lion*
Ship and Castle	*ship and Castell*
George and Vulture	*Jeorg and vulter*
(page 5)	
Burching Lane	*Birchin Lane*
Ship	*Shipe*
Gracechurch st	*gras Church street*
Half Moon	*halef mone*
Bull's Head	*bulls head*
George	*George*
Ship	*Shipe*
Three Tuns	*3 tuns*
Bear	*Bare*
Sun	*Sunne*
Henry the 8th	*Henry the 8*
Monument	*monument*
Swan	*Swane*
Two Golden Boys suporting a basket of fruit	*2 golden boys suporting a basket of frut*
Bishopsgate st	*Bishops geat streat*
Ship	*Shipe*
Queen's Head	*quens head*
Bugle Horn	*bugell horne*
Fenchurch st	*fan Church streat*
Mitre	*miter*
King James the first head	*King James the first head*
Ship	*the Shipe*
just without Aldgate	*just without allgeat*
Magpie	*Magpey*
Minories	*the minoris*
Fountain	*fountain*
Rose	*Rose*
Hurt st	*Hurt Street*
Three Tuns	*3 tuns*
Leadenhall st	*Leadinhall streat*
Nag's Head	*nagshead*
King James the 1st Head	*King James the 1st head*
Golden Griffin	*Golden grifon*
Rose and Crown	*Rose and Croune*
Tower st	*Tower strreat*
Bull's Head	*Bull head*
Dolphin	*Dolphin*
Ship (opens in Bare Lane and Water Lane)	*Shipe taveren openeth in to Bare Lane and Water Lane*
St Martin Legrand	*St Marten Legrand*
Swan	*Swane*
Fountain	*fountain *to page 6*

Pye Corner	*Pey Corner*
Bear	*Bare*
White Hart	*Whitehart*
Smithfield	*Smythfeald*
Bell	*Bell*
George	*Georg*
Swan	*Swan*
Crown	*Crowne*
(page 6)	
St John st	*St John Streat*
Charles the 1st's Head	*Charles the 1st head*
Boar's Head	*Borse head*
Queen Elizebeth's Head	*quean Elizebeths head*
Clerkenwell Green	*Clakenwell Green*
St John of Jeruslem	*St John of Jeruslem*
Castle	*Castell*
Islington	*Isleington*
Angel	*Aingell*
Sadlers Spa [Sadlers' Wells]	*Sadlers spaw Tavren*
without Cripplegate	*without Cripellgeat*
Castle	*Castell*
Crown	*Croune from this mark * in page the 5th*
at Moorgate	*at more geat*
Sun	*sunne*
Whitecross st	*whit Crose streat*
Swan	*Swane*
Red Cross st	*Red Cros Streat*
Red Cross	*Red Crose*
Feathers	*fethers*
Wood St	*Wood streat*
Sun	*Sunne*
Castle	*Castell*
Three Tuns	*3 Tunns*
Bull's Head	*Bulls head*
Lad Lane	*Lad Lane*
St John the baptists head	*St John baptis hed*
Aldermanbury	*Alderman bury*
Swan	*Swan*
Newgate to Holborn Conduit	*newgeat to holbron Cundet*
Fountain	*fountain*
Castle	*Castell*
Bull's Head	*Bull head*
Cross Keys	*Crose Keys*
Coleman st	*Collmanstret*
Whip and Grapes	*whipe and graps*
Star	*Star*

Cateaten st	*Catteaten streat*
King's Arms	*Kings Arms*
	*from this * in page the first*
(page 7)	
Coventry st	*Coventrey streat*
Crown	*Croune*
Panton st	*panton streat*
Crown	*Croune*
Oxenden st	*oxenton streat*
King's Head	*Kings head*
Leicester Fields	*Lester fealds*
Sun	*Sunne*
Angel	*Anengell*
Jermyn st	*Jeurmies streat*
Ship	*Ship*
Pall Mall	*pell mell*
Rose	*rose*
Crown	*Croune*
George	*Georg*
St Martin's Lane	*St Martens Lane*
Crown & Sceptre	*Croune and septer*
Fleece	*flees*
Bedford st	*Bedford stret*
Cross Keys	*Cros Keys*
Primrose st Soho	*<primros> streat Soho*
Three Tuns	*3 Tunns*
Drury Lane	*Drury Lane*
Golden Horseshoe	*golden Hors shue*
Angel	*Aingell*
Rose	*Rose*
Spotted Dog	*Spotted dog*
Katherine st	*Kathrine streat*
King's Arms	*Kings Arms*
Globe	*Globe*
Rose	*Rose*
Fountain	*fountain*
Lichfield st	*Lichfeald streat*
Ship	*Shipe*
Knightsbridge	*Knitesbrige*
Ship	*Swanne*
Salutation	*Salutation*
Fox	*fox*
Hart	*hart*
(page 8)	*to pag * 11*
Leathbury	*Leathbury*
Hart	*hart*

Bartholomew Lane	*Bartholimey Lane*
Bugle Horn	*Bugell horne*
Half Moon	*half mone*
Threadneedle st	*Thredneadl streat*
Antwerp	*Antwarp*
Crown	*Crowne*
Globe	*Globe*
Sun	*Sunn*
Ship	*Shipe*
Angel	*Aingel*
Broad st	*brodestreat*
Black Swan	*Black Swanne*
(page 9)	
Catherine st	*Cathrin Street*
Ship	*Shipe*
Coopers' Arms	*Cooppers Arms*
Wapping	*Wapping*
King James the first's head	*King Jeams the first head*
Fox	*fox*
Hoop & Grapes	*hoope & graps*
Gun	*Gunne*
Anchor	*Anker*
Bull's head	*Bulls head*
Crown	*Croune*
Mitre	*miter*
Wapping & Spring Hund	*Corner Wapping & Spring Hund*
Prince George	*Prince Georgs*
Wapping Wall st	*Waping wall st*
Crown	*Croune*
Vine	*Vinne*
Shadwell Dock st	*Shadwell Docke Street*
Whale	*Whalle*
Corkehill st	*Corke hill Streat*
Red Lion	*Red Lion*
Ratcliffe Highway	*Ratlif heyn way*
King's head	*Kings head*
Ratcliffe Cross st	*Ratlif Crosstreat*
Ship	*Shipe*
Lions st	*Liones streat*
Green Dragon	*green Dragon*
Globe Alley	*Globe Aley*
Sun	*Sunne*
Lanehouse Causeway	*Lanehous Causway*
White Horse	*whit hors*
Blackwall	*Blackwall*
Globe	*Globe*

East India Company's Arms	*Est Inde Companeys Armes*
(page 10)	
Stepney	*Stepney*
Angel	*Aingell*
[2 more]	*and 2 more*
Tottenham Court	*<Tatnam Court*
Hercules Pillars	*Herculus Pillors*
Rose	*Rose>*
and at Marylebone?	*And at marabone*
Rose Tavern	*Rose Tavern*
(page 11)	*from page * 7*
St Alban's st St James's Market	*St Albans streat St Jeamses market*
Crown & Sceptre	*Croune and Septer*
Charles st	*Charles streat*
King's Head	*Kings head*
St James's Square	*St Jeames Square*
Crown	*Croune*
Clare Market (the new market)	*Clare markett the new market*
Bull's Head	*Bulls head*
Vere st	*Vear St*
Sun	*Sunne*
Horton st	*horton streat*
Peacock	*peacoke*
Three Tuns	*3 tunns*
Wish/Wick? st	*wish streat*
Three Tuns	*3 tons*
Covent? Garden	*Comment garden*
Clare st	*Clare streat*
Angel	*Aingell*
Swan	*Swane*
Little Lincolns Inn Field	*Littell Linikers inn feald*
Grange	*Graing*
Head	*hed taveron*
St Giles's church to Holborn Conduit	*St Giles's Church to holborn Cundit*
the Angel	*<the Angel>*
White Lion	*Whit Lion*
Noah's Ark	*Nose Arke*
King Charles 2nd head	*King Charles 2nd head*
Ship	*Ship*
Bear	*<Bare>*
Turnstile	*Turne stile*
Sun	*Sunne*
Griffin	*Grifen*
Castle	*Castell*
Three Tuns	*3 tunns*
Globe	*Globe*

Castle (Fetter Lane end)	*Castle fetter Lane End*
St Dunstan	*St Dunston*
Cross Keys	*Crose Keys*
Bull's Head	*Bulls head*
Crown	*Croune*
Luton st Hatton Garden	*Luton str. haton garden*
Globe	*globe*
(page 12)	
Long Aker	*Long Aker*
Bull's Head	*Bull hed*
Vine	*Vine*
Bloomsbury market	*Blomesbury market*
Rose	*the rose*
Nag's Head	*nageshead*
Goat	*<Gooat>*
George	*<Georg>*
Red Lion Fields	*Red Lion fealds*
Red Lion	*Red Lion*
Dolphin	*<dolphin>*
Grays Inn Lane	*grasin lane*
Castle	*Castel*
3 or 4 number unknown	*<3 or 4> the number unknown*
Bishopsgate without	*Bishops Geat without*
White Lion	*< White lion*
Horn	*horne*
Great James	*Great James*
Queen's head - these within the gate	*Queenes head these within the gate*
Magpye	*magpye*
White Hart	*White hart*
Raven	*raven*
King's Head	*kings head>*
(8 names added by Richd Brookland Jn)	*<Richd Brookland Jnr>*
Whitechapel	*whit Chappell*
Crown	*Croune*
Castle	*Castell*
James 2nd's Head	*Jeames 2nd head*
Charles 2nd Head	*Charles 2nd head*
Grape	*Grape*
Aingell	*Aingell*
White Harte	*Whitt hartt*
Magpie	*<magpy>*
[added by?] Richard Brookland	*Richd Brookland*
Half Moon	*Half moon*
Standard	*Standard*
White Lion	*white lion*
(page 13)	

On Southwark side [of the Thames]	*one Southwark side*
Lambeth	*Lambeth*
Royal Oak	*Royall oake*
Vine	*Vine*
Spring Gardens	*Spring gardenes Tavren*
Fountain	*fountain*
Swan	*Swanne*
White Lion	*Whit Lion*
King's Arms	*Kings Arms*
Cupits? Bridge	*Cupits brig*
Narrow-wall st	*narow-wall streat*
Swan	*Swan*
Newington church to London Bridge	*newington Church to London Brig*
Hawks?	*haukes*
Unicorn	*unicorn*
Bush	*Bush*
Three Tuns	*3 tunns*
King's Arms	*Kings Arms*
Ship	*Shipe*
Bull's Head	*bulls head*
Crown	*Croune*
Two Cocks	*2 Cocks*
King Henry 8th Head	*King Henery 8 head*
St Tole's st	*St Toles streat*
Ram's Head	*Rames head*
Ship	*Shipe*
Lodge	*Loge*
Three Tuns	*3 tunns*
Burnsby? st	*baronbe? streat*
St Christopher	*St Christover*
King's Arms	*Kings Armes*
Horleydown	*howlydown*
Bunch of Grapes	*Bunch of graps*
Mill st	*mill streat*
Bunch of Grapes	*bunch of graps*
Fleur de Lis	*fleurdelise*
Redriff	*Redrife*
Ox & Bell	*ox and bell*
Shepherd & Dog	*Sheperd and dog*
Shad Thames st?	*Bridhamson? Shadtems streat*
Birdhamson	

This part of the list was not originally paginated; it is on ff.25 to 27.

TAVERNS IN THE COUNTRY TEN MILES ROUND LONDON

Merton	*Murten*

King's Head	*King head*
Wimbledon	*Wimblton*
King's Arms	*Kings Armes*
Deptford	*Deptford*
Castle	*Castell*
Angel	*Aingell*
Sun	*Sunn*
King's head	*Kings head*
Red Lion	*Red Lion*
Greenwich	*grinwitch*
Bull's Head	*Bulls head*
Devil or Anchor	*Divell or Anker*
Ship	*Shipe*
Bear	*Bare*
Blackheath	*Blackheath*
Green Man	*green man*
Bush	*the Bush*
Charlton	*Carlton*
Bugle Horn	*bugell horn*
Camberwell	*Camberwell*
Butchers' Arms	*Buchers Arms*
Bull's Head	*Bulls head*
Tiger & Crown	*Tiger and Croune*
Dulwich	*Dullwitch*
George & Feathers	*Georg and fethers*
King's Head	*Kingshead*
Green Man	*Green man*
Bristol Causeway	*Bristo Casway*
Whithers	*whit hors*
Clapham	*Clapham*
White Hart	*whitt hart*
Tooting (Upper)	*Tooten uper*
King's Head	*Kings head*
Castle	*Castell fetter Lane*
Mitcham	*mishom*
Hart	*hart*
King's Head	*Kings head*
Battersea	*Battersea*
White Lion	*Whitt Lion*
Crown and Raven	*Croune and Raven*
Wandsworth	*wansworth*
Ram	*Rame*
Falcon	*falken*
Half Moon	*half mone*
Bush	*bush*
Spread Eagle	*spred Eagell*

Rose & Crown	*Ros and Croune*
Putney	*puteney*
Bull	*Bull*
White Lion	*Whitt Lion*
Barnes	*Barnes*
White Horse	*whitt hors*
Croydon	*Croyden*
George	*Geord*
Greyhound	*grayhound*
White Lion	*whit Lion*
Anchor	*Anker*
Richmond	*Richmond*
Red Lion	*Ried Lion*
Rose and Crown	*Rose and Crown*
White Horse	*whit hors*
Kingston	*Kingston*
Red Lion &	*Red Lion and*
Nag's head	*Nags head*
Lamb	*Lame*
Sun	*Sune*
Old Lion	*old Lion*
Castle	*castell*
Bull	*Bull*
White Hart (the other side of the bridge)	*whit hart the other sid of the brig*
Bromley	*Brumley*
Swan	*swan*
Hart	*hart*
Welling	*Wellig*
nk x 2	*2 unknowne*
Carshalton	*Ceashalten*
nk x 2	*2 unknown*
Hampton Court	*hamton cort*
Toy	*Toy*
Mitre	*miter*
1 more	*1 more*
Hounslow	*hounslo*
George	*Georg*
Red Lion	*Red Lion*
Highgate	*heygeat*
Angel	*Aingell*
2 more	*2 more*
Hampstead	*hamstead*
King of Bohemia's Head	*King of Beehames head*
Feathers	*<Feathers>*
King's Head	*<Kings head>*
Mile End to Romford	*from mile end to Rumford*

Globe (Mile End)	*globe mile end*
1 more	*1 more*
Bow	*Bow*
King's Head	*Kingshead*
George	*Georg*
Queen's Head	*queans head*
Stratford	*Stratford*
Queen's Head	*queans head*
Swan	*Swan*
Dolphin	*Dolphin*
Ilford	*Elver*
Boar's head	*Bores head*
Angel	*Aingell*
Romford	*Rumford*
Crown	*Crooune*
Hart	*hartt*
Sun	*Sunne*
Cock and bell	*Cock and bell*
?Vintner	*vinler*
Chelsea	*Chellsey*
Magpie	*magpey*
Nag's Head	*naggs head*
Goat	*geoat*
Horse	*hors*
Guy of Warwick	*<Guy of Warwick>*
2 more the names forgotten	*2 more the names forgott*
Fulham	*fullham*
Nag's Head	*nages heaad*
Barge	*Barge*
Hammersmith	*humersmyth*
King's Arms	*King armes*
Goat	*gote [brown ink]*
Red Lion	*<Red Lyon>*
Ship	*Shipe*
Between Hammersmith & Kensington	*betwixt Hamersmyth and Kingisinton*
Anchor	*Anker*
Turnham Green	*Turnomgreen*
King of Bohemia's Head	*King of boheenas head*
The Packhorse	*<The Packhorse 1698>*
Turnham Green and now ?Brentford	*in ditto and now Braonton*
Feather	*fether*
Tuns	*Tunns*
Three Pigeons	*3 pigons*
Red Lion	*Red Lion*
2 forgotten names in Old Brentford	*2 in old Breinford forgott*
Chiswick	*Chiswich*

Feathers	*fethers*
Lamb	*Lamb*
Kensington	*Kingsinton*
Hart	*hart*
Red Lion	*Red Lion*
Greyhound	*grayhoud*
Crown	*Croune*
Acton	*Acton*
nk x 2	*2 unknown*
King's Arms	*<Kings Armes*
Hart	*Mr Watson says the Hart>*
Barnet	*Barnit*
2 the names unknown [list follows]	*2 the names unknown [but see list following]*
Red Lion	*<red Lyon*
King's Arms	*Kings Armes*
Cock	*Cock*
White Hart	*white Hart*
Lamb	*Lamb>*
Kingsbury?	*Kings Land*
King's Arms	*Kings Arms*
Newington	*Newington*
Sun	*sunne*
Tottenham	*Tottnem*
Swan	*Swane*
Hart	*hart*
Edmonton	*Edmonton*
Bell	*Bell*
Enfield	*Enfild*
Rose & crown	*Rose and Croune*
Waltham Cross	*Waltom Cros*
Four Swans	*4 Swans*
Waltham Abbey	*Waltom Abey*
Boar's Head	*Borshead*

It may be modestley Computed to 500
My Friend Mr Watson who lives in Diet street St Giles tels in ? there is 700 Stage
Coaches allowed by Act of Parlament to work in London and the Bills of Mortality
An: 1698

APPENDIX

A list of the principal family relationships described by Thomas Baskerville

Baskerville, Thomas (TB): Hannibal (father), Mary née Baskerville (mother), Nicholas (g'father), Sir Thomas (g'father), Constance née Huntley (g'mother), Mary née Throckmorton, (g'mother)

Baskerville brothers:
1. Sir Thomas (d.1597) m. Mary Throckmorton
      son Hannibal b.1630
2. Nicholas Baskerville d. at Flushing; m. Constance Huntley
      2 daughters & a son: Mary, Constance, William
      (i) Mary Baskerville d.1644 m.(1) John Morgan
            m.(2) Hannibal Baskerville
      (ii) Constance Baskerville m. Henry Lyte of Lytes Cary, son of Sir Thomas (by his first marriage

Baskerville, Hannibal (d. 1668) m. Mary Baskerville
      8 children: Thomas (TB) the writer of the manuscripts
      James bu. Wells, Constance bu. Somerton, 'young'; Gertrude (d.1656);
      Henry (d.1656); Nicholas (d.1656); Robert (d.1654); William
(d.1665)

Huntley brother & sisters:
1. Constance m. (1) Nicholas Baskerville *see above*
      m. (2) Sir John Sydney
      m. (3) Sir Thomas Lyte of Lytes Cary
3. Mary m. George Lyte snr of Leighterton
2. Matthew lord of Boxwell & Leighterton
      daughter Mary m. Mr Alde of Hardwick by Chepstow

Lyte family
1. George Lyte of Leighterton snr m. (2) Mary Huntley 'his first love'
2. Sir Thomas Lyte of Lytes Cary (TB's godfather) m.(1) - Worth
     son Henry m. Constance Baskerville
   m. (2) Constance née Huntley
3. Thomas of Martock
     son Thomas jnr m. Mary Anna Morgan

John Morgan m. Constance née Huntley
     daughter Mary m. Capt John Ivie

Sydney, Sir John m. Constance née Huntley
     daughter Barbara m. Paul Dayrell

Sir Thomas Throckmorton of Tortworth
     daughter Mary d.1632, m. (1) Sir Thomas Baskerville *see above*
     m. (2) Sir James Scudamore

BIBLIOGRAPHY

INTERNET RESOURCES

The main sources used to identify people and houses named by Baskerville available on the internet are abbreviated as follows:

ACAD A Cambridge Alumni Database (ACAD) https://venn.lib. cam.ac.uk

CCEd Clergy of the Church of England Database https:// theclergydatabase.org.uk/jsp

Historic England Historic England https://historicengland.org.uk/listing/ the-list

HoP The History of Parliament https://www. historyofparliamentonline.org/research/members/1660-1690

BHO Institute of Historical Research: British History online:

VCH (county) [vol] *Victoria County History* https://www.british-history.ac.uk/ vch

BHO Foster *Alumni Oxoniensis 1500-1714* ed. Joseph Foster (Oxford, 1891). http://www.british-history.ac.uk/alumni-oxon/1500-1714

BHO Hasted [vol] Edward Hasted, *The History and Topographical Survey of the County of Kent* 12 volumes (1797-1801) https://www.british-history.ac.uk/ survey-kent

BHO Blomefield [vol] Francis Blomefield, *An essay towards a topographical history of the county of Norfolk* 11 volumes (1805-10) https://www.britishhistory.ac.uk/ topographical-hist-norfolk

ODNB Oxford Dictionary of National Biography https://www. oxforddnb.com

The National Library of Scotland georeferenced first Ordnance Survey 1 inch maps have been exceptionally helpful in identifying many place-names. https://maps. nls.uk/geo/explore

Nicholas Kingsley, Landed Families of Britain and Ireland https://landedfamilies. blogspot.com

Google and Wikipedia frequently led to more detailed research

PRINTED SOURCES

Sir Robert Atkyns, *The Ancient and Present State of Glostershire* (1712)

Jeremy Black, *Maps and History* (1997)

C J Bond, 'The Reconstruction of the Medieval Landscape; the Estates of Abingdon Abbey', *Landscape History*, 182 (1979–80)

James Bond, *Monastic Landscapes* (Stroud 2004).

Burford buildings and people in a Cotswold Town (A Catchpole, D Clark, R Peberdy, England's Past for Everyone) ed S Townley, (Phillimore 2008) 93.

James Caulfield, *Portraits, Memoirs, and Characters of Remarkable Persons* (1790-95).

P Clark, *The English Alehouse A social history* (Longman 1983)

Barrie Cox, *English Inn and Tavern Names* (Centre for English Name Studies, 1994)

James D Crawshaw, *The history of Chatham Dockyard* (published by Isabel Garford 1999).

Bob Evans, *Tales from God's Acre - Fifty Sunningwell Lives* (2016)

Alan Everitt 'The English Urban Inn', *Landscape and Community in England* ed A Everitt (Hambledon1985)

— 'Common Land', *The English Rural Landscape* ed. J Thirsk (OUP 2000)

Celia Fiennes, *The Illustrated Journeys of Celia Fiennes* ed Christopher Morris (1982)

Roderick Floud, *An Economic History of the English Garden* (2019)

Helen Gammack, *Kitchen Garden Estate* (National Trust, 2012)

Harrison's Description of England 1577-87, ed. F J Furnivall (1877)

Felicity Heal and Clive Holmes, *The Gentry in England and Wales, 1500-1700* (MacMillan, 1994)

Edward Impey & Paul Belford, 'The lost medieval barn of Abingdon Abbey at Cumnor', *Oxoniensis* (2017)

Johannes Kip: the Gloucestershire Engravings ed Anthea Jones (Hobnob Press, 2021)

Joan Johnson, *The Gloucestershire Gentry* (Alan Sutton, 1989)

Anthea Jones, *The Cotswolds* (Phillimore, 1994)

Jacob Larwood and John Camden Hotten, *English Inn Signs* (Exeter, 1951, 1985)

Peter Laslett, *The World we have Lost* (1965; 1971)

Esther Moir, *The Discovery of Britain, the English Tourists 1540-1840* (1964)

Tim Owen and Elaine Pilbeam, *Ordnance Survey Map Makers to Britain since 1791* (Ordnance Survey, Southampton. London HMSO 1992)

F.S. Thacker, *The Thames Highway: a History of the Locks and Weirs* (1920)

The Cambridge History of Travel Writing ed Nandini Das, Tim Youngs (CUP 2019)

Peacham's Compleat gentleman, 1634 ed George S. Gordon, (Oxford 1906)

Remarks and collections of Thomas Hearne, ed C E Doble and others (Oxford Historical Society 48 (Hearne vol 7) 1906).

Henry Savage, *Balliofergus, or, A commentary upon the foundation, founders and affaires of Balliol Colledge gathered out of the records* (written about 1660 in England).

The remains of Thomas Hearne: Reliquae Hernianae ed J Bloss - revised ed J Buchanan-Brown (1965)

John Taylor, *Travels and Travelling 1616-1653* ed J Chandler (enlarged edition, Hobnob Press 2020)

The four visitations of Berkshire made and taken by Thomas Benolte, Clarnceuc, anno 1532; by William Harvey, Clarnceux, anno 1566; by Henry Chiting, Chester herald, and John Philipott, Rouge dragon, for William Camden, Clarenceux, anno 1623; and by Elias Ashmole, Windsor herald, for Sir Edward Bysshe, Clarenceux, anno 1665-66 ed W. Harry Rylands , London [The Harleian Society] (1907-8).

The Observant Traveller, Diaries of Travel in England, Wales and Scotland in the County Record Offices of England and Wales, ed. Robin Gard (HMSO 1989)

Margaret Willes, *The Domestic Herbal* (Bodleian Library 2020)

Anthony A Wood *Athenae Oxonienses* ed. Philip Bliss (1813)

ACKNOWLEDGEMENTS

THE DISCOVERY of Thomas Baskerville for me was made while preparing a talk on the gentry for the Gloucestershire Gardens and Landscape Trust, and finding Joan Johnson had quoted from his journeys in the county. Further investigation led not only to the original manuscript transcribed by the Historic Manuscripts Commission, but to two other manuscripts, and John Chandler at this point did more than encourage, he helped in practical ways obtain copy of the two manuscripts in the British Library. (The third manuscript in the Bodleian Libraries was easier for me to access.) Throughout the project John has been willing to advise and suggest, and a big debt is owed to him, as also for his painstaking work as the publisher. He drew all the illustrative maps. It is good to have this opportunity to thank him formally.

I am grateful to John Blair for sharing his work on Thomas Baskerville, and for alerting me to the original copy of the broadsheet (facing page 1) which Abingdon school holds; he also obtained permission to pass a photographic copy on to me and for its publication in this book. Robert Evans told me of Blair's interest in Baskerville and shared other information, as well as offering encouragement. Consequently I approached Matthew Ravden of 'Baskerville', built on the site of Bayworth manor house, who showed me the site of the excavation and shared photographs of it, also information about Paula Levick who carried out the excavation.

The copy of the Kip engraving of Chepstow bridge is made available by Gloucestershire Archives and the Gloucestershire Gardens and Landscape Trust; Andrew Parry of Gloucestershire Archives carried out the scanning. The British Library is thanked for scanning a manuscript page for me. The source of other illustrations is indicated beneath each. The staff of the Bodleian Libraries Special Collections are thanked for help in making the Rawlinson manuscripts and the catalogue available.

To my son, Peter Newman, I am grateful for much encouragement and for his imagining Thomas Baskerville with his large hat and Baskerville of Bayworth arms on the horse blanket, riding over ink lines seeking 'delicate prospects' from the hill.

Transcribing Baskerville's not always neat and legible writing has brought me to feel that I know him personally, and my hope is that his delightfully frank and natural observations will give many people pleasure as well as information about English places in the seventeenth century. I fear there will have been mistakes in the transcriptions (and interpretations) and responsibility is mine, shared perhaps with Thomas Baskerville.

INDEX

PLACE-NAMES, especially of smaller places or hamlets, were not standardised when Thomas Baskerville was travelling through England, but a cursory glance at the spellings itemised in the index shows he often had a doubtful grasp of the names he encountered. Occasionally he noted that he asked the name of the place he was in, and presumably did not see it written down. Nonetheless, his routes can be traced on the map today. The current form of a place-name is indexed, with Baskerville's variant spellings in brackets, identified by historic county. Based in Berkshire and Oxfordshire, and close to Gloucestershire, the counties Baskerville knew well have since undergone a series of changes and adjustments to their boundaries. Personal names can be difficult to trace for a further reason: he rarely used a Christian name; names with more than local significance have been indexed. Also indexed are the names of London streets and of places within ten miles of London where taverns were listed, but not the analysis of numbers of taverns in each, which is alphabetical.

County names and abbreviations are as follows:
Beds: Bedfordshire; Berks: Berkshire; Bucks: Buckinghamshire; Cambs: Cambridgeshire; Derby: Derbyshire; Dorset; Essex; Glamorgan; Glos: Gloucestershire; Hants: Hampshire; Herefs: Herefordshire; Herts: Hertfordshire; Hunts: Huntingdonshire; Kent; Leics: Leicestershire; Lincs: Lincolnshire; Mddx: Middlesex; Mon: Monmouthshire; Norfolk; Northants: Northamptonshire; Notts: Nottinghamshire; Oxon: Oxfordshire; Salop: Shropshire; Som: Somerset; Suffolk; Surrey; Warwicks: Warwickshire; Wilts: Wiltshire; Worcs: Worcestershire; Yorkshire: East Riding, North Riding, West Riding.

TRAVEL LITERATURE FROM HOBNOB PRESS

Our developing series of titles about roads and travellers includes these:

John Leland Itinerary: a Version in Modern English edited by John Chandler
John Leland's Itinerary is one of the key documents of English local history, offering eye-witness descriptions of hundreds of towns and villages, castles, monasteries and gentry houses during the reign of Henry VIII, by one of the most intelligent and learned observers of his era. But it is not straightforward – Leland became insane before he had time to organise his notes into a coherent and systematic account of his journeys. He left for posterity a jumbled mass of material, written partly in Latin, partly in robust Tudor English, to be plundered, damaged and in some cases lost by later antiquaries, and not published until the eighteenth century. John Chandler's modern English version, based on the standard edition by Lucy Toulmin Smith of 1906-10, was first published in 1993 and has been long out of print. In it he identified place and personal names, and rearranged everything of topographical interest into historic English counties, with maps and a detailed introduction. For this new edition he has corrected the text, added parts of the material relating to Leland's travels in Wales, revised the introduction, and established a reliable chronology for the surviving accounts of five journeys which Leland undertook between 1538 and 1544. While Leland's actual words will continue to be quoted by historians of the places he visited, this rendering into modern English offers an accessible and absorbing window on the world of our towns and countryside almost five centuries ago. April 2022, liv, 529pp, maps, paperback, £25.00, ISBN 978-1-914407-29-1

John Taylor, Travels and Travelling, 1616-1653, edited by John Chandler
John Taylor (1578-1653), known in his lifetime and ever since as the 'Water-Poet', wrote some two hundred pamphlets on every conceivable subject of interest to his contemporaries. A native of Gloucester who became a London waterman, he employed his ebullient wit and facility with words to make a reputation, if not a fortune, from his writing in prose and verse. His descriptions of the fourteen journeys he made between 1616 and 1653 around Britain (and twice to the continent), are not only entertaining to read, but an important source for anyone interested in travel, places and society before, during and just after the Civil Wars.

This expanded edition of a work first published in 1999 includes the two foreign adventures and a group of pamphlets describing carriers, coaches, inns and taverns, with brief introductions to each work, annotations and an index of places and people. October 2020, 512pp, paperback, £18.95, ISBN 978-1-906978-91-4.

The Grand Tour Diaries of William Guise, from Lausanne to Rome edited by Paul and Jane Butler

William Guise, later Sir William Guise, 5th Baronet of Elmore, travelled in Switzerland and Italy in 1764 in the company of Edward Gibbon, the historian. Two journals chronicling in great detail the first part of their tour, from Lausanne to Florence, Rome and other Italian cities, and the cultural sites and artefacts that they saw, have survived in the archives of Elmore Court, Gloucestershire, which was the Guise family home. Despite their historic and cultural interest, there has until now been no full transcription of these journals (totalling 83,000 words) apart from some references to them in an edition of Gibbon's diaries. As well as perceptive comments and opinions on the architecture, statues, pictures and other works of art which they saw, there are extensive references to military matters and fortifications; to the politics and governance of the towns of Northern Italy and to travel and lodging issues. The journals illustrate the serious nature of the Grand Tour as undertaken by Guise and his better known travelling companion, Edward Gibbon. March 2022, xviii, 190pp, illustrated (some colour) hardback, £25.00, ISBN 978-1-914407-30-7

Stage Coaches Explained, the Bristol Example, by Dorian Gerhold

Groundbreaking study of all aspects of coaching between Bristol, Bath and London, and Bristol and other destinations, by the acknowledged authority on pre-railway road transport. A scholarly but readable treatment which penetrates the romantic veneer to provide the key to understanding the stagecoach system as a whole. October 2012, 326 pages, illustrations, maps and tables, paperback, £17.95, ISBN 978-1-906978-15-0 (originally titled Bristol's Stage Coaches).

For full details of all HOBNOB PRESS titles and ordering information please visit **www.hobnobpress.co.uk**